ATOMS AND EDEN

Atoms and Eden

CONVERSATIONS ON
RELIGION AND SCIENCE

Steve Paulson

OXFORD
UNIVERSITY PRESS

2010

OXFORD
UNIVERSITY PRESS

Oxford University Press, Inc., publishes works that further
Oxford University's objective of excellence
in research, scholarship, and education.

Oxford   New York
Auckland   Cape Town   Dar es Salaam   Hong Kong   Karachi
Kuala Lumpur   Madrid   Melbourne   Mexico City   Nairobi
New Delhi   Shanghai   Taipei   Toronto

With offices in
Argentina   Austria   Brazil   Chile   Czech Republic   France   Greece
Guatemala   Hungary   Italy   Japan   Poland   Portugal   Singapore
South Korea   Switzerland   Thailand   Turkey   Ukraine   Vietnam

Published by Oxford University Press, Inc.
198 Madison Avenue, New York, New York 10016

www.oup.com

Oxford is a registered trademark of Oxford University Press

Library of Congress Cataloging-in-Publication Data
Paulson, Steve, 1960–
Atoms and Eden : conversations on religion
and science / Steve Paulson.
p. cm.
ISBN 978-0-19-974316-2
1. Religion and science.
2. Scientists—Interviews.
3. Scholars—Interviews. I. Title.
BL241.P38   2010
202'.4—dc22
2010004043

1 3 5 7 9 8 6 4 2
Printed in the United States of America
on acid-free paper

Contents

ATOMS AND EDEN

Introduction

THE DEBATE OVER SCIENCE AND RELIGION is like catnip for anyone wanting to spout off about the improbability of God or the arrogance of scientists. The public seems to have an insatiable appetite for this debate. Consider some of the books that have popped up on the best-seller list, whether by the atheists Richard Dawkins, Sam Harris, and Christopher Hitchens, or by defenders of religion, such as Francis Collins and Timothy Keller. These polemical tracts have fired up lots of people, but too often this debate is treated as a contest over who can score the most points rather than as a chance to explore some profound questions. Sorting out the relationship between science and religion *is* one of the great intellectual dramas of our time. We need to go beyond the hot-button issues that tend to grab headlines—like stem cell research or creationism—and explore the murkier, more confusing questions about our place in the universe. Is it just a crazy, cosmic stroke of luck that we're here at all? Or do human beings have some larger, mysterious purpose?

Traditionally, philosophers and theologians have presided over these questions about meaning and purpose, but many scientists are no longer willing to cede this territory to religion. The cutting edges of science—from cosmology and evolutionary biology to neuroscience—are now tackling the most profound questions of our existence. Even the soul is under scientific scrutiny. Or at least the soul as it's defined by modern science: the self-aware mind with its keen sense of morality and free will.

Is the human mind just a massive collection of neurons and chemicals in our brains, as most neuroscientists believe? Or is the mind connected to some larger sea of consciousness—an infinitely vast, even divine intelligence? These questions can provoke fierce and bitterly fought arguments between materialists and religious thinkers. And the rest of us often struggle with a difficult issue: Can science and religion coexist in this scientific age? If so, where exactly do we draw the boundary between them?

I have come to the science and religion debate full of intellectual curiosity. My interest goes back to my years of teenage angst, when I struggled rather helplessly with the big, messy questions about God and life's meaning. Later, I stuffed my existential crisis into some deep recess of my brain and got on with my life and career. Then a funny thing happened. As a public radio interviewer, I started exploring these ideas with prominent scientists, philosophers, and religious thinkers. In 2006, a journalism fellowship gave me a few months to focus on this subject with single-minded zeal. I read piles of books and did dozens of interviews about science and religion for the syndicated radio show *To the Best of Our Knowledge*. I would come home after these interviews scratching my head and muttering out loud, "So what does Karen Armstrong mean when she talks about God?" Or "How does consciousness fit into the evolution of the brain?" My two children started ducking out of the room when "science and religion" popped up in conversation at the dinner table.

I soon discovered that I wasn't the only one in the grip of this subject. Our radio interviews about science and religion generated more listener response than anything we had ever done. One of the first interviews I did on the science and religion debate, with the eminent biologist E. O. Wilson, elicited dozens of passionate and vehement letters. One listener wrote, "Wilson's practical, calm and clinical views of the universe and faith felt spiritual. As someone who is not religious, yet who feels almost continually in awe of cosmic forces and the almost shocking power of coincidence, I felt like I was in church." Another listener dissented: "Wilson's idea of heaven is so preposterous that I assume a man of his intelligence was simply being facetious or sarcastic." Dozens of listeners weighed in with opinions on all sorts of contentious matters: the afterlife, atheism, the Holy Ghost, and whether religion is really about faith or experience. This particular interview, along with others that followed, tapped into deeply held beliefs and resentments. Longer transcripts of my interviews ran in *Salon* magazine. These typically sparked hundreds of letters from readers and—to my surprise—a fair amount of vitriol aimed directly at me. Clearly, the debate over science and religion touches a raw nerve in our culture.

At the most obvious level, this is an argument between atheists and religious believers, between hardened materialists and spiritual seekers. Once you scratch the surface, these divisions aren't so clear. I've come to realize that many of the current debates in science and religion turn on how we define certain key words, like "God," "transcendence," and "religion." A great deal also rides on how much of reality we think can be explained by another loaded word, "science."

Take the case of Albert Einstein. He died more than half a century ago, but there's a huge debate right now between religious believers and atheists over who gets to claim Einstein, the most famous scientist of the last century. Einstein himself made a number of provocative and rather cryptic comments about religion. He called himself "a deeply religious nonbeliever." He said, "Science without religion is lame; religion without science is blind." Most famously, he proclaimed, "God does not play dice with the universe." Who is this God that Einstein invoked? Was he simply using the word "God" as a synonym for order and harmony in the universe?

I have asked a number of scientists, theologians, and Einstein scholars, and I've heard many different responses. "Einstein clearly was an atheist in the sense that he didn't believe in a personal God," Richard Dawkins says. "He used the word God as a metaphoric name for that which we don't yet understand, for the deep mysteries of the universe." The Nobel Prize–winning physicist and fellow atheist Steven Weinberg believes Einstein was just using poetic language when he talked about religion, which Weinberg considers a mistake. "Clearly, what Einstein meant by God is so vague and so far from conventional religion, it seems to me a misuse of the word," Weinberg says. "The concept of God historically has had a fairly definite meaning. God was conscious. God was powerful. God was benevolent to some extent. If you're not going to use God to mean something like that, then you shouldn't use the word."

Walter Isaacson, Einstein's biographer, has a very different perspective. He claims that Einstein was a deist who knew exactly what he was doing when he talked about "God" and "religion." "When he was asked whether he was just using the word God symbolically, he said, no, he wasn't," Isaacson told me. "He talked about having a cosmic religion. He thought there was a spirit manifest in the laws of the universe, and that was his notion of God."

These conflicting views about Einstein illustrate some of the fault lines in today's debate over science and religion. Hard-core atheists like Dawkins and Weinberg speak of religious faith as the irrational belief in a supernatural being. Dawkins says the existence of God is itself a scientific question, which isn't surprising, given his understanding of God as a cosmic magician who intervenes in the physical world. Yet that definition of religion simply doesn't apply to a nontheistic tradition like Buddhism. Even in the monotheistic religions, some scholars argue that religion is not really a matter of belief in the supernatural.

The historian Karen Armstrong told me that the great religious sages—including the Buddha, Confucius, and Jesus—didn't care about theology or big metaphysical systems. She regards the supernatural aspects of religion, like miracles and the afterlife, as mere window dressing. Armstrong says religion is a search for transcendence, but "transcendence isn't necessarily sited in an external god, which can be a very unspiritual, unreligious concept." She is trying to carve out a different understanding of religion, one that has no inherent conflict with science. For her, the religious sensibility is something akin to poetry.

What to make of belief is a matter of contention. In his book *The Religious Case against Belief*, the religious scholar James Carse writes: "Being a believer does not in itself make one religious; being religious does not require that one be a believer." Actual religious experience may have only a loose connection to a particular belief system. There's some fascinating brain research supporting this understanding of religion. Andrew Newberg, a neuroscientist, has done brain imaging studies of experienced Buddhist monks and Franciscan nuns. He asked the Buddhists to meditate and the nuns to pray while he measured the blood flow in their brains. He discovered that they had nearly identical neural responses. Both lost their sense of self, mainly by blocking out sensory information in the parietal lobe, which led to a feeling of oneness—what mystics describe as the "oceanic state." Yet their metaphysical systems are entirely different. The Franciscans pray to God, whereas the Buddhists have no concept of God. Their belief systems are the entry points into what they actually experience, which is quite similar. The main difference Newberg found is that the Franciscan nuns' prayers activated the language parts of the brain, whereas the Buddhist monks' meditation stimulated the visual areas.

Skeptical but Open-Minded

One of the great privileges of being a radio interviewer is that I get to ask questions that I rarely ask even close friends—like, what do you think about God? Or how do you find meaning in your own life? I find these questions fascinating, and they have led me down some unexpected paths as I've puzzled over the relationship between science and religion. One line of questioning typically brought me to other, seemingly unrelated fields of inquiry. For instance, as I struggled to grasp the meaning of "transcendence," I kept asking theologians and religious thinkers about their personal understanding of God, which in turn led me to conflicting ideas about faith and religious experience. My interviews with atheists often raised questions about the scope of science and whether certain realms of reality are simply beyond the capacity of science to explain. I soon found myself exploring contentious theories about quantum physics, the origins of the universe, and perhaps the most difficult question of all—the relationship between mind and brain.

I consider myself both skeptical and open-minded. Skeptical because I have a hard time believing any single theory, and I try to poke holes in it—whether it's a Buddhist theory of substrate consciousness or an atheist's strict materialism. But I'm also open to the possibility that any number of theories *could* be right—reincarnation of souls, the existence of God, or the neurochemical model of the mind. These are wildly different ideas—in fact, they can't all be true—and yet I cannot honestly dismiss any out of hand.

My goal for this collection of interviews is to expand the public conversation about science and religion. Too often it's framed as a battle between evolutionists and creationists. Or given the recent prominence of "the new atheists"—Dawkins, Harris, and Hitchens—it's seen as a debate between atheism and faith. If there's an underlying agenda to this book, it's my conviction that we cannot grasp the relationship between science and religion without examining it from many different angles. We must consider the research findings and theoretical insights from different scientific disciplines, including evolutionary biology, quantum physics, cosmology, and neuroscience. We should also have a solid grounding in theology, religious history, and what William James called "the varieties of religious experience."

We need a wide-ranging, nuanced understanding of both science *and* religion. It's often assumed that a thorough understanding of science is all we need to resolve these questions. But without a clear understanding of the word "God," for instance, we won't get very far. This is one reason Richard Dawkins and Karen Armstrong always talk past each other. They define God in completely different ways. We must also have a historically informed understanding of how to read sacred texts. This is urgent for pragmatic reasons, with religious zealots quoting the Quran or the Bible to justify acts of violence. It's also intellectually crucial. There are dramatically different ways to interpret stories that seem to defy the laws of nature, whether the creation story in Genesis, the Resurrection of Jesus, or Muhammad's Night Journey. Atheists should not assume that religion demands the faithful read these stories literally. On the other hand, religious believers should avoid using Scripture as a stick to bash modern science. And those believers who want to reconcile science and religion ought to consider the intellectual problems that result from invoking miracles.

I started digging into some very difficult questions. Did the Big Bang really spring forth spontaneously, ex nihilo? For decades this has been the prevailing scientific view among cosmologists and astrophysicists. This model also fits easily into some Jewish and Christian accounts of creation, though not the Buddhist view. Now some astrophysicists are backpedaling, suggesting there must have been prior moments of creation—perhaps earlier universes that set off the Big Bang in our own universe 13.7 billion years ago. If you go back far enough, science has a way of turning into a highly speculative realm that's not so different from metaphysics.

I also found scientists grappling with deep philosophical questions about meaning and purpose. Did the unfolding of the universe, and then the evolution of life on Earth, follow a preordained drive toward ever greater complexity and ultimately highly intelligent creatures like human beings? Highly regarded scientists like Simon Conway Morris and Paul Davies make this argument, though most scientists reject it, suspecting it to be an underhanded attempt to sneak God back into science. The predominant view among evolutionary biologists is that human existence is just a lucky evolutionary accident. For those who don't believe in God or any sort of cosmic purpose, meaning is for us mere mortals to forge in our own imperfect ways. Owen Flanagan, a materialist philosopher, calls this "the *really* hard problem" in philosophy. Yet the prospect of a world without inherent purpose is simply unacceptable to religious believers. One response is to disregard modern science and embrace theories like creationism and intelligent design. For others, the task is to reconcile their belief in an underlying purpose with the latest scientific thinking. Some religious scholars have argued that the emergence of *Homo sapiens* was an inevitable part of the evolutionary process.

My other questions are more explicitly religious, though some begged for scientific explanation. What exactly happened in the minds of great mystics like Francis of Assisi and Theresa of Ávila during their moments of divine rapture? If neuroscientists could examine St. Francis with today's imaging machines, could they pinpoint the changes in his brain during his ecstatic experiences? Did these mystics simply conjure up God in their heads, or did they actually talk to Him? There's an even bigger problem: How can we understand transcendent reality if God is ineffable—beyond language, even beyond our limited human brains to comprehend?

I don't claim to have found answers to any of these questions, but I have heard many provocative theories and compelling ideas. Without quite realizing it, I started asking spiritual questions in my own quirky way, though I never joined a church or ashram, and I don't meditate or pray. I suppose I'm not that different from many people of my generation. Raised to question authority, we have trouble following the prescribed guidelines of any religious institution. Though we turned away from organized religion, we still yearn for a spiritual dimension in our lives, for some sense of the sacred that fits our largely secular outlook.

I start with a few basic assumptions. I believe the Bible and other sacred texts were written by people—not God—in specific historical circumstances.

Perhaps those people were divinely inspired; I don't know. It is clear that scientific discoveries have steadily encroached on many domains once ruled by religion. By now, the old scriptural accounts of creation simply don't hold up when taken as literal truth. I also don't believe any single religious tradition has the inside track on ultimate truth. That's worth mentioning because most of the prominent religious thinkers in the science and religion debate are Christians, and some have a tendency to discuss religion in strictly Christian terms. Though I was raised a Christian, I have a hard time believing that faith in Jesus is required for salvation or a fully realized spiritual life. That's a grim stroke of fate for the millions of people around the world who have never heard of Jesus.

So what's a scientifically literate, rationally minded person—someone impatient with religious doctrine but open to spiritual experience—supposed to think about religion in the twenty-first century? That's the underlying question posed in this book. You will find a remarkable range of responses in these interviews: distinguished scientists who believe in miracles, like Francis Collins and Simon Conway Morris; a Buddhist scholar, Alan Wallace, who thinks reincarnation can be tested by science; the eminent primatologist Jane Goodall, who talks openly about her paranormal experiences; as well as hard-core materialists like Richard Dawkins and Daniel Dennett, who are adamant that human beings have no cosmic purpose. You might be surprised by the views of certain scientists who don't believe in God: For instance, the pioneering biologist E. O. Wilson, a fierce critic of creationism, calls himself a "provisional deist"; a prominent atheist, Sam Harris, will not rule out the possibility of life after death; and the cosmologist Paul Davies believes there's a grand design to our bio-friendly universe, even though he sees no room for God in that design.

You might also be surprised by the views of certain religious thinkers, like Karen Armstrong's contention that belief in a personal God makes as little sense as belief in Santa Claus. Elaine Pagels, a scholar of the Gnostic Gospels, isn't so quick to dismiss the concept of a personal God, but she's intent on showing that pivotal stories in early Christianity, such as the Immaculate Conception and the Resurrection, can be explained without recourse to supernaturalism. Then there's a philosopher of consciousness, Ken Wilber, who believes it's time we move beyond the mythic and magical claims of religion. Wilber draws on mystical traditions from around the world to make a case for tapping into a higher, transpersonal realm of reality.

I do not mean to suggest that there's no conflict between science and religion, or that everyone wants to reconcile them. Many don't. In fact, there's only one thing that both creationists and Richard Dawkins agree on: You cannot accept both the Bible and the scientific account of evolution. They just disagree over which to believe. Plenty of other people are tired of the shouting match between strident atheists and religious fundamentalists. This highly charged rhetoric obscures the vast ground in the middle—those people who have no trouble believing in God *and* modern science. The historian Ronald Numbers argues that the conflict between science and religion has been greatly exaggerated. He dismisses the whole idea of warfare between science and religion extending back to the Renaissance and points out that the giants of the scientific revolution—Copernicus, Newton, Galileo, Boyle, and Kepler—were all theists.

The Great Debate

In 1997 one of America's most famous scientists, Stephen Jay Gould, tried to broker a truce between science and religion by claiming they are two utterly distinct realms of understanding, or in his terminology, "nonoverlapping magisteria" (NOMA). "The net of science covers the empirical realm: what is the universe made of (fact) and why does it work this way (theory)," he wrote in *Rocks of Ages*. "The net of religion extends over questions of moral meaning and value." This attempt to divide the world into fact and meaning has shaped the debate over science and religion for the past decade. My guess is that Gould's NOMA is the position unconsciously held by many religious believers—at least those who don't take sacred texts as literal truth. They have no problem accepting the world of science while also praying to God in times of distress.

Gould's views on religion echo those of Charles Darwin. Darwin refused to call himself an atheist, as I discovered during a visit to the Darwin Correspondence Project in Cambridge, England. I spent one fascinating afternoon poring over Darwin's letters and inspecting the comments he scribbled in the margins of his books. Paul White, a senior editor at the Darwin Correspondence Project, showed me several letters Darwin wrote to worried religious believers who asked the famous scientist if they could remain good Christians once they accepted his theory of evolution. These letters are crucial for deciphering Darwin's own views on religion, because his books reveal next to nothing of his own beliefs (or lack thereof). His letters suggest that Darwin saw no fundamental incompatibility between evolution and faith. When asked about his own faith, he replied, "An agnostic would be the most correct description of my state of mind."

By now, the science and religion debate has moved beyond Gould's NOMA. Many of the scholars I interviewed—both secular and religious— reject Gould's concept of NOMA. "He dodged the question. That's no answer at all," says E. O. Wilson. "I think it's nonsense," adds fellow biologist Richard Dawkins. Plenty of people on the religious side agree. "It's never been true," says Alan Wallace. "Religion, whether we like it or not, is making many truth claims about the natural world as well as the transcendent world."

Gould may have proposed his NOMA for purely pragmatic reasons. As an outspoken critic of creationism, he could have made a tactical decision that the best way to keep evolution in the classroom was to declare that it had nothing to do with religion. "The politics is very straightforward," Dawkins says. "The science lobby, which is very important in the United States, wants those sensible religious people—the theologians, the bishops, the clergymen who believe in evolution—on their side." Dawkins himself takes a far more controversial stance, claiming that God is incompatible with evolution. He acknowledges that this position is politically explosive, but he considers it intellectually honest. Of course, this argument plays directly into the hands of critics of evolution; they have always claimed that Darwinism leads to atheism. Dawkins admits that his views could undermine the legal case for teaching evolution. As Ronald Numbers points out, "Our public schools are supposed to be religiously neutral. If evolution is in fact inherently atheistic, we probably shouldn't be teaching it in the schools." Plenty of other scholars have no problem reconciling evolution with religion. In fact, John Haught, a Catholic theologian, calls Darwin "a gift to theology." He says evolutionary biology has forced modern theologians to clarify their thinking by rejecting outdated arguments about God as an intrusive designer of life.

I have found that combative atheists like Dawkins and Sam Harris occupy a special place in this discussion. Many scholars who study science and religion—and this includes both believers and nonbelievers—loathe them. Dawkins and company are often dismissed as shrill, divisive, and ignorant of theology. There's no doubt that the "new atheists" have an outsized influence in this debate. Dawkins in particular has a huge following, especially among people who are fed up with what they regard as America's excessive religiosity. In my view, atheists like Dawkins, Harris, and Weinberg have the great virtue of pushing religious believers to clarify their thinking. They ask tough questions: What exactly do the faithful mean when they use words like "mystery" and "transcendence"? Does God really respond to prayer, and if so, how does God interact with the physical world? Why should we consider the Christian and Muslim stories about Jesus and Muhammad to be any more credible than the ancient Greek stories about Zeus?

For all the talk about the new atheists, they are not simply a card-carrying cohort who all believe the same things. Philosopher Daniel Dennett, for instance, appreciates religion's capacity to provide much-needed comfort, whereas Dawkins and Harris see nothing but trouble stemming from religious faith. Opinions also vary on the thorny question of consciousness, which could emerge as the make-or-break issue in the science and religion debate. Virtually all religious traditions assume the mind is more than the brain. If we can communicate with God, or if there really is life after death, then consciousness must go beyond the purely physical mechanics of the brain. Not surprisingly, theologians typically point to the mind as something that science will never fully explain. Atheists themselves, however, are all over the map on this question.

Dennett says science will have no trouble figuring out the relationship between the brain and the mind. As he told me, "There are lots of puzzles, but there aren't any mysteries." Dawkins isn't nearly so certain: "Consciousness is the biggest puzzle facing biology, neurobiology, computational studies and evolutionary biology. It is a very, very big problem." Another leading atheist, Steven Pinker, doubts that science will ever unravel the mystery of consciousness by studying neurons and brain chemistry. In fact, he says this is why he went into cognitive psychology and not neurobiology. For Pinker, studying brain tissue is the wrong level of analysis. To understand the mind, he says you have to look at higher levels of mental organization. Then there's Harris, who may be the fiercest critic of religion of them all. Yet he's also a longtime Buddhist meditator who is quite open to spirituality and—to my astonishment—even told me about his own telepathic experiences. He's a neuroscientist, which makes his comments about the mind all the more intriguing. "Consciousness poses a unique problem," he says. "I'm actually quite skeptical of our ever being able to resolve that question: what the real relationship between consciousness and matter ultimately is."

Who Is under Attack?

What's so striking about the current debate over science and religion is that both sides, paradoxically, claim to be under attack. Polls consistently show that the vast majority of Americans are religious. A Pew Research Center poll found that 96 percent of Americans believe in God or some form of supreme being. Both Dawkins and Harris claim that atheists are despised. "The status of atheists in America today is on a par with that of homosexuals fifty years ago," Dawkins writes in *The God Delusion*. Harris concurs. In *Letter to a Christian Nation*, he says, "Atheists are the most reviled minority in the United States. Polls indicate that being an atheist is a perfect impediment to running for high office in our country (while being black, Muslim or homosexual is not)." The polling numbers would seem to support their claims. Of course, both of their atheist manifestos also spent months on the best-seller list, which suggests that plenty of people have no qualms about living in a godless world.

Yet many religious thinkers also feel under attack. Modern science has dismantled the biblical account of creation. It has undermined most religious claims about supernatural events, and it has left those professing belief in divine miracles sounding credulous and irrational. "In the opinion of most people, science has won those battles, and God should by now really be quite dead," Oxford University theologian Keith Ward writes in *Pascal's Fire*. "Believers and theologians have been reduced to a defensive silence about

God, and are rather apologetic about even mentioning the word." Another theologian, John Haught, agrees. In his book *Is Nature Enough?* he points to the prevailing belief among intellectuals that science can explain all of reality: "Scientific naturalists are still a small minority in the world's overall population, but their influence is out of proportion to their numbers. Generally speaking, their beliefs quietly determine what is intellectually acceptable in many of our universities."

So how can both atheists and theologians claim to be under siege? The truth is, both are under fire. There is no doubt that American politicians criticize religion at their peril. Every four years, we see aspiring presidential candidates trying to polish their religious credentials by visiting churches and talking up their faith. California congressman Pete Stark actually made news headlines when he announced that he doesn't believe in a supreme being. According to the American Humanist Association, Stark is the highest-ranking elected official—and the first congressman—to publicly admit to being an atheist. Even the vast majority of scientists and opinion leaders who defend evolution in school controversies are careful to treat religion with respect, and for good reason. Despite overwhelming evidence, most Americans still don't believe the standard Darwinian account of evolution. According to a recent CBS News poll, 51 percent of Americans believe God created humans in their present form, and another 27 percent think He guided the process. A minuscule 13 percent believe God had no role in evolution.

What I say here is hardly news. We all know that politicians must tread carefully around religion, and that the antievolution lobby—creationists and intelligent design activists—will do whatever they can to poke holes in evolutionary theory. So how is religion also under attack? This is a far subtler point to make, but you often see it in leading newspapers. References to God are typically confined to the religion column, unless religion pops up in politically charged stories about creationism or Islamic suicide bombings. In discussions of science and religion, it's a one-way street: Religion is often dissected by scientists, but religious critiques of science are rarely featured, except in occasional antiscience rants by religious fundamentalists. In leading newspapers, the materialist paradigm is firmly entrenched. The implicit message is that you can go to church on Sunday—and even pray to God if you want—but don't try suggesting that some aspects of the natural world may fall outside the explanatory power of modern science. You will get hammered by the scientific establishment, though it will be done so matter-of-factly as to hardly raise an eyebrow.

The Big Questions

What are the pivotal questions that shape the science and religion debate? Here's a short list of what I consider "the big questions." Incidentally, all of these questions challenge Gould's clear dichotomy between science and religion.

1. How did our universe come into existence?
2. Is the universe "designed" for life?
3. Is there any underlying purpose to human existence?
4. Does any part of the mind operate independently of the physical mechanics of the brain?
5. Are there any dimensions of reality beyond the capacity of science to explain?
6. What are the roots of religious belief?
7. How should we understand the miraculous, supernatural events described in sacred texts?
8. Do we need God to experience transcendence or the sacred?

It is possible that scientists will answer some of these questions. For instance, they may find the precise neurotransmitters, synapses, and neurons that create our thoughts and mental experiences. It is also possible that scientific inquiry has certain intractable limits, and no matter how much we learn about the physical mechanics of the brain, neuroscience and cognitive science may never explain the rich, highly subjective experience of love or the quirky dreams we have.

Other questions seem almost beyond the scope of science. Will we ever know what caused the Big Bang, or why the basic laws of physics seem so finely tuned to form galaxies, stars, planets, and, ultimately, life on Earth? As the physicist Freeman Dyson once said, "It's almost as though the universe knew we were coming." Religious believers are quick to say it's all part of God's plan. Now, leading cosmologists are proposing all kinds of fascinating and far-out theories to explain the structure of the universe, including parallel universes, the multiverse, and even the "participatory universe," in which the awareness of intelligent beings—through the bizarre property of backward-in-time causation—actually shaped the laws of physics billions of years *earlier*. Frankly, much of this speculation seems to fall more in the realm of science fiction. Let's face it, part of the fascination with cosmology—and the more general debate over science and religion—is that it allows us to play with some wild ideas.

What about the quintessential religious question: Is there meaning and purpose to human existence? Gould considered this to be precisely the kind of concern that should fall outside the realm of science. Until recently, it did. Indeed, Dawkins considers it pointless and even improper to ask the question of why we are here. But in the past few years, a few scientists have looked to science itself for answers. Simon Conway Morris, a biologist, believes that evolutionary convergence points to the rise of *Homo sapiens* as an inevitable development, not just a lucky accident resulting from random genetic mutations. Paul Davies, a cosmologist, breaks a long-standing scientific taboo by talking openly about teleology. Are we witnessing the birth of a new scientific paradigm, or are these scientists just grasping at straws, desperate for cosmic purpose to ease their existential angst?

The debate over science and religion is contentious partly because the terms of the debate are so fuzzy. Words like "God" and "religion" can take on different meanings, depending on who uses them. This isn't just semantic game playing; words really do matter. In fact, there's a fascinating movement among some secular scientists and philosophers to appropriate the word "religion." Although they don't believe in God, these "religious naturalists" are impatient with the hard-core atheists who simply dismiss religion. For a cell biologist like Ursula Goodenough, reveling in the awe and wonder of nature is a spiritual act, not unlike the religious experience of rapture. The philosopher Loyal Rue has made the point even more explicit with the title of his book *Religion Is Not about God*. Another cosmologist, Joel Primack, wants to debunk Weinberg's claim that human beings are insignificant specks in a meaningless universe. The biologist and complexity theorist Stuart Kauffman goes even further. He doesn't just want to reclaim "religion"; he's out to transform the very meaning of the word "God." Kauffman's notion of the sacred is rooted in science—specifically, in the unpredictable properties of biology. In his book *Reinventing the Sacred*, he describes God as "the ceaseless creativity in the universe," and he argues that life, meaning, and consciousness all emerge from this creative universe.

Diverse Viewpoints

Shortly before this book went to press, I gave a talk about consciousness to a group of hard-nosed cognitive scientists at the University of Wisconsin. I played excerpts from various interviews I had done, intending to show the dizzying array of theories about the connection between mind and brain. After I played a clip from Alan Wallace about his notion of an underlying "substrate consciousness," a psychologist, clearly annoyed, called out from the back of the room (and I'm paraphrasing only slightly): "Why should I listen to this nonsense when there's no scientific evidence to support what he's saying? I've spent my entire career studying the mind. Why should I care about some Buddhist's speculation about quantum physics and conscious-ness?"

This is a fair question that deserves an answer. His complaint exposes a major fault line within the larger debate over science and religion. How do we decide which theories are credible? Should everyone be given the stage to trumpet any crackpot theory? No, I don't think every theory deserves a pub-lic hearing. That's why I included no young Earth creationists or intelligent design advocates in this book. Their science simply isn't credible. I deliber-ately avoided doing interviews merely to expose faulty logic and shoddy arguments.

Where there is genuine uncertainty, though, I make a plea for the spirit of open-minded inquiry. The materialists may assume that all mental experi-ence rises from the neurochemistry of the brain, but the truth is, no one knows what generates consciousness. It's still a mystery. It seems foolish to assume that the dominant scientific paradigm about the mind is the only possible explanation. Who knows what future discoveries may reveal about the mind? It's no accident that a few maverick scientists like Stuart Kauffman and Roger Penrose are looking outside the reigning paradigm to consider alternative explanations for consciousness, including a possible connection to quantum mechanics. Yes, it's highly speculative—they say so themselves—but they doubt that today's neuroscience paradigm will unlock the deepest mysteries of the mind.

So much of what we believe to be real stems from our unquestioned assumptions. A neuroscientist who studies brain plasticity may assume that neuronal activity explains all conscious experience. A Buddhist monk who has spent decades in deep meditation may just as easily assume that his experience of satori taps into some sort of universal consciousness. I think it's entirely possible that certain aspects of reality will remain beyond the reach of science—or at least the science we know today. I have heard remarkable and highly plausible accounts of energy healing, uncanny dreams, and near-death experiences that defy scientific explanation. To say they cannot possibly be real because they can't be replicated in a laboratory or a double-blind study seems narrow-minded.

We come back to the question of evidence. Science demands confirmation through repeatable experiments or observations and has little use for anecdotal evidence. But many spiritual beliefs stem from personal experience, perhaps an otherworldly vision or an occurrence so remarkable that it doesn't seem accidental. If you ask a spiritual believer why she believes in a transcendental reality, she will often point to profound personal experiences as empirical evidence. Her experience may not stand up as credible scientific evidence, but that doesn't mean it can't reflect an underlying reality. I should add one caveat: Even if we do grant the possibility of such extraordinary occurrences, they still don't prove the existence of God. Talking about God is typically an interpretive attempt to make sense of personal spiritual experience.

The interviews in this book reflect a remarkably diverse range of viewpoints about the relationship between science and religion, reason and faith. I've talked with Christians, Jews, Muslims, and Buddhists, as well as atheists and agnostics of various stripes. Why did I choose these particular scientists, philosophers, historians, and theologians? The quick answer is that many are among the world's leading figures in the science and religion debate. I simply couldn't put together this collection without voices like Karen Armstrong and Paul Davies, Richard Dawkins and Daniel Dennett, Francis Collins and Steven Weinberg. Over the years, they have shaped the public discussion about science and religion. But the real answer is that I found all the people included in this book engaging—indeed, fascinating—in one way or another. Though you will find many disagreements—and in some cases, diametrically opposing views—I find all their perspectives worthy of consideration and argument.

I have also tried to broaden the way the science and religion debate is framed with this particular selection of interviews. Questions about how to read religious texts—and more generally, what to make of sacred and transcendent experience—usually fall outside this discussion. I see these questions as central to any meaningful discussion of religion. Atheist critiques of religion invariably refer to the seemingly preposterous stories of miracles in sacred texts, and they tend to equate religion with unreason and irrationality. Of course, religious believers draw different lessons from sacred texts, and they often have a subtler understanding of faith and God. In my view, any serious examination of science and religion must wrestle with the meaning of religion itself.

Each interview in this book stands on its own. Readers will have no problem skipping around to read the selections that seem most intriguing. There are echoes and responses in adjoining chapters—for instance, Karen Armstrong's response to Sam Harris's critique of religion; Daniel Dennett and Alan Wallace's debate over the meaning of reductionism in science; Steven Weinberg's dissent from Paul Davies's theory of a "designer" universe; and conflicting ideas from Robert Wright, Elaine Pagels, and Nidhal Guessoum over how to interpret sacred texts. These interviews reflect my quest to understand the relationship between science and religion. This book grew out of genuine curiosity and my own questions about consciousness, evolution, cosmology, God, and mystical experience. It has been an exhilarating experience to talk with such profound and provocative thinkers. If the experience of reading these interviews is even half as stimulating for the reader, then I have accomplished what I set out to do.

E. O. Wilson

FOR A MAN WHO IS OBSESSED with tiny critters, Edward O. Wilson has a strange knack for stirring up controversy about life's biggest questions. The Harvard University biologist is a renowned expert on insects, coauthor of the Pulitzer Prize–winning book *The Ants*. His seminal 1975 book *Sociobiology* laid the groundwork for the new field of evolutionary psychology, and it made Wilson a scientific luminary—and a major intellectual force in America. That book, along with its Pulitzer Prize–winning sequel, *On Human Nature*, argued that many human behaviors—including aggression, altruism, and hypocrisy—are shaped by evolution.

Wilson's tilt toward nature in the age-old nature/nurture debate may have put him on the map, but it also made plenty of enemies. Fellow Harvard biologists Stephen Jay Gould and Richard Lewontin denounced sociobiology, saying it provided a genetic justification for racism and Nazi ideology. Wilson's classes were picketed. In one famous incident, demonstrators at a scientific meeting stormed the stage where he was speaking and dumped a pitcher of water over his head, chanting, "Wilson, you're all wet!"

Over the years, sociobiology—once so controversial—became a widely accepted branch of science. Ultimately, Wilson won the National Medal of Science for his scholarship. His popularity soared when he emerged as a champion of biodiversity and a passionate advocate for endangered species. His 1992 book *The Diversity of Life* became a best-seller. He stirred up more trouble in the late 1990s with another book, *Consilience*. This was his attempt to outline a unified theory of knowledge, which had the effect of elevating science at the expense of religion and the arts. In his view, knowledge of the world ultimately comes down to chemistry, biology, and—above all—physics; people are just extremely complicated machines. Wendell Berry, among other critics, railed against Wilson's scientific reductionism, calling it a "modern superstition."

Wilson is retired, although he still spends plenty of time at his Harvard lab. He continues to write and lecture. He recently edited a collection of Charles Darwin's books titled *From So Simple a Beginning* and wrote his first novel, *Anthill*. In person, Wilson is a courtly Southerner. He's an affable man who laughs easily and—unlike many scientists—is quite willing to speculate on the most cosmic questions. This was evident when he stopped by my radio studio before giving a sold-out lecture at the University of Wisconsin. We talked about Darwin and the growing rift between science and religion, as well as Wilson's take on religion—his "provisional deism" and personal horror of an eternal afterlife in heaven.

■ ■ ■ ■

What were the personal and intellectual qualities that made Darwin such a great scientist?
A relentlessly inquiring mind, a love of natural history acquired as a child, the extraordinary opportunity presented by the voyage of the *Beagle* to travel around the world at exactly the right age when the mind is opening, the opportunity in the scientific world to make a major discovery, and—I should not overlook—being a country squire with no economic pressures.

Did he have any particular agenda when he set out on his voyage on the *Beagle*?
I don't think so. He was a deeply religious man. He hadn't thought about evolution at all. What he was was an all-purpose observer, with a particular interest in natural history, and of course in beetles, which were the love of his life.

It's worth pointing out that when Darwin first set out on the *Beagle*, he brought his own Bible. He had to overturn his whole upbringing to come up with this revolutionary idea.

Darwin departed England a devout Bible literalist. After failing his effort to become a doctor, he had in fact trained as a minister at Cambridge University. As he says in his autobiography, he would even pull out the Bible to settle some argument with other members of the ship's crew. But then as the trip went on, for reasons Darwin really never disclosed but I don't think had to do with the idea of evolution, he gradually dropped his Christian beliefs. Becoming a man of the world and much more aware of other cultures and religious beliefs, he realized that the stories of the Bible were basically no different from the stories of these other religions.

But what really turned him against religion was the doctrine of damnation. He said if the Bible is true, you must be redeemed in Christ and be a believer in order to go to heaven. And others will be condemned. And that includes my brothers and all my best friends. And he said that is a damnable doctrine. Those are his words.

Darwin's own transformation from devout Christian to nonbeliever obviously raises significant questions in our own time. It raises a very provocative question: If you fully accept the theory of evolution by natural selection, does that logically lead you to atheism?

Well, it does up to the origin of the mind and spirit. And one of the Vatican's scientific spokesmen, incidentally, just recently turned thumbs down on intelligent design. Pope John Paul II took the position that evolution's been pretty well proved, and certainly was acceptable as God's way of creating the diversity of life. But the human soul was injected by God. So that's a kind of compromise position that a lot of devoutly religious people have taken.

But that begs the question, when did the soul enter? I mean, if you accept evolution, at some point humans evolved out of something that came before. So do all creatures have some kind of soul? Or do only humans have a soul?

Yeah, that's the dilemma. Of course, there is no reconciliation between the theory of evolution by natural selection and the traditional religious view of the origin of the human mind.

Are you saying we have to choose between science and religion?

Well, you have to choose between the scientific materialist view of the origin of the mind on the one side, and the traditional religious view that the spirit and the mind are independent of the process of evolution and eventually noncorporeal, capable of leaving the body and going elsewhere.

This is not a view that all scientists subscribe to. Stephen Jay Gould famously talked about how science and religion are two entirely separate spheres. And they really didn't have anything to do with each other.

Yeah, he threw in the towel.

He dodged the question.

He dodged the question, famously. That's no answer at all. That's evasion. I think most scientists who give thought to this with any depth—who understand evolution—take pretty much the position that I've taken. For example, in the National Academy of Sciences, which presumably includes many of the elite scientists in this country, a very large number would fully accept the scientific view. I know it's 80 percent or more who said, on the issue of the immortality of the soul, they don't care.

It would seem that religion and science have two entirely different ways of understanding the world. Science is founded on reason and deduction and empirical study. Religion, on the other hand, is grounded in faith—often a leap of faith, in mystery, in living with the nonrational part of your mind. Are those two utterly alien ways of looking at the world? Or is there any common ground?

The only common ground that I see is the one that was approached by Darwin himself. Religious belief itself is an adaptation that has evolved because we're hardwired to form tribalistic religions. Religion is intensely tribalistic. A devout Christian or Muslim doesn't say one religion is as good as another. It gives them faith in the particular group to which they belong and that set of beliefs and moral views.

What about the sense of awe, of wonder? That's something you hear about all the time among religious people. You hear about it from some scientists as well.

Well, you do. You hear about it from me. Awe is hard to put into words. But it certainly involves a sense of the mightiness and splendor and almost indecipherable intricacy of something greater than ourselves. A lot of religious mysticism arises directly from it. But it's equally experienced by the secularist whose mind opens to the splendor and intricacy of the material universe.

I've talked with some atheists who have suggested what they really need is a spiritual atheism. They need the sense of awe. They're competing with religious traditions, with very powerful stories, that have been passed down through the ages.

Yeah, that's true.

Does the scientist, does the nonbeliever, need that as well? Can the nonbeliever have that?

The answer to the second question is yes. The answer to the first question—do they have it?—is usually no. The problem with secular humanism is that it does lack it. I think it was Camille Paglia who talked about Foucault and the almost religious awe that the French poststructuralist philosophers once had in France. She compared it to the power of the Judeo-Christian tradition and said 3,000 years of Yahweh beats one generation of Foucault.

Would you be comfortable saying that science can have a sacred dimension?

Sacred, yes, in the sense of spirituality. This would be based upon a deeper understanding of just how intricate and surprising the universe is. The story of the origin of life on this planet—the time scale, the magnitude of it, the complexity of how it has been put together—all of that engenders in me even more awe than I ever felt as a devout Southern Baptist growing up.

You grew up in a religious family?

Oh yes, I grew up fundamentalist. I grew up as a Southern Baptist with strict adherence to the Bible, which I read as a youngster. As a child, I was warned by counselors and routine religious training that the truth was in the Bible. Redemption was only in Christ, and the world is full of satanic force. Satan himself perhaps—but certainly his agents, witting and unwitting—would try to make me drop my belief. I had that instilled in me. You have to understand how powerful the religious drive is—the instinct which I consider tribalist but probably necessary—in most societies for continuing day-to-day business.

That's an interesting perspective. Basically, you're saying it's necessary but it's wrong.

Well, you see, that's the dilemma of the twenty-first century. Possibly the greatest philosophical question of the twenty-first century is the resolution of religious faith with the growing realization of the very different nature of the material world. You could say that we evolved to accept one truth—the religious instinct—but then discovered another. And having discovered another, what are we to do? You might say it's just best to go ahead and accept the two worldviews and let them live side by side. I see no other solution. I believe they can use their different worldviews to solve some of the great problems—for example, the environment. But generally speaking, the difficulty in saying they can live side by side is a sectarianism in the world today, and traditional religions can be exclusionary and used to justify violence and war. You just can't deny that this is a major problem.

To return to your personal history, when did you reject that early fundamentalist belief? When did you start to question the literal interpretation of the Bible?

One thing I did was grow up as an ardent naturalist. I never grew out of my bug period. By the time I got to college, I was steeped in natural history and biology. I didn't learn much else in the high schools of Alabama, but I was really steeped in that.

By the time you got to college, had you rejected your religious background?

In college, I did begin to get a good education. As soon as I got to the University of Alabama, I discovered evolution and the new synthesizers of evolutionary theory. I read them all. This was an epiphany. I realized that all I had loved about the natural world, and all I had learned, now made sense. And that's what converted me.

So you spent your whole youth out in the fields, observing nature, but in some ways it didn't add up because you hadn't understood evolution.
It didn't. And it can't. That's the problem. You cannot explain the patterns of diversity in the world, the geography of life, the endless details of distribution, similarity and dissimilarity in the world, by any means except evolution. That's the one theory that ties it together. It is very hard to see how traditionalist religious views will come to explain the meaning of life on this planet.

Let me follow up on this because I've heard you call yourself a deist.
Yeah, I don't want to be called an atheist.

Why not?
You know, being a good scientist, and having been drawn up short so many times on my own theories and speculations—as all honest scientists are—I don't want to exclude the possibility of a creative force or deity. I think that would be a mistake to say there is no God or supernatural force. As the theologian Hans Kung once said, how are we to explain there is something and not nothing? Well, that's a question I'm happy to leave to the astrophysicist—where the laws of the universe came from and what is the meaning of the origin of existence. But I do feel confident that there is no intervention of a deity in the origin of life and humanity.

That is the distinction between theism and deism.
That is the distinction. So I am not a theist, but I'll be a provisional deist.

To be a deist, you're saying maybe there was some creator, some presence, that set in motion the laws of the universe.

Maybe. That has not yet been discounted as a hypothesis. That's why I use the word "provisional."

It's fascinating because everything you have said up until now suggests that you should be an atheist. Why hold out the specter that maybe there was some divine presence that got the whole thing going?
Well, because there's a possibility that a god or gods—I don't think it would resemble anything of the Judeo-Christian variety—or a super-intelligent force came along and started the universe with a Big Bang and moved on to the next universe. I can't discount that.

Let's just play this out for a minute. If there was this creative . . . whatever you want to call it . . .
Intelligence.

This intelligence that got our universe going, what happened to that intelligence? Did it go off to the next universe?
That's what I mean. That's exactly what I said. (*Laughs*)

Thirteen billion years ago, it left and went somewhere else?
Well, they are now either lurking on the outer reaches of the universe, watching with some amusement as the eons passed, to see how the experiment worked out, or they moved on. Who can say?

I think this is actually of great importance when we're talking about science and religion. There are a lot of people who discount the literal interpretation of the Bible because it does not square with modern science. And even "God" is such a loaded word. What if we put that word aside? Can we talk about energy or some sort of cosmic force?
That's why I say I leave this to the astrophysicist.

Not the religious scholars?
Oh, of course not. They don't know enough. Literally. I hope I'm not being insulting. But you can't talk about these subjects now without knowing a great

deal of theoretical physics, particularly astrophysics and developments in astronomy concerning the origins and evolution of the universe. But one thing we may very well be able to understand from start to finish—we haven't done it yet—is the origin of life on this planet. And that's what counts for human beings. Where we came from. And it's beginning to look—it's looking pretty persuasively—that we are in fact ultimately physical and chemical in nature, and that we evolved autonomously on this planet by ourselves. There's no evidence whatsoever that we're being overseen or directed in our evolution and actions by a supernatural force.

This raises another question. I know evolutionary biologists disagree on this point—whether there is some inevitable progress in the course of evolution. In other words, once the simplest forms of life appeared on Earth, was it inevitable that eons down the road, some highly intelligent creature would evolve—like humans?

Yeah, philosophers love this question, and scientists like to stay away from philosophers. To get involved is like a bird landing on tangled feet. Let me see if I can square away the idea of progress. If you define progress as an increase in complexity—say, going from a simple bacterium-like organism up to an advanced animal or human society—there's no question that evolution has progressed. But if you see it as some kind of teleological force that is moving evolution along, that there will be progress in the universe from A to Z, you cannot see that in evolution. Progress is basically a human concept.

On the other hand, if you subscribe to the evolutionary viewpoint, but you also want to find some larger purpose, it would seem to be comforting that evolution moves toward greater complexity. It will keep evolving into something that's bigger and greater.

Well, I'm an existential conservative. I take the view that the human species has evolved to be a biological part of this biosphere. We belong in this biosphere. We are intimately connected to it. Our physiology, our psychology. This planet can actually be a paradise if we use our intelligence to make it so. That, to me, would be progress.

You're saying humans have purpose here.

Yeah, they have purpose to live long and be happy.

More than that. They have purpose to be good stewards of this Earth.

I believe so, yes. When you unpack happiness into satisfaction, fulfillment, vision, awe, a sense of higher purpose and quality, we have that ability. And I think it will be reached not by traditional religious faith but by knowledge and human self-understanding.

There are some people who talk about evolution as a kind of secular religion. The philosopher Michael Ruse has made this argument. He talks about "evolutionism." If you want to identify the characteristics of a religion—a complete, all-encompassing worldview, with an origin story—you can find that in the theory of evolution.

Maybe Michael, who is a friend of mine, was talking about me. I often write in a spiritual tone, particularly on issues like biophilia—our relationship to the natural world, which is now a well-founded psychological principle. But let me say something about scientists, including those who work on evolution. Basically, they don't worry about things like this. They're not uplifted in this manner. They are journeymen doing this. They realize that the commerce of science is original discovery. That's our silver and gold. When you talk with them, they won't have a conversation like the one we're having now. They'll talk about the latest findings on ecosystems or the organization of California tidal pools. They go home, and watch television, and maybe go fishing. But basically, they are journeymen. There are relatively few people who are doing anything like a spiritual search.

You're saying scientists, for the most part, don't have existential crises?

That's correct. Most are not religious. They're quite happy with what they have. Therefore, scientism—or science as an alternative religion—is not, in my opinion, a valid comparison. I don't see it as having the qualities of a religion, in terms of obeisance to a supreme being or of an urge to proselytize.

Suppose, miraculously, there was proof of a transcendental plane out there. Would you find that comforting?

Sure. Let me take this opportunity to dispel the notion, the canard, that scientists are against transcendentalism, that they want to block any talk of it, particularly intelligent design. If any positive evidence could be found of a supernatural guiding force, there would be a land rush of scientists into it. What scientist would not want to participate in what would be one of the greatest discoveries of all time? Scientists are simply saying—particularly in reference to intelligent design—that it's not science and it's garbage until some evidence or working theory is produced. And they are suspicious because they see it coming from people who have a religious agenda.

I guess I'm asking a slightly different question of you personally. Would you like there to be evidence of God? Forget about this as a great scientific discovery. Just personally, given your background, would that be thrilling? Would that be comforting?

Well, it would certainly give you a lot of material to study and think about the rest of your time. But you didn't ask me the right question.

What's the right question?

Would I be happy if I discovered that I could go to heaven forever? And the answer is no. Consider this argument. Think about what is forever. And think about the fact that the human mind, the entire human being, is built to last a certain period of time. Our programmed hormonal systems, the way we learn, the way we settle upon beliefs, and the way we love are all temporary. Because we go through a life's cycle. Now, if we were to be plucked out at the age of 12 or 56 or whenever, and taken up and told, "Now you will continue your existence as you are. We're not going to blot out your memories. We're not going to diminish your desires." You will exist in a state of bliss—whatever that is—forever. And those who didn't make it are going to be consigned to darkness or hell. Now think, a trillion times a trillion years. Enough time for universes like this one to be born, explode, form countless star systems and planets, then fade away to entropy. You will sit there watching this happen millions and millions of times and that will just be the beginning of the eternity that you've been consigned to bliss in this existence.

This heaven would be your hell.

Yes. If we were able to evolve into something else, then maybe not. But we are not something else.

Francis Collins

AS THE DIRECTOR OF THE NATIONAL INSTITUTES of Health and the former head of the Human Genome Project, Francis Collins is one of America's most visible scientists. He holds impeccable scientific credentials—a medical degree as well as a doctorate in physics—and has a distinguished track record as a gene hunter. He's also an evangelical Christian, someone who has no qualms about professing his belief in miracles or seeing God's hand behind all of creation. The cover of his book illustrates this unusual mixture; the book's title, *The Language of God*, is superimposed on a drawing of the double helix. "The God of the Bible is also the God of the genome," he writes. "He can be worshiped in the cathedral or in the laboratory."

Collins wants to stake out the middle ground between Darwinian atheists and religious fundamentalists. "Both of these extremes don't stand up to logic, and yet they have occupied the stage," he told me. "We cannot let either side win." Unlike so many of those players most invested in this culture war, Collins sees no inherent conflict between science and religion. Yet his approach is likely to alienate plenty of people on both sides of the debate. His frequent references to God's almighty power might be difficult for secularists to swallow. His scathing critique of both young Earth creationism and intelligent design may turn off the religious fundamentalists who can't tolerate evolution.

The Language of God offers an unusually personal look at a leading scientist's search for meaning. Collins recounts his struggles with faith, as well as his daughter's rape by a man who broke into her apartment and held a knife to her throat. This trauma became a test of faith and a lesson in how suffering can lead to personal growth. His book also recaps his scientific triumphs, including his discovery of the long-sought gene that causes cystic fibrosis. Later, he stood by Bill Clinton's side when the president announced that the mapping of the human genome was complete. It turns out that Collins worked with the president's speechwriter to help craft a religious spin on this scientific breakthrough. "Today," Clinton said, "we are learning the language in which God created life."

I spoke with Collins about various scientific and religious matters—the existence of miracles, the mind of God, the ethics of stem cell research, and Collins's conversion to Christianity at the age of 27.

■ ■ ■ ■

You've said you were once an "obnoxious atheist." What changed you? Why did you turn to religion?
I became an atheist because as a graduate student studying quantum physics, life seemed to be reducible to second-order differential equations. Mathematics, chemistry, and physics had it all. And I didn't see any need to go beyond that. Frankly, I was at a point in my young life where it was convenient for me to not have to deal with God. I kind of liked being in charge myself. But then I went to medical school, and I watched people who were suffering from terrible diseases. And one of my patients, after telling me about her faith and how it supported her through her terrible heart pain, turned to me and said, "What about you? What do you believe?" And I stuttered and stammered and felt the color rise in my face, and said, "Well, I don't think I believe in anything." But it suddenly seemed like a very thin answer. And that was unsettling. I was a scientist who was supposed to draw conclusions from the evidence, and I realized at that moment that I'd never really looked at the evidence for and against the possibility of God.

In your book you describe this as a "thoroughly terrifying experience."
It was. It was like my worldview was suddenly under attack. So I set about reading about the various world religions, but I didn't understand their concepts and their various dogmas. So I went down the street and met with a

Methodist minister in this little town in North Carolina and asked him a number of blasphemous questions. And he smiled and answered a few of them but said, "You know, I think you'd learn a lot if you'd read this book on my shelf. It was written by somebody who has traveled the same path—a scholar who was an atheist at Oxford and tried to figure out whether there was truth or not to religion." The book was *Mere Christianity* by C. S. Lewis. And within the first three pages, I realized that my arguments against faith were those of a schoolboy.

So that one book totally changed your life?
Absolutely. It was as if he was reading my mind. As I read his arguments about the moral law—the knowledge of right and wrong, which makes no sense from the perspective of basic evolution and biology but makes great sense as a signpost to God—I began to realize the truth of what he was saying. Ultimately, I realized I couldn't go back to where I was. I could never again say atheism is the only logical choice for a scientifically trained person.

You also write about a seminal experience you had a little later, when you were hiking in the Cascade Mountains in Washington.
Nobody gets argued all the way into becoming a believer on the sheer basis of logic and reason. That requires a leap of faith. And that leap of faith seemed very scary to me. After I had struggled with this for a couple of years, I was hiking in the Cascade Mountains on a beautiful fall afternoon. I turned the corner and saw in front of me this frozen waterfall, a couple of hundred feet high. Actually, a waterfall that had three parts to it—also the symbolic three in one. At that moment, I felt my resistance leave me. And it was a great sense of relief. The next morning, in the dewy grass in the shadow of the Cascades, I fell on my knees and accepted this truth—that God is God, that Christ is His son, and that I am giving my life to that belief.

You went on to become a hotshot gene hunter at the University of Michigan. Your lab made some important discoveries about the genes that cause several diseases. Did you keep your religious faith secret from your fellow scientists?

No, I didn't. I don't think I was particularly outspoken about it. But I was never secretive either. And I did at times offer to meet with medical students who wanted to discuss science and faith, and whether they were compatible. But certainly, the academic environment is not particularly welcoming to open discussions of this sort. There's a bit of an unwritten taboo that you can talk about almost anything else in terms of the search for truth, but maybe you ought not to talk about religion. It might offend somebody.

A lot of scientists say religious faith is irrational. Your fellow biologist Richard Dawkins calls it "the great cop-out." How do you respond to these critics of religion?
Certainly this has been one of the more troubling developments in the last several decades. I think that commits an enormous act of hubris, to say— because we're now so wise about evolution and how life-forms are related to each other—that we have no more need of God. Science investigates the natural world. If God has any meaning at all, God is outside of the natural world. It is a complete misuse of the tools of science to apply them to this discussion.

So God is outside of space and time?
I would say so. And God is certainly outside of nature. So for a scientist to say, "I know for sure there is no God," seems to commit a very serious logical fallacy. Frankly, I think many of the current battles between atheists and fundamentalists have really been started by the scientific community. This is an enormous tragedy of our present time, that we've given the stage to the extremists.

Why do you say those arguments have been started by scientists? Because some of these scientists—like Dawkins—have said the theory of evolution leads to atheism?
That's been a very scary statement coming back towards the religious community, where people have felt they can't just leave that hanging in the air. There has to be a response. If you look at the history of the intelligent design movement, you will see that it was a direct response to claims coming from

people like Dawkins. They could not leave this claim unchallenged—that evolution alone can explain all of life's complexity. It sounded like a godless outcome.

So, one response then is simply to dismiss evolution—to say it doesn't hold up as science.
I think that's what many well-intentioned, sincere believers have done. The shelves of many evangelicals are full of books that point out the flaws in evolution, discuss it only as a theory, and almost imply that there's a conspiracy here to avoid the fact that evolution is actually flawed. All of those books, unfortunately, are based upon conclusions that no reasonable biologist would now accept. Evolution is about as solid a theory as one will ever see.

Obviously, you're saying you should not read the Bible literally, especially the story of Genesis.
That also seems very threatening to many believers who have been led to believe that if you start watering down any part of the Bible, including a literal interpretation of Genesis 1, then pretty soon you'll lose your faith and you won't believe that Christ died and was resurrected. But you cannot claim that the Earth is less than 10,000 years old unless you're ready to reject all of the fundamental findings of geology, cosmology, physics, chemistry, and biology. You really have to throw out all of the sciences in order to draw that conclusion.

Intelligent design is a more sophisticated critique of evolution. The core argument is that certain natural phenomena, such as human blood clotting and the eye, are irreducibly complex; you can't get these through incremental genetic mutations. What's wrong with this argument?
It's a very interesting argument, but I fear there's a flaw. The intelligent design argument presumes that these complicated, multicomponent systems—the most widely described one is the bacterial flagellum, a little outboard motor that allows bacteria to zip around in a liquid solution—that you couldn't get there unless you could simultaneously evolve about 30 different proteins. And until you had all 30 together, you would gain no advantage. The problem is it

makes an assumption that's turning out to be wrong. All of those multicomponent machines, including the flagellum, do not come forth out of nothingness. They come forth very gradually by the recruitment of one component that does one fairly modest thing. And then another component that was doing something else gets recruited in and causes a slightly different kind of function. And over the course of long periods of time, one can in fact come up with very plausible models to develop these molecular machines solely through the process of evolution as Darwin envisaged it. So intelligent design is already showing serious cracks. It is not subject to actual scientific testing.

This is what's often called "the God of the gaps." You use God to explain certain things that science can't explain. You're saying these arguments end up hurting religious people because once science does explain these things, it discredits religion.

And that has happened down through time. When God is inserted in a place where science can't currently provide enough information, then sooner or later, it does. My God is bigger than that. He's not threatened by our puny minds trying to understand how the universe works. And He didn't design evolution so that it had flaws and had to be fixed all along the way. My God is this amazing creator who, at the very moment that the Big Bang occurred, already had designed how evolution would come into place to result in this marvelous diversity of living things.

This gets at what I think is actually the more serious challenge that evolution poses to religious faith—the whole business of random genetic mutations. Certainly, many evolutionists have argued that there is no inherent meaning to the course of evolution. It could end up any which way, and the fact that human beings ever evolved was blind luck. Without the asteroid that wiped out the dinosaurs 65 million years ago, it seems unlikely that large mammals, and eventually humans, would have ever evolved. Isn't this a problem for religion?

I don't think so. I can see the arguments that you just voiced and why they trouble people. But they are based upon the idea that God has the same limitations that we do. We cannot contemplate what it is like to be able to affect the future, the present, and the past all at once. But God is not so limited. What appears random to us—such as an asteroid hitting the Earth—need not have been random to Him at all. And in that very moment of creation, being as He is, outside of the time limitations, He knew everything, including our having this conversation. As soon as you accept the idea of God as creator, then the randomness argument essentially goes out the window.

Are you saying that God set the natural laws in motion so that somehow, billions of years later, humans would evolve? There was intent, there was purpose to humans evolving, and God made it so?

That is part of my faith—to believe that God did have an interest in the appearance, somewhere in the universe, of creatures with intelligence, with free will, with the moral law, with the desire to seek Him.

Is this to say that God set in motion the asteroid that wiped out the dinosaurs so that human beings could eventually evolve?

Oh goodness, that's getting into more specific details than I would dare to imagine. But I would say that God had a plan for creatures like us. Need they have looked exactly like us? Does "in His image" mean that God looks like us and has toenails and a belly button? Or is "in His image" an indication of the spirit, the moral law, the sense of who we are, the consciousness? In which case perhaps it didn't matter so much whether that ended up occurring in mammals or some other life-form.

What do you say to those evolutionists—people like E. O. Wilson and Dan Dennett—who look to evolutionary reasons for why human beings have come to believe in religion? They say religion is clearly a very powerful bonding force. It unites people. Even moral values like altruism have a genetic component. It may have evolved to help people related to you because there's a shared genetic interest.

I have trouble with the argument that altruism can be completely explained on evolutionary grounds. Evolutionists now universally agree—I think Dawkins and Wilson and Dennett would all agree—that evolution does not operate on the species. It operates on the individual. If that's the case, then it does seem that in any given circumstance, the individual's evolutionary drive should be to preserve their ability to reproduce at all costs. They're simply—as Dawkins has described them—a way of propagating DNA. That's what we are. But that's not what I see in my own heart. And it's not what I see in those around me. I see Oskar Schindler, who sacrificed his own potential for long-term survival by saving Jews—not even people of his own faith. When I see Mother Teresa dedicating herself to help others, not even of her own tribe, we admire that. What is that all about? If I'm walking down the banks of a river and I hear someone who's drowning calling for help—even if I'm not a good swimmer—I feel this urge that I should try to help, even at the risk of my own life. Where is that coming from?

But you and I have grown up with certain moral lessons. We've been told that we should help people. This is the right thing to do. Couldn't you argue that doing good and helping people is just part of cultural evolution?

You could argue that, but if it was just a cultural tradition, you ought to be able to find some cultures where it is not present. If you read the appendix of C. S. Lewis's wonderful book *The Abolition of Man*, he comes to the conclusion that there is this wonderful, monotonous repetition of morals across the world and across history. You are to reach out to those who are less fortunate. You are to aid the widow, you are to help the orphan. All of these altruistic things seem to be a universal feature of human beings. And yet they're a scandal to evolutionary biology because they motivate people to do things that are exactly the opposite of what evolution would require.

The subtitle of your book refers to "evidence for belief." What do you find to be the most compelling evidence that there is, in fact, a supreme being?

First of all, we have this very solid conclusion that the universe had an origin, the Big Bang. Fifteen billion years ago, the universe began with an unimaginably bright flash of energy from an infinitesimally small point. That implies that before that, there was nothing. I can't imagine how nature, in this case the universe, could have created itself. And the very fact that the universe had a beginning implies that someone was able to begin it. And it seems to me that had to be outside of nature. And that sounds like God.

A second argument: When you look from the perspective of a scientist at the universe, it looks as if it knew we were coming. There are 15 constants—the gravitational constant, various constants about the strong and weak nuclear force, et cetera—that have precise values. If any one of those constants was off by even one part in a million, or in some cases, by one part in a million million, the universe could not have actually come to the point where we see it. Matter would not have been able to coalesce, there would have been no galaxy, stars, planets, or people. That's a phenomenally surprising observation. It seems almost impossible that we're here. And that does make you wonder—gosh, who was setting those constants anyway? Scientists have not been able to figure that out.

What I find interesting about your argument is that, in many ways, it lines up with the deist position—that God created everything to begin with, set in motion the laws of nature, and didn't intervene after that. And yet, I don't think that's your position.
No, it's not.

You are talking about a God who intervenes in the world—the presence of a personal God.
Right. I haven't quite finished my list of evidences. I started with the deist ones—which are the Big Bang and the anthropic principle—very strong arguments, by the way. But that doesn't get you to a personal God. The argument that gets me is the one I read in those first few pages of *Mere Christianity*, which is the existence of the moral law, something good and holy, that in our hearts has somehow written that same law about what is good and what is evil and what we should do. That doesn't sound like a God that wandered off once the universe got started and is now doing something else. That sounds like a God who really cares about us and wishes somehow to have a relationship with us.

But you've also said that God exists outside of nature, outside of space and time. So how can God intervene in our lives? How can God come into our hearts?

By saying that He's outside of space and time, I didn't mean that there is some wall around the natural that God is not also part of. I guess I should have said that God is not limited by space and time. So I have no trouble with that concept at all—that God both knows the future and yet can hear my prayer as I'm seeking to find out what I should do in a given situation.

Do you think God answers your prayers?

I've never heard God speak. Some people have. I don't think prayer is really a way that you try to manipulate God's intentions and talk Him into something. I don't think He's going to find me a parking space when I'm having trouble finding one. Prayer is really a way that you try to get in touch with God. And in the process, you learn something about yourself and your own motivations, often discovering things about yourself that you don't necessarily want to discover.

I guess I'm trying to figure out if you think God intervenes in the affairs of human beings. Virtually all of your arguments so far suggest He does not. God stays out of the realm of humanity.

I think God can intervene. That's what the great miracles are. Certainly God intervened in the person of Jesus Christ and in the most amazing miracle of all, the Resurrection. But I don't think God pops up in lots of circumstances and turns around the course of events or alters the way in which nature is going to behave. I think those are reserved for special moments, of special significance, with a special lesson involved.

Well, I have to ask you about a couple of the best-known miracles in the Bible. Do you believe in the Virgin Birth?

I do.

And the Resurrection? Do you believe that what was resurrected was the physical body of Jesus?

Physical body? We should be careful in terms of exactly what you mean by that. Does that mean the cellular structure was exactly the same as it was when he was alive? I don't know. But I believe that he was resurrected in physical form and seen by witnesses whom he spoke to before he then ascended. That is the absolute cornerstone of the Christian faith.

But how can you as a scientist accept some of these ideas in the Bible that cut so directly against the laws of nature?

I have no trouble at all. Again, the big decision is, do you believe in God? If you believe in God, and if God is more than nature, then there's no reason that God could not stage an invasion into the natural world, which—to our limited perspective—would appear to be a miracle.

Yet this does seem to be a case where religion and science are in fundamental conflict. Everything we know from science says this is not possible. The Virgin Birth is not possible. The resurrection of a dead person—no matter how special—is not possible. It's never happened in the history of the world, as far as we know.

Again, that would be the perspective if one had decided up front that the only worldview that can be brought to bear on any circumstance is the scientific one. In that situation, all miracles have to be impossible. If, on the other hand, you're willing to accept the spiritual worldview, then in certain rare circumstances—I don't think they should be common—the miraculous could have a nonzero probability.

So far, we haven't talked about your work as head of the Human Genome Project. Why do you call the human genome "the language of God"?

Well, it's a metaphor. It's one that was used by President Clinton on June 26, 2000, when the announcement was made that the draft of the human DNA sequence was now in hand. I think it's a thought-provoking way to consider this whole question: Where did all this come from, anyway? If you accept my premise—that God was actually the author of the evolutionary process, that it was His way of speaking life into being—then you can think of the genome, the DNA, as God's language. And for the believer, it's also a small glimpse into God's mind.

Geneticists are sometimes accused of "playing God," especially when it comes to genetic engineering. There are various thorny bioethical issues. What's your position on stem cell research?

Stem cells have been discussed for ten years, and yet I fear that much of that discussion has been more heat than light. First of all, I believe that the product of a sperm and an egg, which is the first cell that goes on to develop a human being, deserves considerable moral consequences. This is an entity that ultimately becomes a human. So I would be opposed to the idea of creating embryos by mixing sperm and eggs together and then experimenting on the outcome of that, purely to understand research questions. On the other hand, there are hundreds of thousands of such embryos in freezers at in vitro fertilization clinics. In the process of in vitro fertilization, you almost invariably end up with more embryos than you can reimplant safely. The plausibility of those ever being reimplanted in the future—more than a few of them—is extremely low. Is it more ethical to leave them in those freezers forever or throw them away? Or is it more ethical to come up with some sort of use for those embryos that could help people? I think that's not been widely discussed.

So your position is that they should be used for research if they already exist and they're never going to be used to create a human life?

I think that's the more ethical stance. And I say this as a private citizen and not as a representative of the U.S. government, even though I've been employed by the federal government at the National Institutes of Health. Now let me say, there's another aspect of this topic that I think is even more confusing—a different approach which is more promising medically. It's this thing called somatic cell nuclear transfer, which is where you take a cell from a living person—a skin cell, for instance. You take out its nucleus, which is where the DNA is, and you insert that nucleus into the environment of an egg cell, which has lost its nucleus. Now think about this. We have a skin cell, and we have an egg cell with no nucleus. Neither of those would be things that anybody would argue has moral status. Then you give a zap of electricity and you wait a couple of days. And that environment convinces that skin cell that it can go back in time and it can become anything it wants to be. That is an enormously powerful opportunity, because the cell would then be received by that same person who happened to need, say, neurons for their Parkinson's disease or pancreas cells for their diabetes without a transplant rejection.

Isn't this the process that is otherwise known as cloning?
Yeah, it's called cloning, which is a very unfortunate term because it conjures up the idea that you're trying to create a copy of that human being. And at this point, you're doing nothing of the sort. You're trying to create a cell line that could be used to substitute for something that a person desperately needs. It would only become a cloned person if you then intentionally decided to take those cells and reimplant them in the uterus of a recipient woman. And that, obviously, is something that we should not and must not do and probably should legislate against. But until you get to that point, it's not clear to me that you're dealing with something that deserves to be called an embryo or deserves to be given moral status.

Is the question of when life begins a scientific question or a religious question?
It's a religious question. I mean, science can tell you what happens in terms of the mechanics of DNA coming out of the sperm and the egg and joining together to make a full set of chromosomes. And science can tell you all the steps that happen with various genes getting turned on and off and various cell types appearing. But none of that really tells you what your question is: At what point does this acquire the status of a human being as a moral entity? When does life begin? When does the soul enter? That's a religious question. Science is not going to be able to help with that.

Sam Harris

THREE-QUARTERS OF ALL AMERICANS BELIEVE the Bible is God's word, according to a Pew Research Center poll. Numbers like that make an outspoken atheist like Sam Harris either foolhardy or uncommonly brave.

In 2004, when he launched a full-scale attack on religious belief in his book *The End of Faith*, Sam Harris was an unknown. That changed overnight when his book shot up the *New York Times* best-seller list and later went on to win the 2005 PEN Award for Nonfiction. Since then, *The End of Faith* has earned an avid following among atheists and lapsed churchgoers; it's the kind of book that gets passed around from one friend to another to another. Here, finally, was someone willing to do the unthinkable: denounce religious faith as irrational—murderous, even.

The heart of Harris's book is a frontal assault on Islam and Christianity, with page after page of quotations from the Quran imploring the faithful to kill infidels and a chilling history of how Christian leaders have punished heretics. He argues that much of the violence in today's world stems directly from people willing to live and die by these sacred texts.

In perhaps his most daring rhetorical gambit, Harris seeks to undermine religion by denouncing not just jihadists and fundamentalists but moderates. "Religious moderates are, in large part, responsible for the religious conflict in our world," he writes, "because their beliefs provide the context in which scriptural literalism and religious violence can never be adequately opposed." He especially chastises moderates for refusing to criticize Scripture-quoting extremists; for him, they are guilty of legitimating fundamentalism.

All this would seem to make Harris a hero among atheists. To a large degree, it has. Yet some atheists can't stomach the end of Harris's book, where he plays up the virtues of spirituality and mysticism, as well as serious meditation. He is a longtime practitioner of Buddhist meditation—an outgrowth of the many years he spent studying the contemplative traditions of both East and West. Although he's scathing about monotheism, he's far gentler in his assessment of Eastern religions. For all his insistence on reason and scientific study, Harris is surprisingly open—as I discovered in this interview—to paranormal experiences like telepathy and even the possibility of consciousness existing outside the human brain.

Harris completed a doctorate in neuroscience, studying the neural basis of belief and disbelief. He keeps most of the details of his personal life vague. When I asked about his research, he said he preferred not to say where he's working on it "to keep the scary people away from the lab." It appears that Harris's academic future may have to compete with his writing career. His follow-up book, *Letter to a Christian Nation*, was also a best-seller. It was his response to the thousands of angry letters he received from devout Christians about his first book.

■ ■ ■ ■

Your book *The End of Faith* has become one of the touchstones for atheists across America. Because you don't seem to have any qualms about denouncing the Bible or the Quran, you've emerged as perhaps America's critic-in-chief of religious faith. Is that a role you willingly embrace?
Well, I did not embrace it consciously. In fact, it's ironic that some of the most vituperative criticism I've gotten has come from atheists because, in the last chapter of my book, I talk about meditation and mystical experience. While I'm a very strident critic of religious faith, my argument doesn't totally line up with the biases that atheists tend to have.

But 90 percent of your book is a rather strident attack on religion. One reviewer described it as "nuclear assault" on religion. I'm wondering why

you chose to write this way. Maybe this is just how you feel. Or was it a strategic decision to write such a polemical attack on religion?

No, it was not in any sense strategic. It was really my immediate response to the events of September 11—the moment it became apparent to me that we were meandering into a religious war with the Muslim world and were not going to call it as such, and paradoxically, in our efforts to console ourselves, we were becoming increasingly deranged by our own religious certainty. We have a society in which 44 percent of the people claim to be either certain or confident that Jesus is going to come back out of the clouds and judge the living and the dead sometime in the next 50 years. It just seems to me transparently obvious that this is a belief that will do nothing to create a durable civilization. And I think it's time someone spoke about it.

Is that what especially worries you—the apocalyptic thinking that crops up in certain religions, whether we're talking about Islam or Christianity? Or is it much broader than that—what you see to be the intellectual dishonesty in a lot of religious discussions?

My concern can be parsed out on many levels. The most basic is that our world has really been shattered unnecessarily by competing religious certainties. People who believe their religious propositions strongly are doing so for bad reasons and on insufficient evidence. There's just nothing that a fundamentalist Christian and a fundamentalist Muslim can say to one another to revise their mutual understanding of the world, because they do not have a mutual understanding of the world. Their core beliefs have been taken off the table and have become resistant to conversation. So now we have Muslims tending to side with other Muslims in geopolitical conflicts, and Christians tending to side with other Christians. And this breeds conflict that would not otherwise occur. I think it is a profoundly widespread and disempowering myth, particularly among secularists and religious moderates, that these people would be killing each other anyway—killing each other over land or scarce resources.

That certainly is the other argument—what we're seeing in the Middle East is more political than religious. Religion may be used to buttress

ɔlitical arguments. **But ultimately, if you take, say, Hamas, the**
ɪere is against Israel. **It's not an argument about faith.**

that's misreading the situation. When you ask why these people cannot
live ɪ̇appily together on the same piece of land, the answer is a religious one.
Muslims and Jews see the world differently because of their incompatible
religious claims—literally, claims upon certain real estate. And they view the
disposition of this real estate in biblical or Quranic terms. That's a deal breaker.
More specifically, when you look at the style of violence on the Muslim side—
the suicide bombing—that can really only be made sense of in religious terms.
Once you accept some of the core propositions of Islam—once you accept the
metaphysics of martyrdom and the principle of jihad—then it becomes
perfectly reasonable that a mother could celebrate the suicidal atrocities committed by her son, because she thinks he's gone to paradise and he's killed
infidels in the process. And he's paved the way for the whole family to get to
paradise. If you actually believe these things, this behavior becomes quite
understandable.

You really go after Islam and Christianity and Judaism. Why are you
especially critical of monotheistic religions?
Part of that is just a matter of how much mad work is being done in the name
of those faiths at this moment. I would rank them in order of Islam and Christianity and then Judaism coming up a distant third. But there's also something
intrinsic to monotheism itself which is problematic. Monotheism tends to be
far more rigid than other approaches to faith and far less able to incorporate
the incompatible religious certainties of other groups. The Hindus, worshiping
a dizzying profusion of gods, can accept an extra god when they come upon
it. And so there are Hindus who talk about Jesus being an avatar of Vishnu,
for instance.

You're saying with monotheism, the whole notion of the heretic or the
infidel is much more of an issue than it would be in other religions where
there is not just one god.
Yeah. When you look at the doctrine of Islam, and you consider the state of
Muslim discourse in the twenty-first century, it is hard to imagine a doctrine

that is less susceptible to modernity and pluralism. There are many apologists for Islam saying it's a religion of peace and Muslims are tolerant of other religions. I really think we owe it to ourselves and to future generations to be very clear and rigorous about what is actually believed by mainstream Muslims. What we recently saw in Afghanistan—this man who converted to Christianity and was up for execution, and then got spirited away to Italy as the only accommodation that could be made—that really is the true face of Islam. It really is punishable by death to wake up one morning and decide you no longer want to be a Muslim. The crime of apostasy, the disavowal of your religion, is a capital offense. We're not waging a war of ideas that's even addressing issues like this.

But doesn't it matter where we're talking about? I mean, Indonesia, the most populous Muslim country in the world, for the most part doesn't have this more extreme version of Islam.

For the most part. There are cells in Indonesia that are considered al Qaida affiliates. And you'd be hard-pressed to find a Muslim country, even Turkey, that does not have elements that should be troublesome to us. But it's true, the character of Islam is different in different societies. And that's a good thing. I think we can attribute that to the fact that most people do not take their religion as seriously as they might. But when you look at the theology, the truth is, the Quran really does nothing more eloquently than vilify the infidel. It's absolutely plain in the pages of the Quran that the responsibility of Muslims is to convert, subjugate, or kill the infidel. This is not a document that's well designed for a pluralistic world or a global civil society. Unless the Muslim world can find some way of reforming this theology, or find some rationale by which to ignore the better part of it—as Christians have tended to do, albeit imperfectly—we have a recipe for disaster on our hands.

What about the Bible? Do you see this as a recipe for religious intolerance?

Oh, I do. There's no document that I know of that is more despicable in its morality than the first few books of the Hebrew Bible. Books like Exodus and Deuteronomy and Leviticus, these are diabolical books. The killing never stops. The reasons to kill your neighbor for theological crimes are explicit and preposterous. You have to kill people for worshiping foreign gods, for working on the Sabbath, for wizardry, for adultery. You kill your children for talking back to you. It's there and it's not a matter of metaphors. It is exactly what God expects us to do to rein in the free thought of our neighbors.

Now, it just so happens, however, that most Christians think there's something in the New Testament that fully and finally repudiates all of that. Therefore, we do not have to kill homosexuals. We don't have to kill adulterers. And that's a very good thing that most Christians think it. Now, most Christians actually are not on very firm ground theologically to think that. It's not an accident that St. Thomas Aquinas and St. Augustine thought we should kill or torture heretics. Aquinas thought we should kill them, Augustine thought we should torture them. And Augustine's argument for the use of torture actually laid the foundations for the Inquisition. So it's not an accident that we were burning heretics and witches and other people in Europe for five centuries under the aegis of Christianity. But Christianity is at a different moment in its history.

But isn't this a problem mainly when you read the Bible or the Quran literally? Doesn't the conversation change once you stop reading sacred Scriptures literally? If you understand, for instance, the historical context—when Judaism or Christianity was first emerging, they were religions competing with other religions. Doesn't that free you up to appreciate their spiritual teachings?

I'd be the first to agree that it's better not to read these books literally. The problem is, the books never tell you that you're free not to read them literally. In fact, they tell you otherwise, explicitly so. Therefore, the fundamentalist is always on firmer ground theologically and—I would argue—intellectually than the moderate or the progressive. When you consult the books, you do not find more reasons to be a moderate or a liberal. You find more reasons to be a fundamentalist. I agree, it is a good thing to be cherry-picking these books and ignoring the bad parts. But we should have a twenty-first-century conversation about morality and spiritual experience and public policy that is not constrained by superstition and taboo. In order to see how preposterous our situation really is, you need only imagine what our world would be like if we had people believing in the literal existence of Zeus. I defy anyone to come forward with the evidence that puts the biblical God or the Quranic God on fundamentally different footing than the gods of Mt. Olympus. There are historical reasons why Zeus is no longer worshiped and the God of Abraham is. But there are not sound epistemological or philosophical or empirical reasons.

There's no doubt many awful things have been done in the name of religion over the centuries. But of course, there have also been many wonderful religious people. I would argue, for instance, that Martin Luther King Jr. has been the most important moral leader in America over the last century. I think it would be impossible to make sense of what he did without talking about his faith. It seems to me his Christian faith compelled him to be an activist and it's what gave him strength in very difficult times. What do you make of those kinds of people who've been inspired because of their faith?

I agree, King was an incredible person who did heroic and necessary work. A couple of answers here. There's no evidence that those things can only be done in the name of faith, whereas there is considerable evidence that really terrible acts of violence are being done only because of what people believe about God. For instance, while there are Christian missionaries working in sub-Saharan Africa doing heroic work to relieve famine, there are also secular people, like Doctors Without Borders, who work alongside them, doing the same kind of work and not doing it because they think Jesus was born of a virgin. They're not preaching the sinfulness of condom use the way Catholics and Christian ministers tend to do. So while Christian missionaries are helping people, they're also helping to spread AIDS with their sexual taboos and their prudery. So that's one issue.

I'm also breaking a taboo. I'm rejecting the idea that all of our religions are equally wise and emphasize compassion to the same degree. This is just clearly not true. Martin Luther King, to some significant degree, was animated by Christianity. But when you look at why he preached nonviolence to the degree that he did, he didn't get that from Christianity. He got it from Gandhi.

And Gandhi got it from the Jains. Jainism is a religion of India that preaches this doctrine of nonviolence. To argue that that's the true face of Christianity is really misleading. Christianity also gives you the Jesus of the *Left Behind* novels who's going to come back and just hurl sinners into the pit. And the God who's going to punish homosexuals for eternity.

That's highly debatable, though. If you're a Christian and you look at the figure of Jesus, you can easily read his core message as being about love and compassion and caring, particularly for the outcasts of society.
That is Jesus in half his moods speaking that way. But there's another Jesus in there. There's a Jesus who's just paradoxical and difficult to interpret, a Jesus who tells people to hate their parents. And then there is the Jesus—while he may not be as plausible given how we want to think about Jesus—but he's there in Scripture, coming back amid a host of angels, destined to deal out justice to the sinners of the world. That is the Jesus that fully half of the American electorate is most enamored of at this moment.

Let me follow up on that, because a lot of people say the problem is that religion has been hijacked by the extremists—people who've distorted the basic religious teachings of peace and love. But this, as far as I can tell, is not your view. You say religious moderates are largely responsible for religious conflict.
Well, I think religious moderation is a politically correct discourse about all religions truly being benign in their essence and just being hijacked by people who are psychologically unstable or political megalomaniacs. This is a false view. And it's giving cover to religious extremists. This respect for faith, this taboo against criticizing faith, prevents us from saying the necessary things that we must say against religious fundamentalism.

But wouldn't it make more sense to support the religious moderates, the people who really do not support those fundamentalists? Otherwise, you are removing the middle ground. In essence, if you take away the moderates, you're pitting fundamentalists against secularists. And a lot of people don't buy that dichotomy. I'm thinking of all the people

in the United States who've rejected the dogmas of the churches they grew up in but who still believe there is some transcendent reality out there.

It depends on what you mean by transcendent reality. I believe there's a transcendent reality out there, but that belief doesn't give me the slightest inclination to pay lip service to the God of the Bible or to deny the immoral message that comes through in many books of the Bible. I just think it's a myth we finally have to put to rest that our morality is necessarily linked to these scriptural traditions. The Bible is just not a good lens through which to view our present circumstance, given all that we've learned in the last 2,000 years. So questions of stem cell research, questions of social equity are not best processed through a reading of the Bible, however liberal you want to be.

We've been talking about how intolerant so many religious people can be. But aren't you asking us to be very intolerant of religion?

It may sound paradoxical, but it's not. I'm advocating a kind of conversational intolerance. It's really the same intolerance we express everywhere in our society when someone claims that Elvis is still alive, or that aliens are abducting ranchers and molesting them. These are beliefs that many people have. But these beliefs systematically exclude them from holding positions of responsibility. The person who's sure that Elvis is still alive and expresses this belief candidly does not wind up in the Oval Office or in our nation's boardrooms. And that's a very good thing. But when the conversation changes to Jesus being born of a virgin or Muhammad flying to heaven on a winged horse, then these beliefs not only do not exclude you from holding power in society; you could not possibly hold power, in a political sense, without endorsing this kind of thinking.

It should be terrifying to us, because many of these beliefs are not just quaint and curious, like beliefs in Elvis. These are beliefs about the end of history, about the utility of trying to create a sustainable civilization for ourselves—specifically, beliefs in eschatology. These are maladaptive. For instance, if a mushroom cloud replaced the city of New York tomorrow morning, something like half the American people would see a silver lining in that cloud because it would presage to them that the end of days are upon us.

I want to step back for a moment and talk about your own background. Did religion play any part in your childhood?
Not really. I had a very secular upbringing. But when I became about 16 or 17, I got very interested in spiritual experience and the possibilities of seeing the world in a fundamentally different sense.

Did you pursue those spiritual interests?
Yeah, I've spent a lot of time studying meditation and sitting on meditation retreats where you're in silence for the entire duration, whether it's one month or three months, just practicing meditation for sometimes 18 hours a day. I've done this mostly in a Buddhist context, but not exclusively. And I've spent a lot of time studying religion and the contemplative traditions within Christianity and Judaism and Islam.

So you don't see Buddhism as being limiting in the same way as the monotheistic religions you've been criticizing?
Well, I certainly see it as limiting insofar as it's a religion. You can make the argument that Buddhism, specifically, is not best thought of as a religion. And certainly many Western Buddhists say that Buddhism is not a religion. But that doesn't change the fact that something like 99 percent of the Buddhists in this world practice Buddhism as a religion in the same superstitious way that most religions are practiced. Now, it doesn't have the same liabilities of Islam or Christianity. You can't get the same kind of death cult brewing in Buddhism, or at least not as readily. And that's why we don't see Tibetan Buddhist suicide bombers.

You know, the Tibetans have suffered a terrible occupation under the Chinese. Many people estimate that 1.1 or 1.2 million Tibetans have died as a result of that occupation. We should see Tibetan Buddhists blowing themselves up on Chinese buses, if all religions are equivalent. But we don't see that. What we do see in Tibetan Buddhism—which is impossible to even imagine in Islam at the moment—we see Tibetans who have been tortured for decades in Chinese prisons, coming out and saying things like, "My greatest fear while I was in prison was that I would lose the strength of my compassion and come to hate my torturers." Now, that said, there's nothing in Buddhism that's held dogmatically that I would support. It's just that all dogmas are not equal and don't have equal behavioral consequences.

It sounds like you've been meditating for years and often quite seriously. Have you ever felt bliss or rapture while you've meditated?

Oh yeah. The problem with those states, however, is that they are transitory. They are conditioned by concentration. And when your mind is no longer concentrated on your object of meditation—whether you're focusing on Jesus or a mantra or the state of rapture itself—when thoughts again intervene and you're no longer concentrated in the same way, the state goes. And one of the real pitfalls of the contemplative life is to crave those states. You can become a kind of drug addict of your own meditative process where you mistake those states as being the goal of meditation.

One thing I find so fascinating about your book is that you're out there as an atheist. Yet you also say life has a sacred dimension. You talk about the value of spirituality and mystical experiences. It's interesting that you put all that in the same pot.

Yeah, many atheists felt it should not have been in the same pot. But I think it's necessary to just be honest. These are some of the most beautiful and most profound experiences that human beings can have. And therefore we're right to want to understand them and to explore that landscape.

But it does raise the question, what do you mean by "spiritual"? And what do you mean by "mystical"?

By "spiritual" and "mystical"—I use them interchangeably—I mean any effort to understand and explore happiness and well-being itself through deliberate uses of attention. Specifically, to break the spell of discursive thought. We wake up each morning, and we're chased out of bed by our thoughts, and then we think, think, think, think all day long. And very few of us spend any significant amount of time breaking that train of thought. Meditation is one technique by which to do that. The sense that you are an ego, busy thinking, disappears. And its disappearance is quite a relief.

Well, it's interesting to hear this description of mysticism, because I don't think that's how most people would see it. I mean, most people would play up the more irrational side. Yes, you're losing yourself, but you're plunged into some larger sea of oneness, of perhaps transcendent presence. Obviously, you're staying away from that whole supernatural way of thinking.

Well, it's very Buddhist of me to do that. The Buddhists tend to talk in terms of what it's not. They talk about it being no self, they talk in terms of emptiness. But the theistic traditions talk in terms of what the experience is like. There, you get descriptions of fullness and rapture and love and oneness. And to some degree, I've had experiences that can be characterized that way. But there are pitfalls in using that language. People tend to reify these states and make metaphysics out of it. It's not like you learn about physics by being a mystic.

I want to ask you about one sentence from your book *The End of Faith*. You say, "Whatever is true now should be discoverable now." It sounds like you're putting inordinate faith in science. Are you willing to acknowledge that there might be plenty of things we still don't understand scientifically that could very well be true?

There's no scientist who would hesitate to acknowledge that. This is one of the ironies of religious discourse. Religious people talk in terms of their own humility and talk of the intellectual arrogance of science, whereas the situation is totally reversed. Every scientist worth his Ph.D. will admit that we have no idea how the universe, or why the universe, came into existence. We have no idea why there is everything rather than nothing. And most of what is there to be discovered has not been discovered.

Let me mention one case in point. There is a wealth of anthropological literature about sorcery in Africa and Latin America, and there are plenty of personal testimonies about the power of witchcraft. From the scientific

worldview, this looks like sheer nonsense. Yet I'm wondering if it might be possible that science someday will be able to explain what now seems supernatural.

Oh yeah, I think the only way to explain it is with a scientific frame of mind. Now, scientists tend to be dogmatically opposed to looking at this kind of phenomenon—at telepathy, for instance—because there's been so much fraud and wishful thinking. Science generally has been eager to divest itself of the spookiness of this area. But I think that kind of phenomenon is fascinating and worth looking into. And it may be that minds have some effect upon the physical world that we currently can't explain. But the way we will explain it is scientifically.

It sounds like you're open-minded to the possibility of telepathy—things that we might classify as psychic. You're saying it's entirely possible that they might be true and science at some point will be able to prove them.

Yeah, and there's a lot of data out there that's treated in most circles like intellectual pornography that attests to there being a real phenomenon here. I just don't know. But I've had the kinds of experiences that everyone has had that seem to confirm telepathy or the fact that minds can influence other minds.

Tell me about one of those experiences.

Oh, just knowing who's calling when that person hasn't called you in years. The phone rings and you know who it is and it's not your mother or your wife or someone who calls you every day. I've had many experiences like that. I know many people who've had even more bizarre experiences. But that does not rise to the level of scientific evidence. The only way to determine if it really exists is to look in a disinterested and sustained way at all of the evidence.

You are a neuroscientist. Do you think there's any chance that human consciousness can survive after death?

I just don't know. One thing I can tell you is that we don't know what the actual relationship between consciousness and the physical world is. There are good reasons to be skeptical of the naive conception of a soul. We know that almost everything we take ourselves to be subjectively—all of our cognitive powers, our ability to understand language, our ability to acknowledge anything in our physical environment through our senses—this is mediated by the brain. So the idea that a brain can die and a soul that still speaks English and recognizes Granny is going to float away into the afterlife, that seems to be profoundly implausible. And yet we do not know what the relationship between subjectivity and objectivity ultimately is. For instance, we could be living in a universe where consciousness goes all the way down to the bedrock so that there is some interior subjective dimension to an electron. So I'm actually quite skeptical of our ever being able to resolve that question—what the real relationship between consciousness and matter ultimately is.

That's interesting. Most evolutionary biologists would say consciousness is rooted in the brain. It will not survive death. You are not willing to make that claim.

I just don't know. I'm trying to be honest about my gradations of certainty. I think consciousness poses a unique problem. If we were living in a universe where consciousness survived death, or transcended the brain so that single neurons were conscious—or subatomic particles had an interior dimension— we would not expect to see it by our present techniques of neuroimaging or cellular neuroscience. And we would never expect to see it. And so we have a problem. There are profound philosophical and epistemological problems that anyone must confront who's trying to reduce consciousness to the workings of the brain. This discourse is in its infancy, and who knows where it's going to go?

Karen Armstrong

KAREN ARMSTRONG IS A ONE-WOMAN publishing industry, the author of more than 20 books on religion. When her breakthrough book *A History of God* appeared in 1993, this British writer quickly became known as a leading historian of spiritual matters. Her work displays a wide-ranging knowledge of religious traditions—from the monotheistic religions to Buddhism. What's most remarkable is how she carved out this career for herself after rejecting a life in the church.

At age 17, Armstrong became a Catholic nun. She eventually left the convent after seven years. "I had failed to make a gift of myself to God," she wrote in her memoir, *The Spiral Staircase*. While she despaired over never feeling the presence of God, she also bristled at the restrictive life imposed by the convent, which she described in her first book, *Through the Narrow Gate*. When she left in 1969, she had never heard of the Beatles or the Vietnam War, and she had lost her faith in God.

Armstrong went on to work in British television, where she become a well-known secular commentator on religion. Then something strange happened. After a TV project fell apart, she rediscovered religion while working on two books, *A History of God* and a biography of Muhammad. Her study of sacred texts finally gave her the appreciation of religion she had longed for—not as a system of belief but as a gateway into a world of mystery and the ineffable. Her book *Muhammad: A Biography of the Prophet* also made her one of Europe's most prominent defenders of Islam.

Armstrong now calls herself a "freelance monotheist." It's easy to understand her appeal in today's world of spiritual seekers. As an ex-nun, she resonates with people who have fallen out with organized religion. She has little patience for literal readings of the Bible, and argues that sacred texts yield profound insights if we read them as myth and poetry. She is especially drawn to the mystical tradition, which—in her view—has often been distorted by institutionalized religion. Although her books have made her enormously popular, it isn't surprising that she's also managed to raise the ire of both Christian fundamentalists and atheists.

In her book *The Great Transformation*, Armstrong writes about the religions that emerged during the "axial age," a phrase coined by the German philosopher Karl Jaspers. This is the era when many great sages appeared, including the Buddha, Socrates, Confucius, Jeremiah, and the mystics of the Upanishads. I interviewed Armstrong in the middle of her grueling U.S. book tour. She dislikes flying in small airplanes, so her publisher hired a car service to drive her from Minnesota to Wisconsin, where I spoke with her before she met with a church group. When she got out of her car, I was greeted by a rather short and intense woman, somewhat frazzled by last-minute interview requests. Once she was settled, her passion for religion came pouring out. She was full of surprises. She dismissed the afterlife as insignificant, and she drew some intriguing analogies: Just like there's good and bad sex and art, there's good and bad religion. Religion, she says, is hard work.

■ ■ ■ ■

Why are you so interested in the axial age?
Because it was the pivot, or the axis, around which the future spiritual development of humanity has revolved. We've never gone beyond these original insights. And they have so much to tell us today because very often in our religious institutions we are producing exactly the kind of religiosity that people such as the Buddha wanted to get rid of. While I was researching this book, they seemed to be talking directly to us in our own troubled time.

What religions emerged during the axial age?

From about 900 to 200 B.C.E., the traditions that have continued to nourish humanity either came into being or had their roots in four distinct regions of the world. So you had Confucianism and Taoism in China; Hinduism, Buddhism, Jainism in India; monotheism in Israel; and philosophical rationalism in Greece.

You're saying all these different religions developed independently of each other. But there was a common message that emerged roughly around the same time.

Yes. Without any collusion, they all came up with a remarkably similar solution to the spiritual ills of humanity. Before the axial age, religions had been very different. They had been based largely on external rituals which gave people intimations of greatness. But there was no disciplined introspection before the axial age. The axial sages discovered the inner world. And religions became much more spiritualized because humanity had taken a leap forward. People were creating much larger empires and kingdoms than ever before. A market economy was in its very early stages. That meant the old, rather parochial visions were no longer adequate. And these regions were torn apart by an unprecedented crescendo of violence. In every single case, the catalyst for religious change had been a revulsion against violence.

So what was the spiritual message that rejected violence?

First of all, they all insisted that you must give up and abandon your ego. The sages said the root cause of suffering lay in our desperate concern with self, which often needs to destroy others in order to preserve itself. And so they insisted that if we stepped outside the ego, then we would encounter what we call Brahman or God, Nirvana or the Tao.

You say one of the common messages in all these religions was what we now call the Golden Rule. And Confucius was probably the first person who came up with this idea.

All these sages, with the exception of the Greeks, posited a counterideology to the violence of their time. The safest way to get rid of egotism was by means of compassion. The first person to promulgate the Golden Rule, which was the bedrock of this empathic spirituality, was Confucius 500 years before Christ. His disciples asked him, "What is the single thread that runs through all your teaching and pulls it all together?" And Confucius said, "Look into your own heart. Discover what it is that gives you pain. And then refuse to inflict that pain on anybody else." His disciples also asked, "Master, which one of your teachings can we put into practice every day?" And Confucius said, "Do not do to others as you would not have them do to you." The Buddha had his version of the Golden Rule. Jesus taught it much later. And Rabbi Hillel, the older contemporary of Jesus, said the Golden Rule was the essence of Judaism.

Now, there is the question of whether all of these were actually religions. I mean, the philosophies of the ancient Greeks—Socrates and Plato—were not religious at all. Buddhism is essentially a philosophy of mind. And I suppose you could see Confucianism as essentially a system of ethics.
That's a very chauvinistic Western view, if I may say so. You're saying this is what we regard as religion, and anything that doesn't measure up to that isn't. I think a Buddhist or a Confucian would be very offended to hear that he or she was not practicing a religion.

Well, explain that. What is religion?
Religion is a search for transcendence. But transcendence isn't necessarily sited in an external god, which can be a very unspiritual, unreligious concept. The sages were all extremely concerned with transcendence, with going beyond the self and discovering a realm, a reality, that could not be defined in words. Buddhists talk about Nirvana in very much the same terms as monotheists describe God.

That's fascinating. So in Buddhism, which is nontheistic, the message or the experience of Nirvana is the same as the Christian God?
The experience is the same. The trouble is that we define our God too closely. In my book *A History of God*, I pointed out that the most eminent Jewish, Christian, and Muslim theologians all said you couldn't think about

God as a simple personality, an external being. It was better to say that God did not exist because our notion of existence was far too limited to apply to God.

Didn't a lot of people say God is beyond language? We could only experience the glimmer of God.

That's what the Buddha said. You can't define Nirvana, you can't say what it is. The Buddha also said you could craft a new kind of human being in touch with transcendence. He was once asked by a Brahman priest who passed him in contemplation and was absolutely mesmerized by this man sitting in utter serenity. He said, "Are you a god, sir? Are you an angel or a spirit?" And the Buddha said, "No, I'm awake." His disciplined lifestyle had activated parts of his humanity that ordinarily lie dormant. But anybody could do it if they trained hard enough. The Buddhists and the Confucians and the greatest monotheistic mystics did with their minds and hearts what gymnasts and dancers do with their bodies.

You're saying these ancient sages really didn't care about big metaphysical systems. They didn't care about theology.

No, none of them did. And neither did Jesus. Jesus did not spend a great deal of time discoursing about the trinity or original sin or the incarnation, which have preoccupied later Christians. He went around doing good and being compassionate. In the Quran, metaphysical speculation is regarded as self-indulgent guesswork. And it makes people, the Quran says, quarrelsome and stupidly sectarian. You can't prove these things one way or the other, so why quarrel about it? The Taoists said this kind of speculation where people pompously hold forth about their opinions was egotism. And when you're faced with the ineffable and the indescribable, they would say it's belittling to cut it down to size. Sometimes, I think the way monotheists talk about God is unreligious.

Unreligious? Like talk about a personal God?

Yes, people very often talk about him as a kind of acquaintance, whom they can second-guess. People will say God loves that, God wills that, and God despises the other. And very often, the opinions of the deity are made to coincide exactly with those of the speaker.

Yet we certainly see a personal God in various sacred texts. People aren't just making that up.

No, but the great theologians in Judaism, Christianity, and Islam say you begin with the idea of a god who is personal. But God transcends personality as God transcends every other human characteristic, such as gender. If we get stuck there, this is very immature. Very often people hear about God at about the same time as they're learning about Santa Claus. And their ideas about Santa Claus mature and change in time, but their idea of God remains infantile.

What about the supernatural, though? Do you need any sense of the miraculous or of things that cannot be explained by science?

I think religions hold us in an attitude of awe and wonder. People such as the Buddha thought miracles were rather vulgar—you know, displays of power and ego. If you look at the healing miracles attributed to Jesus, they generally had some kind of symbolic aspect about healing the soul rather than showing off a supernatural power. Western people think the supernatural is the essence of religion, but that's rather like the idea of an external god. That's a minority view worldwide. I really get so distressed on behalf of Buddhists and Confucians and Hindus to have a few Western philosophers loftily dismissing their religion as not religious because it doesn't conform to Western norms. It seems the height of parochialism.

I think these questions are tremendously important now because more and more people, especially those with a scientific bent, say we don't need religion anymore. Science has replaced religion. You know, religion used to explain all kinds of things about the world. But science for the most part does that now. And people who are not religious say they can be just as morally upright.

They can. I fully endorse that. I don't think you need to believe in an external god to obey the Golden Rule. In the axial age, when people started to concentrate too much on what they're transcending to—that is, God—and neglected what they're transcending from—their greed, pompous egotism, cruelty—then they lost the plot, religiously. That's why God is a difficult religious concept. I think God is often used by religious people to give egotism a sacred seal of divine approval, rather than to take you beyond the ego.

As for scientists, they can explain a tremendous amount. But they can't talk about meaning so much. If your child dies, or you witness a terrible natural catastrophe such as Hurricane Katrina, you want to have a scientific explanation of it. But that's not all human beings need. We are beings who fall very easily into despair because we're meaning-seeking creatures. And if things don't add up in some way, we can become crippled by our despondency.

So would you say religion addresses those questions through the stories and myths?
Yes. In the premodern world, there were two ways of arriving at truth. Plato, for example, called them mythos and logos. Myth and reason or science. We've always needed both of them. It was very important in the premodern world to realize these two things, myth and science, were complementary. One didn't cancel the other out.

Well, what do you say to the scientists, especially the Darwinists—Richard Dawkins would be the obvious case—who are quite angry about religion? They say religion is the root of much evil in the world. Wars are fought and fueled by religion. And now that we're in the twenty-first century, they say it's time that science replace religion.
I don't think it will. In the scientific age, we've seen a massive religious revival everywhere but Europe. And some of these people—not all, by any means—seem to be secular fundamentalists. They have as bigoted a view of religion as some religious fundamentalists have of secularism. We have too much dogmatism at the moment. Take Richard Dawkins, for example. He did a couple of religious programs that I was fortunate enough to miss. It was a very, very one-sided view.

Well, he hates religion.

Yeah, this is not what the Buddha would call skillful. If you're consumed by hatred—Freud was rather the same—then this is souring your personality and clouding your vision. What you need to do is to look appraisingly and calmly on other traditions. Because when you hate religion, it's also very easy to hate the people who practice it.

This does raise the question, though, of how to read the sacred Scriptures.

Indeed.

Because there are all kinds of inflammatory things that are said. For instance, many passages in both the Bible and the Quran exhort the faithful to kill the infidels. Sam Harris, in his book *The End of Faith*, has seven very densely packed pages of nothing but quotations from the Quran with just this message. "God's curse be upon the infidels"; "slay them wherever you find them"; "fighting is obligatory for you, much as you dislike it." And Harris's point is that the Muslim suicide bombings are not the aberration of Islam. They are the message of Islam.

Well, that's simply not true. He's taken parts of those texts and omitted their conclusions, which say fighting is hateful for you. You have to do it if you're attacked, as Muhammad was being attacked at the time when that verse was revealed. But forgiveness is better for you. Peace is better. But when we're living in a violent society, our religion becomes violent, too. Religion gets sucked in and becomes part of the problem. But to isolate these texts as though they expressed the whole of the tradition is very mischievous and dangerous at this time when we are in danger of polarizing people on both sides. And this kind of inflammatory talk, say about Islam, is convincing Muslims all over the world who are not extremists that the West is incurably Islamaphobic and will never respect their traditions. I think it's irresponsible at this time.

But many people would say you can't just pick out the peaceful and loving passages of the sacred Scriptures. There are plenty of other passages that are frightening.

I would say there are more passages in the Bible than the Quran that are dedicated to violence. I think what all religious people ought to do is to look at their own sacred traditions. Not just point a finger at somebody else's, but our own. Christians should look long and hard at the Book of Revelation. And they should look at those passages in the Pentateuch that speak of the destruction of the enemy. They should make a serious study of these. And let's not forget that in its short history, secularism has had some catastrophes.

Certainly, the major tragedies of the twentieth century were committed by secularists—Stalin, Hitler, Mao.
And Saddam Hussein, a secularist supported by us in the West for ten years, even when he gassed the Kurds. We supported him because he was a secularist. If people are resistant to secularism in Iraq now, it's because their most recent experience of it was Saddam. So this kind of chauvinism that says secularism is right, religion is all bunk—this is one-sided and I think basically egotistic. People are saying, "My opinion is right and everybody else's is wrong." It gets you riled up. It gives you a sense of holy righteousness, where you feel frightfully pleased with yourself when you're sounding off, and you get a glorious buzz about it. But I don't see this as helpful to humanity. And when you suppress religion and try and get rid of it, then it's likely to take unhealthy forms.

That's when fundamentalism starts to appear.
Yes, because fundamentalism has developed in every single one of the major traditions as a response to secularism that has been dismissive or even cruel, and has attempted to wipe out religion. And if you try to repress it—as happened in the Soviet Union—there's now a huge religious revival in Russia, and some of it's not very healthy. It's like the suppression of the sexual instinct. If you repress the sexual instinct and try to tamp it down, it's likely to develop all kinds of perverse and twisted forms. And religion's the same.

Well, it seems to me you're also saying that to be religious—truly religious—is tremendously hard work. It's far harder than just . . .
. . . singing a few hymns.

. . . or just reading the Scriptures literally. You can't live that way.

Religion is hard work. It's an art form. It's a way of finding meaning, like art, like painting, like poetry, in a world that is violent and cruel and often seems meaningless. And art is hard work. You don't just dash off a painting. It takes years of study. I think we expect religious knowledge to be instant. But religious knowledge comes incrementally and slowly. And religion is like any other activity. It's like cooking or sex or science. You have good art, sex, and science, and bad art, sex, and science. It's not easy to do it well.

So how should we approach the sacred texts? How should we read them?

Sacred texts have traditionally been a bridge to the divine. They're all difficult. They're not a simple manual—a how-to book that will tell you how to gain enlightenment by next week, like how to lose weight on the Atkins diet. This is a slow process. I think the best image for reading Scripture occurs in the story of Jacob, who wrestles with a stranger all night long. And in the morning, the stranger seems to have been his God. That's when Jacob is given the name Israel—"one who fights with God." And he goes away limping as he walks into the sunrise. Scriptures are a struggle.

Is faith a struggle?

Well, faith is not a matter of believing things. That's again a modern Western notion. It's only been current since the eighteenth century. Believing things is neither here nor there, despite what some religious people say and what some secularists say. That is a very eccentric religious position, current really only in the Western Christian world. You don't have it much in Judaism, for example.

But it's not surprising that religion has become equated with belief, because these are the messages we hear as we grow up, regardless of our faiths.

We hear it from some of them. And I think we've become rather stupid in our scientific age about religion. If you'd presented some of these literalistic readings of the Bible to people in the premodern age, they would have found it rather obtuse. They'd have found it incomprehensible that people really believe the first chapter of Genesis is an account of the origins of life.

So how should we read the story of creation in Genesis?
Well, it's not a literal account because it's put right next door to another account in Chapter 2, which completely contradicts it. Then there are other creation stories in the Bible that show Yahweh like a Middle Eastern god killing a sea monster to create the world. Cosmogony in the ancient world was not an account of the physical origins of life. Cosmogony was usually used therapeutically. When people were sick or in times of vulnerability, they would read a cosmogony in order to get an influx of the divine, to tap in to those extraordinary energies that had created something out of nothing.

That seems to be a question that scientists are struggling with now. Did the Big Bang come out of nothing?
Exactly. And I think some scientists are writing a new kind of religious discourse, teaching us to pit ourselves against the dark world of uncreated reality and pushing us back to the mysterious. They're resorting to mythological imagery: Big Bang, black hole. They have all kinds of resonances because this is beyond our ken.

I'm curious about how these issues have played out in your own life, because you went into a convent at a rather young age—at 17. You lived there for seven years. You've written about how you tried to find God but couldn't. And you left in despair. I don't know if you called yourself an atheist, but you were certainly close to that. And then, as you worked on your book, *A History of God*, you seemed to discover something that you hadn't known before.
I couldn't get on with religion in the convent because it was a very unkind institution. I limped away from it. I wanted nothing to do with religion ever again, but came back to it through the study of other religious traditions— initially, Judaism and Islam. Later, Buddhism, Hinduism, and Confucianism.

So it was actually studying the history and the texts that allowed you to enter into the religious experience.

Yes, once I'd stopped prancing and posturing around on TV, where I was expected to have an inflammatory opinion and to let people have it. All this was pure egotism. I did some early television programs and expressed my secularism very cleverly. I'm slightly down on cleverness, which can be fun and witty at a dinner party and I enjoy that as much as anybody else. But it can be superficial. Once my television career had folded, I was left on my own with these texts. There was nobody to exclaim to derisively about the irrationality of a Greek Orthodox text or the stupidity of a certain Jewish mysticism. I began to read them like poetry, which is what theology is. It's poetry. It's an attempt to express the inexpressible. It needs quiet. You can't read a Rilke sonnet at a party. Sometimes a poem can live in your head for a long time until its meaning is finally revealed. And if you try and grasp that meaning prematurely, you can distort the poem for yourself. And because I'd been cast out from the media world, and was living in a world of silence and solitude, the texts and I started to have a different relationship.

Do you consider yourself a religious person?

Yes. It's a constant pursuit for me. It's helped me immeasurably to overcome despair in my own life. But I have no hard-and-fast answers.

I take it you don't like the question "Do you believe in God?"

No, because people who ask this question often have a rather simplistic notion of what God is.

What about an afterlife?

It's a red herring as far as I'm concerned.

But you must have thought about that question. Does everything end once we die?

I don't know. I prefer to be agnostic on that matter, as do most of the world's religions. It's really only Christianity and Islam that are obsessed with afterlife in this way. It was not a concern in the axial age, not for any of them. I think the old scenarios of heaven and hell can be unreligious. People can perform their good deeds in the spirit of putting their installments in their retirement annuities. And there's nothing religious about that. Religion is supposed to be about the loss of the ego, not about its eternal survival.

But certainly there are a lot of people—both scientists and religious people—who speculate about whether there's some cosmic order. For the evolutionary biologists, the question is whether there's some natural progression to evolution.
Who knows?

And is there an endpoint? From the cosmological perspective, was the universe designed specifically for life? Are those important questions?
Yeah, I think they can be wonderful questions. But they don't occupy me very much. I believe that what we have is now. The religions say you can experience eternity in this life, here and now, by getting those moments of ecstasy where time ceases to be a constraint. And you do it by the exercise of the Golden Rule and by compassion. And just endless speculation about the next world is depriving you of a great experience in this one.

Andrew Newberg

CAN WE ACTUALLY SEE GOD in the brain? Not exactly. But a few enterprising neuroscientists have found ways to detect and measure the varieties of religious experiences. By using brain-scanning technology, they can pinpoint which parts of the brain are activated during prayer and meditation. Although they can't answer the biggest question of all—does God exist?—they are probing one of the deepest mysteries in science: the nature of consciousness.

They are also wading into a thorny issue in the science and religion debate: the connection between brain and mind. Most neuroscientists assume the mind is nothing more than electrochemical surges among nerve cells in the brain. But the neuroscientists who study spirituality tend to be open to the possibility that the mind could exist independently of the brain. Some even question the materialist paradigm of science—the idea that the only reality worth studying is what can be tested, quantified, and reproduced. They wonder whether current scientific methods will ever be able to explain consciousness. But others are skeptical. Stephen Heinemann, president of the Society for Neuroscience, told the *Chronicle of Higher Education*, "I think the concept of the mind outside the brain is absurd."

One of the pioneers in the new field of neurotheology is Andrew Newberg, a physician at the University of Pennsylvania and director of the Center for Spirituality and the Mind. He is the coauthor of several books, including *How God Changes Your Brain* and *Why We Believe What We Believe*. Newberg has conducted a series of brain-imaging studies of various spiritual practitioners, including Franciscan nuns, Buddhists, and Pentecostal Christians who speak in tongues. His lab research has brought some surprising—and curious—results. For instance, during his study of Pentecostals, Newberg was amazed to see one of his own lab assistants start to sing and speak in tongues. It turned out that she had been doing it as part of her own religious practice for almost 10 years. Newberg himself hasn't joined any organized religion, but he has clearly been influenced by various contemplative traditions.

Newberg uses an imaging technique called single photon emission computed tomography, which measures blood flow in various parts of the brain. More blood flow, of course, means more brain activity. In his studies, he has found that there is no single part of the brain that controls religious experience. In fact, a specific religious belief will shape a person's spiritual experience—and what happens in his or her brain. Although his research falls short of proving the presence of God, it does show that engaging our spiritual selves can have profound effects on our biological selves, too.

I spoke with Newberg about his brain-imaging studies, the nature of mystical experiences, and whether scientists will ever crack the mystery of consciousness.

■ ■ ■ ■

Do you think the human brain is hardwired for religious belief?
Well, I think the brain is structured in such a way that we can very easily have religious beliefs and spiritual experiences. But the problem with the term "hardwired" is that it implies that someone or something did the hardwiring. And I'm not sure that I can say that. When we look at how the brain is set up to help us understand our reality, it's very easy to see how we have different types of spiritual experiences and feelings of transcendence. And ultimately, this spills over into our ability to form religious concepts. So our brain is always asking those questions, which often wind up resulting in a spiritual or religious quest.

You've said God may exist but we can only experience God through our brain. Can brain-imaging technology actually tell us much about the experience of the divine?

It certainly can tell us what happens in our brain when we have a religious or spiritual experience. For example, in our study of Franciscan nuns during prayer, our brain scans show what happens in the brain if they experience being in God's presence. What those scans don't prove is whether or not that experience was real in some sort of objective sense—that God really was in the room, communicating with them. At this point in our technology, that is something we can't answer. Whether we will ever be able to answer it, I don't know.

You studied Franciscan nuns who had prayed for decades, and you also studied Tibetan Buddhists who had meditated for many years. What happened when they came into your lab?
We found that the Franciscan nuns activated several important parts of the brain during prayer. One part was the frontal lobe. I've been particularly interested in the frontal lobe, because it tends to be activated whenever we focus our mind on something. This can be very mundane, like focusing on a problem we're trying to solve at work. Or it can be focusing on a phrase from the Bible, which was happening with the Franciscan nuns. They would focus their attention on a particular prayer of great meaning, and they'd begin to feel a lot of unusual experiences. They would lose their sense of self. They would feel absorbed into the prayer itself. They'd no longer see a distinction between who they are and the actual prayer process itself. Some people call it a feeling of connectedness or oneness.

Another part of the brain that changes in the prayer state is the parietal lobe. This is located toward the back top part of the head. The parietal lobe normally uses our sensory information to create a sense of our self and relates that self spatially to the rest of the world. So it's that part of our brain that enables us to get up out of our chair and walk out the door. We've hypothesized that when people meditate or pray—if they block the sensory information that gets into that area—they no longer get a sense of who they are in relation to the world. They may lose their sense of self, and they feel they become one with something greater—ultimate reality or God.

Do the Buddhists have that same sense of oneness when they meditate? Was the same thing happening in the brain, even though Buddhists don't believe in God?

We did see similar changes. In both prayer and meditation, we see a decrease of activity in this orientation part of the brain. So when the Buddhist meditators feel a blending in or absorption with the visual object—in this case, they're doing a visualization technique—we see a similar change. And it raises some very intriguing issues. How similar are these different practices? Are they associated with similar or different changes in the brain? When these practitioners had the same kind of experience—a feeling of oneness or an experience of focusing the mind—we saw very similar changes in the Buddhist meditators and the nuns. But one difference was the nuns actually activated the language areas of the brain. Of course, that made sense because it was a verbal practice. They were focusing on a prayer, whereas the Buddhist meditators activated the visual areas of the brain because they were focusing on a visual image—a sacred object they would hold in their minds.

This is fascinating. You're saying once you get past a few specific differences, the same kind of thing seems to be going on in the brains of the Buddhists and the nuns. Both have a sense of oneness and that oceanic feeling that the mystics have talked about for centuries, even though their metaphysical systems are quite different.
Exactly. And part of why I've been doing this research for the last 10 years is to see where the similarities are. I think one of the great equalizers, in many respects, is the human brain. If you go anywhere in the world and take a person's brain and slice it up and look at it—as a lot of medical people do—you will see a lot of the same basic structures and connections and functions.

Clearly one thing you've done is to show there's nothing delusional about spiritual or religious experience. This is a normal thing happening in the brain. But I'm wondering if there's anything especially spiritual about these experiences. Could an intensely pleasurable experience—say, sex or great music—produce similar brain activity?
To a certain extent, I think it can. When we look at how the brain works, it has a limited set of functions. So if one has a feeling of euphoria—whether one gets that through sex or religion or watching your team win the championship—it's probably going to activate similar areas of the brain. There's a

continuum of these experiences. People can describe a religious experience as being anything from a mild sense of awe to a profound mystical experience, where the person changes fundamentally how they understand the whole world. Now, religious or spiritual experiences do seem to be among the more complex sets of experiences. When somebody meditates, it involves a lot of different parts of the brain. There's not just a religious part of the brain. And that makes sense when you look at the richness and diversity of these experiences.

But I think you're also asking one of the most important questions: Are we really capturing something that's inherently spiritual? This is a big philosophical question. If the soul or the spirit is really nonmaterial, how does it interact with us? Of course, the human brain has to have some way of thinking about it. Perhaps the most interesting finding I could have would be to see nothing change on the brain scan when one of the nuns has an incredible experience of transcendence and connectedness with God. Maybe then we really would capture something that's spiritual rather than just cognitive and biological.

You also did a study of some Pentecostal Christians who speak in tongues. What happened when you hooked them up to your brain-imaging technology?

Well, this was a fascinating study for me personally. One of the problems I have with the meditation studies and the nun studies is that what they're doing is all internal. So you see them sitting in a room, but you're missing the big fireworks. It's a much more fascinating experience to watch people who speak in tongues. They're moving and dancing and making vocalizations that are incomprehensible to the rest of us. And we found some very unique differences from all the meditation states that we'd seen. We saw an actual decrease of activity in the frontal lobes. They are not really focusing their attention on the practice of speaking in tongues. They actually lose their attention. They feel they are no longer in control of what's happening to them. And we think that may be associated with this drop of activity in the frontal lobes.

When the Franciscan nuns prayed, they activated the language part of the brain. Was that true with the people who spoke in tongues?

We did not observe that. That also is intriguing. Speaking in tongues is a very unusual kind of vocalization. It sounds like the person is speaking a language, but it's not comprehensible. And when people have done linguistic analyses of speaking in tongues, it does not correspond to any clear linguistic structure. So it seems to be distinct from language itself. That's interesting, because we did not see activity in the language areas of the brain. Of course, if somebody is a deep believer in speaking in tongues, the source of the vocalizations is very clear. It's coming from outside the person. It's coming through the spirit of God.

So what did you find most significant about that study?
The most fascinating result was that it represented a very different type of spiritual and religious state than what we saw during prayer or meditation. We saw very different changes in the brain. Different types of religious practices and beliefs seem to be associated with different changes in the brain.

I have to ask, do you meditate?
I don't do a formal type of meditation. A lot of why I got into this research area in the first place was because of my own exploration of how we understand reality. I was very intrigued by what our brain, what our mind could find out about our world. It started out as a very Western-based, scientific approach. But as I proceeded down this path, my own thinking became much more contemplative and in many ways became a meditation type of practice. So while I personally don't do a formal Tibetan Buddhist or Zen meditation, I do look at contemplative practices. And it's given me a better understanding of what people are actually doing when they engage in these practices.

We have to recognize the limitations of science. It's great for understanding that a certain medication is helpful for patients with a certain disease, but it may not be helpful for trying to crack the nut of human consciousness. And we may really need to develop a new kind of science—or at least a new approach to science—that would keep the strengths that science already has but add a new layer to it that has to do with subjective experiences and contemplative approaches.

One thing that's difficult about this whole subject is the language we use. We've used words like "transcendent" and "mystical" and "spiritual." Do they all mean the same thing?

Well, throughout this discussion we've been talking about spiritual and religious experiences in the same way. And that may or may not be accurate. I've come to realize that everyone defines those experiences a little bit differently. So if I asked 15 people, "What does spirituality or God mean to you?," I would probably get a different answer from each person. But a lot of people will describe spirituality as having something to do with a sense of the self connected to some greater reality. Whether they ultimately call that a spiritual realm or some deeper interconnectedness of all things in the universe, there's that kind of similarity.

There is a history of defining some of these words in very specific ways. Didn't William James define "transcendence" as something quite rare— experiences that are not reproducible?

That's true. People talk about transcendence as being indescribable or ineffable. And they've tried to use certain kinds of ideas or emotions to describe it. But that's part of the problem. A lot of these experiences are indescribable. It's like trying to explain what love is—what it means to say you love your spouse or your child. How does one describe that? We can talk about words, but it's harder to get at what exactly that experience is about.

Well, it raises interesting questions. In the William James definition, the Buddhist meditators and Franciscan nuns in your lab were not having a transcendent, once-in-a-lifetime experience. This must be a problem for you as a neuroscientist. I'm sure you would love to see this kind of experience in your lab, but it's highly unlikely you'll ever get a brain scan with someone who has one of these truly profound experiences.

That's true. That is a great challenge for us to figure out how to capture this very rare, mystical experience. The way we've established our research is to look at a whole continuum. So even though the imaging studies we've done haven't specifically measured or captured a mystical experience, the changes that we see support an overall model that we've been developing over the years. Different parts of the brain may be involved when someone has one of those truly unique, life-altering kinds of experiences.

Would you be willing to speculate here? Suppose you could somehow record what the medieval mystics like Meister Eckhart or St. Francis talked about—these truly big, profound experiences? What's your guess as to what happened in their brains when they had those experiences?

I think the orientation part of the brain would be profoundly affected. So while we're seeing decreased activity in this orientation part of the brain during prayer, for example, I think if somebody had a true mystical experience, we would see a vastly greater change—to the point where there would be a complete loss of their sense of self in relation to the world. Now, one other aspect of the overall function of the brain that we haven't mentioned is the autonomic nervous system that regulates our arousal and our quiescent responses in the body. What we have hypothesized is that in these peak states, there is a simultaneous activation of both this very profound sense of arousal and alertness and also a deep sense of oceanic bliss and calmness. Maybe someday, if we're fortunate enough, that could actually be captured on a brain scan.

There's a fundamental mystery in all of this research you've been describing. A religious person might call a mystical vision a gift from heaven, while a neuroscientist would say it's just an electrochemical surge firing in the brain. Is there any way to resolve this question?

Well, I think there is. We really need to look not just at what science has to say, but what the subjective nature of these experiences are, what the spiritual side has to say. And it's been my goal to get people to look at both of these perspectives. What is the reality of those experiences? That's really what the question is. Is it really a spiritual reality, or is it just a biological one?

This is essentially the question that divides atheists from religious believers.

Exactly. I think it's something that could be answered at some point. But it really requires a philosophical and consciousness perspective, as well as a biological perspective. What we have to be careful about is explaining away those experiences just because we capture something in the brain that's associated with these experiences. It's possible that we might be able to explain it away at some point, but at this time, I don't think we can.

I often get asked: Could we just develop a drug that makes people spiritual? Well, that already exists. If you look at shamanic cultures throughout the world, many use different substances that don't diminish their experiences at all. It doesn't become just a drug-induced state that affects their physiology. It's their way of opening up their brain as a window into the spiritual realm. Again, I think it ultimately comes down to the belief systems that we hold.

Would it ever be possible to devise some kind of brain-imaging test to get at the question of whether there is some reality outside of us? That's really what we're talking about: some larger intelligence—God or some divine presence. Could we determine whether there's something that's not just in our brains?
I think it would be very difficult. I never want to say never, but the problem is that all of science is something that we as conscious observers look at and interpret. So we never really get outside of our own mind to look at what's out there in reality. On the other hand, let's say we get lucky enough to see an experience where someone does feel they get beyond the brain, where they feel intimately interconnected with the universe or with God. And we see whether or not that is always associated with something going on biologically or whether there's ultimately something that happens beyond simply the biological. That's why I think we always need to consider both the scientific perspective, but also what consciousness is all about and how the conscious mind interprets the world. I think it's possible, but it's very complicated. Could we design an experiment to do that? I think it's very hard to do without making a lot of assumptions that ultimately will explode the research and foul us up in our science.

There's a basic metaphysical question here: Does consciousness exist outside the brain? Do you want to weigh in on this?
Well, at this point, there isn't an answer. I'm open to both possibilities. I don't think we have enough information to be able to say one way or the other.

John Haught

EVOLUTION REMAINS THE THORNIEST ISSUE in the ongoing debate over science and religion. For all the yelling between creationists and scientists, there is one perspective that's largely absent from public discussions about evolution. We rarely hear from religious believers who accept the standard Darwinian account of evolution. It's a shame, because there is an important question at stake: How can a person of faith reconcile the apparently random, meaningless process of evolution with belief in God?

The simplest response is to say that science and religion have nothing to do with each other—to claim, as Stephen Jay Gould famously did, they are "nonoverlapping magisteria." Perhaps that response seems too easy, a politically expedient ploy to pacify both scientists and mainstream Christians. Maybe evolutionary theory, along with modern physics, really does pose a serious challenge to religious belief. To put it another way, how can an intellectually responsible person of faith justify that faith—and even belief in a personal God—after Darwin and Einstein?

That's the question John Haught has set out to answer by proposing a "theology of evolution." Haught is a Roman Catholic theologian at Georgetown University and a prolific author. His books include *God after Darwin, Is Nature Enough?* and *God and the New Atheism*. He's steeped in evolutionary theory as well as Christian theology. Haught believes Darwin is actually "a gift to theology." He says evolutionary biology has forced modern theologians to clarify their thinking by rejecting outdated arguments about God as an intrusive designer. Haught reclaims the theology of his intellectual hero, Pierre

Teilhard de Chardin, a Jesuit priest and paleontologist who died more than half a century ago. Teilhard believed that we live in a universe evolving toward ever-greater complexity and, ultimately, to consciousness.

Haught is an intriguing figure in the debate over evolution. He was the only theologian to testify as an expert witness in the landmark 2005 Dover trial that ruled against teaching intelligent design in public schools. He testified against intelligent design, arguing that it's both phony science and bad theology. But he is also a fierce critic of hard-core atheists like Richard Dawkins and Daniel Dennett, who claim that evolution leads logically to atheism. He says both sides place too much faith in science. "Ironically," Haught writes, "ID advocates share with their ideological enemies, the evolutionary materialists, the assumption that science itself can provide ultimate explanations."

I talked with Haught about the new atheists, Albert Camus, and how evolutionary biology can be a complement to faith. We also spoke about why science is ultimately not equipped to answer questions about love, consciousness, and the Resurrection.

■ ■ ■ ■

Your book *God and the New Atheism* is a critique of Richard Dawkins, Christopher Hitchens, and Sam Harris. You claim that they are pale imitations of great atheists like Nietzsche, Camus, and Sartre. What are they missing?
The only thing new in the so-called new atheism is the sense that we should not tolerate tolerance of faith because, by doing so, we open people's minds to any crazy idea—including very dangerous ideas like those that led to the terrorist attacks of 9/11. In every other respect, this atheism is similar to the secular humanism of the modern period, which said that faith is incompatible with science, that religion and belief in God are bad for morality, and that theology should be purged from culture and academic life. These are not new ideas. But there were atheists in the past who were much more theologically educated than these. My chief objection to the new atheists is that they are almost completely ignorant of what's going on in the world of theology. They talk about the most fundamentalist and extremist versions of faith, and they

hold these up as though they're the normative, central core of faith. And they miss so many things. For example, they miss the moral core of Judaism and Christianity—the theme of social justice, which takes those who are marginalized and brings them to the center of society. They give us an extreme caricature of faith and religion.

You're saying older atheists like Nietzsche and Camus had a more sophisticated critique of religion?

Yes. They wanted us to think out completely and thoroughly, and with unrelenting logic, what the world would look like if the transcendent is wiped away from the horizon. Nietzsche, Sartre, and Camus would have cringed at "the new atheism" because they would see it as simply dropping God like Santa Claus and going on with the same old values. The new atheists don't want to think out the implications of a complete absence of deity. Nietzsche, as well as Sartre and Camus, all expressed it quite correctly. The implications should be nihilism.

Didn't they see the death of God as terrifying?

Yes, they did. And they thought it would take tremendous courage to be an atheist. Sartre himself said atheism is an extremely cruel affair. He was implying that most people wouldn't be able to look it squarely in the face. And my own belief is they themselves didn't either. Nietzsche, Sartre, and Camus eventually realized that nihilism is not a space within which we can live our lives.

But it seems to me that Camus had a different project. He thought there was no God or transcendent reality, and the great existential struggle was for humans to create meaning themselves, without appealing to some higher reality. This wasn't a cop-out at all. It was a profound struggle for him.

Yes, it was. But his earlier life was somewhat different from his later writings. In *The Stranger* and *The Myth of Sisyphus*, he argues that in the absence of God, there's no hope. And we have to learn to live without hope. His figure of Sisyphus is the image of living without hope. And whatever happiness

Camus thought we could attain comes from the sense of strength and courage that we feel in ourselves when we shake our fist at the gods. But none of the atheists—whether the hard-core or the new atheists—really examine where this courage comes from. What is its source? I think a theologian like Paul Tillich, who wrestled with the atheism of Nietzsche, Sartre, and Camus, put his finger on the real issue. How do we account for the courage to go on living in the absence of hope? As you move to the later writings of Camus and Sartre, those books are saying it's very difficult to live a life without hope. And what I want to show in my own work—as an alternative to the new atheists—is a universe in which hope is possible.

Why can't you have hope if you don't believe in God?
You can have hope. But the question is, can you justify the hope? I don't have any objection to the idea that atheists can be very good and morally upright people. But we need a worldview that is capable of justifying the confidence that we place in our minds, in truth, in goodness, in beauty. I argue that an atheistic worldview is not capable of justifying that confidence. Some sort of theological framework can actually justify our trust in meaning, in goodness, in reason.

For years, we've been bombarded by arguments over religion and evolution. And yet you say theology has not yet come to grips with Darwin. What are theologians missing?
Well, this has been one of the most dramatic events that theology—at least in the West—has ever had to face. The Darwinian story of evolution seems to give people a whole new creation story. You have to remember that our sense of ethics and the divine came into our religious awareness firmly fixed to a static, vertical, hierarchical understanding of the universe. The fact that there's a special place for humans gave us the sense that we were cared for in a special way by divine providence. But if you suddenly switched to a universe that's 13.7 billion years old, and an evolutionary process that takes almost 4 billion years to lead to humans, then it's very difficult for many people to map this new horizontal, temporal, historical unfolding onto the static hierarchy, which was the backbone of spirituality for so many centuries.

So you're talking about more than just the story of Genesis in the Bible. This is a much bigger issue for modern theology.

The story of Genesis has been hyped as the only problem. I think the fundamental difficulty is the new evolutionary world in process—that the world is unfinished and still being created is so different from the cosmology that was the backbone of traditional spirituality.

I would think the biggest challenge that evolutionary theory poses to most religions is the sense that there's no inherent meaning in the world. If you look at the process of evolution—this apparently random series of genetic mutations—it would seem that there's no place for ultimate purpose. Human beings may just be an evolutionary accident.

Yes, in the new scientific understanding of the universe, there are no sharp breaks between lifeless matter and life, between life and mind. It seems to many people that the new evolutionary picture places everything in the context of a meaningless smudge of stuff, of atoms reshuffling themselves over the course of time. The traditional view was that nature emanates from on high, so that when you get down to matter, you have the least important level. Above that there's life and mind and God. But in the new cosmography, it seems that mindless matter dominates the whole picture. And many scientists, like Dawkins and Gould, have said evolution has destroyed the notion of purpose. So one thing I do in my theology is to say that's not necessarily true.

Isn't there a simple response to the materialist argument? You can say "purpose" is simply not a scientific idea. Instead, it's an idea for theologians and philosophers to debate. Do you accept that distinction?

I sure do. But that distinction is usually violated in scientific literature and in much discussion of evolution. From the beginning of the modern world, science decided quite rightly that it wasn't going to tackle such questions as purpose, value, meaning, importance, God, or even talk about intelligence or subjectivity. It was going to look for purely natural, causal, mechanical explanations of things. And science has every right to be that way. But that principle of scientific puritanism is often violated by scientists who think that by dint of their scientific expertise, they are able to comment on such things as purpose. I consider that to be a great violation.

Who are these scientists who extrapolate about purpose from science?
A good example is the Nobel Prize–winning physicist Steven Weinberg. In his book *Dreams of a Final Theory*, he asks, will we find God once science gets down to what he calls the fundamental levels of reality? It's almost as if he assumes that science itself has the capacity and the power to comment on things like that. Similarly, Dawkins, in *The God Delusion*, has stated that science has the right to deal with the question of God and other religious issues, and everything has to be settled according to the canons of the scientific method.

But Dawkins argues that a lot of claims made on behalf of God—about how God created the world and interacts with people—are ultimately questions about nature. Unless you say God has nothing to do with nature, those become scientific questions.
Well, I approach these issues by making a case for what I call "layered explanation." For example, if a pot of tea is boiling on the stove, and someone asks you why it's boiling, one answer is to say it's boiling because H_2O molecules are moving around excitedly, making a transition from the liquid state to the gaseous state. And that's a very good answer. But you could also say it's boiling because my wife turned the gas on. Or you could say it's boiling because I want tea. Here you have three levels of explanation, which are approaching phenomena from different points of view. This is how I see the relationship of theology to science. Of course, I think theology is relevant to discussing the question, what is nature? And what is the world? It would talk about it in terms of being a gift from the Creator, and having a promise built into it for the future. Science should not touch upon that level of understanding. But it doesn't contradict what evolutionary biology and the other sciences are telling us about nature. They're just different levels of understanding.

What do you say to the atheists who demand evidence or proof of the existence of a transcendent reality?

The hidden assumption behind such a statement is often that faith is belief without evidence. Therefore, since there's no scientific evidence for the divine, we should not believe in God. But that statement itself—that evidence is necessary—holds a further hidden premise that all evidence worth examining has to be scientific evidence. And beneath that assumption, there's the deeper worldview—it's a kind of dogma—that science is the only reliable way to truth. But that itself is a faith statement. It's a deep faith commitment, because there's no way you can set up a series of scientific experiments to prove that science is the only reliable guide to truth. It's a creed.

Are you saying scientists are themselves practicing a kind of religion?
The new atheists have made science the only road to truth. They have a belief, which I call "scientific naturalism," that there's nothing beyond nature—no transcendent dimension—that every cause has to be a natural cause, that there's no purpose in the universe, and that scientific explanations, especially in their Darwinian forms, can account for everything living. But the idea that science alone can lead us to truth is questionable. There's no scientific proof for that. Those are commitments that I would place in the category of faith. So the proposal by the new atheists that we should eliminate faith in all its forms would also apply to scientific naturalism. But they don't want to go that far. So there's a self-contradiction there.

Do you accept Stephen Jay Gould's idea of nonoverlapping magisteria—that science covers the empirical realm of facts and theories about the universe, while religion deals with ultimate meaning and moral value?
I think he's too simplistic. I don't think we want to remain stuck in this stand-off position. First of all, Gould defines religion as simply concern about values and meanings. He implicitly denies that religion can put us in touch with truth.

By truth, are you talking about reality?
Yes, I'm talking about what is real, or what has being. The traditions of religion and philosophy have always maintained that the most important dimensions

of reality are going to be least accessible to scientific control. There's going to be something fuzzy and elusive about them. The only way we can talk about them is through symbolic and metaphoric language—in other words, the language of religion. Traditionally, we never apologized for the fact that we used fuzzy language to refer to the real, because the deepest aspect of reality grasps us more than we grasp it. So we can never get our minds around it.

We can't get our minds around this transcendent reality because we're limited by our language and our brains?

We have to refer to it in the oblique and fuzzy but also luxuriant and rich language of symbol and metaphor. But I still think we have the obligation today of asking how our new scientific understanding of the world fits into that religious discourse. I don't accept Gould's complete separation of science and faith. Theology is faith seeking understanding. We have every right to ask what God is doing by making this universe in such a slow way, by allowing life to come about in the evolutionary manner in which Darwinian biology has very richly set forth. So science cannot be divorced from faith. However, I think most people do resort to this nonoverlapping magisteria as the default position. It's an easy approach. It allows you to put all your ducks in a row. But it avoids the really interesting and perhaps dangerous issue of how to think about God after Darwin. In my view, after Darwin, after Einstein—just as after Galileo and Copernicus—we can't have the same theological ideas about God as we did before.

So if you're a person of faith who wants to be intellectually responsible, you can't just shove all this science into a drawer. You do have to deal with it.

Exactly. Theology has always looked to secular concepts to express, for its particular age, what the meaning of God is. For example, in early Christianity, St. Augustine went to Neoplatonism. Later on, Thomas Aquinas did something very adventurous. He went to a pagan philosopher, Aristotle, to renew the understanding of Christianity in his own time. Islamic and Jewish philosophers and theologians have done the same thing. But as we move into our own time, theology has to deal with other concepts in order to make sense of its faith.

Darwin's thought seems to be more important intellectually and culturally than it's ever been. My view is that theology, instead of ignoring or closing its eyes to it, should look it squarely in the face. It has everything to gain and nothing to lose by doing so. In my view, Darwin's thought is a gift to theology.

Why? Because it forces theologians to sharpen their thinking?

Yes. I came to this idea of evolutionary theology long ago when I was still a young man. I read the works of a famous Jesuit paleontologist named [Pierre] Teilhard de Chardin. Teilhard was saying in the early twentieth century pretty much what I'm saying today. In many ways, my vocation as a theologian has been to expand on the work he started. Teilhard was sent by his superiors to study geology and paleontology. He was a priest at the time, trying to figure out what the evolutionary character of life on Earth had to do with his Christianity. He wrote essays synthesizing evolution into a broad understanding of his faith, including a deeper understanding of God. His religious superiors thought these essays were a bit too adventurous. So they shipped him off to China, which is the wrong place to send people who like to dig up old bones. Teilhard got involved in expeditions that uncovered Peking Man and other interesting evolutionary phenomena.

During all this time, 25 or so years in China, he was developing his ideas, synthesizing Christianity and evolution, and writing his major work, *The Phenomenon of Man*, now translated as *The Human Phenomenon*. But he couldn't get it published in his own lifetime, because the Church wasn't ready for it. But after he died, his lay friends flooded the religious world with his publications, and Teilhard ended up having an enormous influence on religious thought. Some major Catholic theologians were steeped in Teilhard's ideas by the time the Second Vatican Council came along. If you read the documents from that council, you can see the imprint of Teilhard's attempt to unify evolution and Christianity.

Teilhard argued that the universe is still evolving. Wasn't that the cosmic process he was trying to explain?

He put the Darwinian story of nature in the larger context of cosmic evolution. He saw the emergence of what he called "more" coming in gradually from the time of the Big Bang. Atoms become molecules. Molecules become cells. Cells become organisms. Organisms become vertebrates with a complex nervous system. Nervous tissue developed and eventually became very complex in humans. He saw this process of growing complexity as something that's still going on. This planet is itself becoming more complex. And the process is accelerating today at an enormous pace because of communications technology, engineering, economics, and politics. The globe is shrinking. We're able to connect instantaneously with other parts of the Earth, in the same way that nerve fibers carry an electronic message from one part of the body to the other. We should place what's happening now in the context of the previous phases of evolution and the cosmos. And we should expect—and hope for— the universe to keep becoming "more."

Earlier, you said cosmic purpose is a question that lies outside of science. But it sounds like you're bringing it into science. If you want to look for purpose—whether it's in evolution or the larger universe—you'll find it in this inexorable drive toward greater complexity.

We have to distinguish between science as a method and what science produces in the way of discovery. As a method, science does not ask questions of purpose. But it's something different to look at the cumulative results of scientific thought and technology. From a theological point of view, that's a part of the world that we have to integrate into our religious visions. That set of discoveries is not at all suggestive of a purposeless universe. Just the opposite. And what is the purpose? The purpose seems to be, from the very beginning, the intensification of consciousness. If you understand purpose as actualizing something that's unquestionably good, then consciousness certainly fits. It's cynical of scientists to say, offhandedly, that there's obviously no purpose in the universe. If purpose means realizing a value, consciousness is a value that none of us can deny.

Are you suggesting there's some kind of cosmic consciousness—a consciousness pervading the universe that has some connection to God?

I'm looking for an explanation that's robust enough to account for the kind of universe that is able, from within itself, to develop and unfold in this ongoing process of complexification. So the idea that some sort of providential presence is accompanying this process seems not at all irrational. And I like to think of God in these terms.

The whole question of consciousness raises all kinds of difficult scientific problems. Virtually all neuroscientists say consciousness is a direct product of the brain. As far as we know, the human brain evolved within the past few million years. This suggests that there was no consciousness before this time.

Certainly, consciousness has a physiological correlate. But here again, I would want to approach the question of consciousness in the same layered way I did with the boiling teapot. Suppose you asked me, why am I thinking right now? I could say, my neurons are firing, the synapses are connecting, the lobes of my brain are activated. And you could spend your whole career, as neuroscientists do, unfolding that level of understanding. But I could also say I'm thinking because I have a desire to know. I want to figure things out. That's an explanation that can't be mapped onto the first because a dimension of subjectivity enters in here. You cannot find it by the objectifying method of neuroscience.

So science as it's now practiced has nothing to say about subjective experience, about what happens in our minds?

I think science, especially neuroscience, does a very good job of saying what has to be working cerebrally and in our nervous systems in order for consciousness to be present. And it can also do a very good job of pointing out what has broken down physically and chemically if my brain is failing to function—for example, in Alzheimer's. But it doesn't have the complete explanation. Many cognitive scientists and brain scientists are saying the same thing. They're almost in despair at times about whether we'll ever be able to jump from the third-person discourse of science to the first-person discourse of subjective consciousness.

Let me try to pin you down a little more. You're saying the scientific method has only so much explanatory power. At least right now, it has

very little to say about subjective experience. That still leaves open the question, is the mind more than the brain? Or does consciousness always have some physical correlate?

Don't get me wrong. I want to push physical explanations as far as possible. I'm a man who loves science. I'm in awe of science. I don't ever want theology to put restraints upon science. I believe every thought we have has a physical correlate. But at the same time, I believe there's something about mind that does transcend, while at the same time fully dwelling incarnately in the physical universe. I see that as a microcosmic example of what's going on in the universe as a whole. So I want a worldview that's wide enough to ask the question, why does the universe not stand still? For example, once radiation came about early in the universe, why didn't the universe say, "Well, we're just fine here. This is a pretty good universe." Instead, there's a restlessness, a tendency of the cosmos to go beyond itself.

We experience this in ourselves. We're just as much a part of the universe as rivers and rocks are. Therefore, we should use what's going on in our own experience as a key to what's happening in the cosmos as a whole. I call this a "wider empiricism." Most modern science has acted as though subjectivity and consciousness are not part of the natural world. It doesn't reflect adequately on why subjectivity enters the universe at all. Why does the universe transcend itself from purely material to living and then to conscious phenomena? Teilhard himself said that what science left out was nature's most important development—human phenomena.

You have carved out an interesting position in this whole debate over science and religion. You are critical of atheists like Richard Dawkins and Daniel Dennett, who believe evolutionary theory leads to atheism. Yet you testified at the 2005 Dover trial against intelligent design. What's wrong with intelligent design?

I testified against it because, first of all, teaching it in public schools is a violation of the establishment clause of the First Amendment. There is something irremediably religious about the idea. Try to deny it though they might, advocates of intelligent design are really proposing a kind of watered-down version of natural theology. That's the attempt to explain what's going on in nature's order and design by appealing to a nonnatural source. So it's not science. I agree with all the scientists who say intelligent design should not be made part of science. It's not a valid scientific alternative to Darwinian ideas. It should not be taught in classrooms and public schools. It's also extremely poor theology. What intelligent design tries to do—and the great theologians have always resisted this idea—is to place the divine, the creator, within the continuum of natural causes. And this amounts to an extreme demotion of the transcendence of God, by making God just one cause in a series of natural causes.

This becomes the "God of the gaps." When you can't explain something by science, you say God did it.

Paul Tillich, the great Protestant theologian, said that kind of thinking was the foundation of modern atheism. Careless Christian thinkers wanted to make a place for God within the physical system that Newton and others had elaborated. That, in effect, demoted the deity as being just one link in a chain of causes that brought the transcendent into the realm of complete secular immanence. The atheists quite rightly said this God is unnecessary.

It seems to me that we need to be clear about what we mean by "religion." You have used that word in various ways. You've even suggested that some scientists are inherently religious because of their quest to understand ultimate causes, even though they may not believe in God. What is your definition of religion?

There are thousands of different definitions of religion. But I like to think of three main ways of understanding it. The first way—and I think almost all of us are religious in this sense—is to define religion as concern about something of ultimate importance. This was Tillich's broad definition: Religion is ultimate concern. Even the atheist who says that science is the only reliable road to truth, and nature is all there is, is setting up something that's ultimate. It's like the top stone of a pyramid that conditions everything else in the pyramid. In our own lives, we all have something like a top stone. If it were suddenly removed, it would cause our lives to fall apart. So we're all religious in that sense. In a narrower sense, religion is simply a sense of mystery. Einstein, for example, was someone who couldn't conceive of people—especially scientists—living without a sense of mystery. There are many scientists—sometimes they're called "religious naturalists"—who are deeply satisfied with the scientific universe that has given us an exhilarating sense of new horizons. That sense can fulfill a person's life.

They want to reclaim the word "religion." And they say hard-core atheists are missing out on the sacred. But they don't want any part of God.
Yeah, but there's a deep division among scientific atheists on this question. People like Dawkins and Weinberg are reluctant to go along with that idea of sacredness. But let me get to my third understanding of religion. That's a belief that this ultimate reality is at heart personal, by which we mean it is intelligent and is capable of love and making promises. This is the fundamental thinking about God in the Quran and the Bible—God is personal. Theologically speaking, personality is a symbol, like everything else in religion. Like all symbols, "personality" doesn't adequately capture the full depth of ultimate reality. But the conviction of the Abrahamic religions is that if ultimate reality were not at least personal—at least capable of everything that humans are capable of— then we cannot surrender ourselves fully to it. It would be an "it" rather than a "thou" and therefore would not reach us in the depth of our being.

But why? There are many people who lead profound spiritual lives who don't accept the idea of a personal God. There are entire religious traditions, like Buddhism, which don't have a concept of God, and certainly not a personal God.
I'm not denying that they're religious. They certainly would fit into the second, and sometimes the first, understanding of religion. Nor am I denying that they are capable of living with deep morality and compassion. I'm just delineating three understandings of faith. It's especially when you come to the belief in a personal God that the question of science and religion becomes most acute.

Einstein is certainly relevant in this context. He called himself a "deeply religious nonbeliever." He talked about having genuine religious feelings when he marveled at the inherent order and harmony in the universe. But

he thought the idea of a personal God was preposterous. He couldn't believe in a God who interfered with natural events or intervened in the lives of people.

Let's look at why Einstein found that idea of God objectionable. Einstein was a man who thought the laws of physics have to be completely inviolable. Nature is a closed continuum of deterministic causes and effects, and if anything interrupted that, it would violate the fundamental scientific worldview that he had. So the idea of a responsive God—a God who answers prayers—would have to violate the laws of physics, the laws of nature. This is why Einstein said the problem of science and religion is caused by the belief in a personal God. But it's not inevitable that a responsive God violates the laws of physics and chemistry. I don't think God does violate those laws.

Let's take the example of prayer. You are a Christian. Do you believe God answers your prayers?

Yes, but I have to go along with Martin Gardner here and ask, what if God answered everybody's prayers? What kind of world would we have? I also have to think of what Jesus said when his disciples asked him to teach them to pray. What he told them, in effect, was to pray for something really big. He called it "the kingdom of God." What that means is praying for the ultimate fulfillment of all being, of all the universe. So when we pray, we're asking that the world might have a future. I believe God is answering our prayers but not always in the ways we want. In the final analysis, we hope and trust that God will show or reveal Himself as one who has been accompanying our prayers and responding to the world all along, but not necessarily in the narrow way that the human mind is able to conjure up.

What do you make of the miracles in the Bible—most important, the Resurrection? Do you think that happened in the literal sense?

I don't think theology is being responsible if it ever takes anything with completely literal understanding. What we have in the New Testament is a story that's trying to awaken us to trust that our lives make sense, that in the end everything works out for the best. In a prescientific age, this is done in a way in which unlettered and scientifically illiterate people can be challenged by this event of Resurrection. But if you ask me whether a scientific experiment could verify the Resurrection, I would say such an event is entirely too important to be subjected to a method which is devoid of all religious meaning.

So if a camera was at the Resurrection, it would have recorded nothing?
If you had a camera in the upper room when the disciples came together after the death and Resurrection of Jesus, we would not see it. I'm not the only one to say this. Even conservative Catholic theologians say that. Faith means taking the risk of being vulnerable and opening your heart to that which is most important. We trivialize the whole meaning of the Resurrection when we start asking, is it scientifically verifiable? Science is simply not equipped to deal with the dimensions of purposefulness, love, compassion, forgiveness—all the feelings and experiences that accompanied the early community's belief that Jesus was still alive. Science is simply not equipped to deal with that. We have to learn to read the universe at different levels. That means we have to overcome literalism not just in the Christian or Jewish or Islamic interpretations of Scripture but also in the scientific exploration of the universe. There are levels of depth in the cosmos that science simply cannot reach by itself.

Richard Dawkins

IN THE ROILING DEBATE BETWEEN SCIENCE and religion, it would be hard to exaggerate the enormous influence of Richard Dawkins. This British scientist is religion's chief prosecutor—"Darwin's Rottweiler," as one magazine called him—and the world's most famous atheist. Speaking to the American Humanist Association, Dawkins once said, "I think a case can be made that faith is one of the world's great evils, comparable to the smallpox virus but harder to eradicate."

Not surprisingly, these kinds of comments have made Dawkins a lightning rod in the debate over evolution. Although he's a hero to those who can't stomach superstition or irrationality, his efforts to link Darwinism to atheism have upset scientists and philosophers, like Francis Collins and Michael Ruse, who are trying to bridge the gap between science and religion. Surprisingly, some intelligent design advocates have actually welcomed Dawkins's attacks. William Dembski, for instance, says his inflammatory rhetoric helps the ID cause by making evolution sound un-Christian.

Dawkins's outspoken atheism is a relatively recent turn in his public career. He first made his name more than 30 years ago with his ground-breaking book *The Selfish Gene*, which reshaped the field of evolution-ary biology by arguing that evolution played out at the level of the gene itself, not the individual animal. Dawkins has retired from his position as Professor of the Public Understanding of Science at Oxford University. Thanks to his tremendous talent for clear and graceful writing, he has done more to popularize evolutionary biology than virtually any other scientist, with the possible exception of Stephen Jay Gould. Dawkins has a gift for explaining science through brilliant metaphors. Phrases like "the selfish gene" and "the blind watchmaker" not only crystallized certain scientific ideas; they entered the English vernacular. His concept of "memes"—ideas themselves evolving like genes—has spawned a new way of thinking about cultural evolution.

In Dawkins's atheist manifesto, *The God Delusion*, he fulminates against religious moderates as well as fundamentalists. He argues that the existence of God is itself a scientific conjecture, one that doesn't hold up to the evidence. He dismisses the entire discipline of theology: "I have yet to see any good reason to suppose that theology (as opposed to biblical history, literature, etc.) is a subject at all."

I spoke with Dawkins about the dangers of unquestioned faith, the politics of the evolution debate, and why atheists are among the most intelligent people in the world.

■ ■ ■ ■

You've written about going to church as a boy. When did you become an atheist?

I started getting doubts when I was about nine and realized that there are lots of different religions and they can't all be right. And which one I happened to be brought up in was an arbitrary accident. I then sort of went back to religion around the age of 12, and then finally left it at the age of 15 or 16.

Did God and religion just not make sense intellectually? Is that why you turned against religion?

Yes, purely intellectually. I was never much bothered about moral questions like, how could there be a good God when there's so much evil in the world? For me, it was always an intellectual thing. I wanted to know the explanation for the existence of all things. I was particularly fascinated by living things. And when I discovered the Darwinian explanation, which is so stunningly elegant and powerful, I realized that you really don't need any kind of supernatural force to explain it.

Why do you call yourself an atheist? Why not an agnostic?

Well, technically, you cannot be any more than an agnostic. But I am as agnostic about God as I am about fairies and the Flying Spaghetti Monster. You cannot actually disprove the existence of God. Therefore, to be a positive atheist is not technically possible. But you can be as atheist about God as you can be atheist about Thor or Apollo. Everybody nowadays is an atheist about Thor and Apollo. Some of us just go one god further.

When you're talking about God, are you really talking about the God of the Bible—Yahweh of the Old Testament?

Well, as it happens, I am because I have an eye to the audience who's likely to be reading my book. Nobody believes in Thor and Apollo anymore, so I don't bother to address the book to them. So, in practice, it's addressed to believers in the Abrahamic God.

In *The God Delusion*, you say atheists are widely reviled, especially in the United States: "The status of atheists in America today is on a par with that of homosexuals fifty years ago." Doesn't it all depend on where you live? I know various cities and academic communities in the United States where it would be a lot harder to be an evangelical Christian than an atheist.

Yes, I should have qualified that. As you rightly said, it is highly respectable to be an atheist in Britain and most of Europe. In America, too—of course, I should have acknowledged and I apologize to my American friends—large parts of America, just about 50 percent of the United States of America, is intelligent and atheistic. Although the figures won't necessarily show that.

It's interesting that you link those two words—"intelligent" and "atheistic." Are you saying the more intelligent you are, the more likely you are to be an atheist?

There's a fair bit of evidence in favor of that equation, yes.

That sounds like an elitist argument. Do you want to cite that evidence?

It's certainly elitist. What's wrong with being elitist, if you are trying to encourage people to join the elite rather than being exclusive? I'm very, very keen that people should raise their game rather than the other way around. As for citing the evidence, a number of studies have been done. The one meta-analysis of this that I know of was published in *Mensa Magazine*. It looked at 43 studies on the relationship between educational level or IQ and religion. And in 39 out of 43—that's all but 4—there is a correlation between IQ/education and atheism. The more educated you are, the more likely you are to be an atheist. Or the more intelligent you are, the more likely you are to be an atheist.

You are quite up front about your goal with *The God Delusion*. You are hoping that "religious readers who open it will be atheists by the time they put it down." Do you really think that will happen?

No, I describe that as presumptuous. It's an ambition. I was hoping, in the best of all possible worlds, that would be the consequence of reading my book. I'm too realistic to think that it's going to happen in very many cases.

What is so bad about religion?

Well, it encourages you to believe falsehoods, to be satisfied with inadequate explanations which really aren't explanations at all. And this is particularly bad because the real explanations, the scientific explanations, are so beautiful and so elegant. Plenty of people never get exposed to the beauties of the scientific explanation for the world and for life. And that's very sad. But it's even sadder if they are actively discouraged from understanding by a systematic attempt in the opposite direction, which is what many religions actually are. But that's only the first of my many reasons for being hostile to religion.

My sense is that you don't just think religion is dishonest. There's something evil about it as well.

Well, yes. I think there's something very evil about faith, where faith means believing in something in the absence of evidence, and actually taking pride in believing in something in the absence of evidence. And the reason that's dangerous is that it justifies essentially anything. If you're taught in your holy book or by your priest that blasphemers should die or apostates should die—anybody who once believed in the religion and no longer does needs to be killed—that clearly is evil. And people don't have to justify it because it's their faith. They don't have to say, "Well, here's a very good reason for this." All they need to say is, "That's what my faith says." And we're all expected to back off and respect that. Whether or not we're actually faithful ourselves, we've been brought up to respect faith and to regard it as something that should not be challenged. And that can have extremely evil consequences. The consequences it's had historically—the Crusades, the Inquisition, right up to the present time where you have suicide bombers and people flying planes into skyscrapers in New York—all in the name of faith.

But don't you need to distinguish between religious extremists who kill people and moderate, peaceful religious believers?

You certainly need to distinguish them. They are very different. However, the moderate, sensible religious people you've cited make the world safe for the extremists by bringing up children—sometimes even indoctrinating children— to believe that faith trumps everything, and by influencing society to respect faith. Now, the faith of these moderate people is in itself harmless. But the idea that faith needs to be respected is instilled into children sitting in rows in their madrasahs in the Muslim world. And they are told these things not by extremists but by decent, moderate teachers and mullahs. But when they grow up, a small minority of them remember what they were told. They remember reading their holy book, and they take it literally. They really do believe it. Now, the moderate ones don't really believe it, but they have taught children that faith is a virtue. And it only takes a minority to believe what it says in the holy book—the Old Testament, the New Testament, the Quran, whatever it is. If you believe it's literally true, then there's scarcely any limit to the evil things you might do.

Yet most moderate religious people are appalled by the apocalyptic thinking of religious extremists.

Of course they're appalled. They're decent, nice people. But they have no right to be appalled because, in a sense, they brought it on the world by teaching people, especially children, the virtues of unquestioned faith.

Are you saying if parents belong to a particular church, they should not teach their children about that religion?

I would say that parents should teach their children anything that's known to be factually true—like "that's a bluebird" or "that's a bald eagle." Or they could teach children that there are such things as religious beliefs. But to teach children that it is a fact that there is one god or that God created the world in six days, that is child abuse.

But isn't much of parenting about teaching values to children? Just as a family of vegetarians will teach their children about the evils of killing animals and eating meat, can't parents who believe in God teach their children the values of a religious upbringing?

Children ask questions. And when a child says, "Why is it wrong to do so and so?" you can perfectly well answer that by saying, "Well, how would you like it if somebody else did that to you?" That's a way of imparting to a child the Golden Rule: "Do as you would be done by." The world would fall apart if everybody stole things from everybody else, so it's a bad thing to steal. If a child says, "Why can't I eat meat?" then you can say, "Your mother and I believe that it's wrong to eat meat for this, that, and the other reason. We are vegetarians. You can decide when you're older whether you want to be a vegetarian or not. But for the moment, you're living in this house, so the food we give you is not meat." That I could see. I think it's child abuse not to let the child have the free choice of knowing there are other people who believe something quite different and the child could make its own choice.

There are an awful lot of people who call themselves religious—or some people prefer to use the word "spiritual"—even though they don't go to church. They aren't part of any organized religion. They don't believe in a personal God. Some don't even like the word "God" because there's so much baggage attached to that word. But they still have some powerful feeling that there is a transcendent reality. They often engage in some spiritual practice in their own lives. Would you call these people "religious"?

That's a difficult question. I might call them religious. It depends on exactly what they do believe. The first chapter of *The God Delusion* talks about Einstein, who often used the word "God." Einstein clearly was an atheist in the sense that he didn't believe in any sort of personal God. He used the word "God" as a metaphoric name for that which we don't yet understand, for the deep mysteries at the foundation of the universe.

But I think most people would call Einstein a deist. He suggested that God may have created the laws of nature, the laws of physics, to get the universe started.

Some people have maintained that position. My judgment, reading what Einstein said, is that he was not a deist. He certainly believed in some sort of deep mystery, as do I. And it is possible to use the word "religious" to describe such a person. On that basis, one could even say that I am a religious person or Carl Sagan was a religious person. But for me, the divide comes with whether you believe there is some kind of a supernatural, personal being. And I think deists, as well as theists, believe that. By that criterion, I don't think Einstein was a deist. He certainly wasn't a theist, although the language he used might lead you to think he was. I think it's misleading to use a word like "God" in the way Einstein did. I'm sorry that Einstein did. I think he was asking for trouble, and he certainly was misunderstood.

Your definition of religious belief seems to involve a personal being. I think a lot of people would disagree. They may consider themselves strongly religious, but they would regard the whole idea of a personal God to be an outdated notion of what religion is.

Well, then I would want to know what they did mean by it. I would take my stand on whether the god or the being—whatever we're talking about—is complicated and improbable and has those attributes of a person—intelligence, creativity, something of that sort. If you believe that the universe was created by a designing intelligence, whether you call that personal or not, that seems to me to be a good definition of God. That's what I don't believe in. And that's what Einstein did not believe in.

Once you get past the biblical literalists, I think most people assume that science and religion are actually quite compatible. Stephen Jay Gould famously argued that they were "nonoverlapping magisteria": Science covers the empirical realm of facts and theories about the observable universe, and religion deals with ultimate meaning and moral value. But you're very critical of this argument, right?

Yes, I think religious belief is a scientific belief, in the sense that it makes claims about the universe which are essentially scientific claims. If you believe the universe was created and inhabited by a supreme being, that would be a very different kind of universe from the sort of universe that wasn't created and does not house a creative intelligence. That is a scientific difference. Miracles. If you believe in miracles, that is clearly a scientific claim, and scientific methods would be used to evaluate any miracle that somebody claimed evidence for.

Suppose, hypothetically, that forensic archaeologists, in an unlikely series of events, gained evidence—perhaps from some discovered DNA—which showed that Jesus did not really have an earthly father, that he really was born of a virgin. Can you imagine any theologian taking refuge behind Stephen Jay Gould's nonoverlapping magisteria and saying, "Nope, DNA evidence is completely irrelevant. Wrong magisterium. Science and religion have nothing to do with each other. They just peacefully coexist." Of course they wouldn't say that. If any such evidence were discovered, the DNA evidence would be trumpeted to the skies.

On the other hand, I think a lot of people have trouble with your claim that the existence of God is itself a scientific question. They would say God is, almost by definition, unknowable and ineffable.

If they mean some kind of supreme intelligence who set up the laws of physics or set up the world so it's compatible with life, I really would have a problem with that. That really is a scientific claim. If you're using the word "God" just to be a synonym for the laws of physics themselves, if God just means no more than Planck's constant or something like that, then I think we're into semantics. If that's the God you believe in, that's fine. But I don't think that's what people who call themselves religious really do mean by it. I think they mean something more like a supreme intelligence, a being who thinks, who creates, who designs.

What about the old adage that science deals with the "how" questions and religion deals with the "why" questions?

I think that's remarkably stupid, if I may say so. What on Earth is a "why" question? There are "why" questions that mean something in a Darwinian world. We say, why do birds have wings? To fly with. And that's a Darwinian translation of the evolutionary process whereby the birds that had wings survived better than the birds without. They don't mean that, though. They mean "why" in a deliberate, purposeful sense. So when you say religion deals with "why" questions, that begs the entire question that we're arguing about. Those of us who don't believe in religion—supernatural religion—would say there is no such thing as a "why" question in that sense. Now, the mere fact that you can frame an English sentence beginning with the word "why" does not mean that English sentence should receive an answer. I could say, why are unicorns hollow? That appears to mean something, but it doesn't deserve an answer.

But it seems to me the big "why" questions are, why are we here? And what is our purpose in life?

It's not a question that deserves an answer.

Well, I think most people would say those questions are central to the way we think about our lives. Those are the big existential questions, but they are also questions that go beyond science.

If you mean, what is the purpose of the existence of the universe, then I'm saying that is quite simply begging the question. If you happen to be religious, you think that's a meaningful question. But the mere fact that you can phrase it as an English sentence doesn't mean it deserves an answer. Those of us who don't believe in a god will say that is as illegitimate as the question, why are unicorns hollow? It just shouldn't be put. It's not a proper question to put. It doesn't deserve an answer.

I don't understand that. Doesn't every person wonder about that? Isn't that a core question, what are we doing in this world? Doesn't everyone struggle with that?

There are core questions like, how did the universe begin? Where do the laws of physics come from? Where does life come from? Why, after billions of years, did life originate on this planet and then start evolving? Those are all perfectly legitimate questions to which science can give answers, if not now, then we hope in the future. There may be some very, very deep questions, perhaps even where do the laws of physics come from, that science will never answer. That is perfectly possible. I am hopeful, along with some physicists, that science will one day answer that question. But even if they don't—even if there are some supremely deep questions to which science can never answer—what on Earth makes you think that religion can answer those questions?

At one point in your book, you say you don't like confrontation. That will surprise a lot of people, because you have become a lightning rod in the science and religion wars. Why do you think you evoke such powerful reactions?

Well, I don't relish confrontation for its own sake. I don't spoil for a fight. I'd much rather have an amicable discussion. But I am a professional academic, and professional academics are used to arguing about all sorts of things. And we argue in a robust way, bringing forth evidence where we can and using our skills of argument to deploy that evidence. So I may come across as passionate. But that doesn't mean I go out of my way to have confrontations in an aggressive way. I don't.

I have to ask you about a letter that I've come across from the intelligent design advocate William Dembski. He thanked you for your outspoken atheism. His letter to you said, "I want to thank you for being such a wonderful foil for theism and for intelligent design more generally. In fact, I regularly tell my colleagues that you and your work are one of God's greatest gifts to the intelligent design movement. So, please, keep at it." What do you make of that?

Yeah, I get that quite a lot. It is a difficult political dilemma that we face. In the United States of America there's a big battle going on, educationally, over teaching evolution in public schools. Science is definitely under attack. And evolution is in the frontline trench of that battle. So a science defense lobby has sprung up, which in practice largely means an evolution defense lobby. Now, it is true that if you want to win a court case in the United States where it's specifically on the narrow issue of should evolution be taught in the public schools, if somebody like me is called as a witness and the lawyer for the other side says, "Professor Dawkins, is it true that you were led to atheism through the study of Darwinian evolution?" I would have to answer, "Yes." That of course plays into their hands, because any jury is likely to have been brought up to believe that atheists are the devil incarnate. And therefore, if Darwin leads to atheism, then obviously we've got to throw out Darwinism. Well, that is exactly what Dembski is getting at. He claims to like the things that I say because I am playing into his hands by allowing people like him to make the equation between Darwinism and atheism.

But it's not just Dembski. I've heard this from various scientists—hard-core evolutionists—who wish you would tone down your rhetoric, quite frankly.
That is absolutely true.

They say this hurts the cause of teaching evolution. It just gives fire to the creationists.
Exactly right. And they could be right, in a political sense. It depends on whether you think the real war is over the teaching of evolution, as they do, or whether, as I do, you think the real war is between supernaturalism and naturalism. If you think the war is between supernaturalism and naturalism, then the war over the teaching of evolution is just one skirmish, just one battle, in the war. So what the scientists you've been talking to are asking me to do is to shut my mouth. Because for the sake of what I see as the war, I'm in danger of losing this particular battle. And that's a worthwhile political point for them to make.

Well, I think a lot of these scientists really do accept Stephen Jay Gould's idea of nonoverlapping magisteria. These are hard-core evolutionists, but they say religion is an entirely different realm. So you, with your inflammatory rhetoric, just muddy the waters and make life more difficult for them.
That is exactly what they say. And I believe that actually is the political reason for Gould to put forward the nonoverlapping magisteria in the first place. I

think it's nonsense. And I'll continue to say that I think it's nonsense. But I can easily see, politically, why he said that and why other scientists follow it. The politics is very straightforward. The science lobby, which is very important in the United States, wants those sensible religious people—the theologians, the bishops, the clergymen who believe in evolution—on their side. And the way to get those sensible religious people on your side is to say there is no conflict between science and religion. We all believe in evolution, whether we're religious or not. Therefore, because we need to get the mainstream orthodox religious people on our side, we've got to concede to them their fundamental belief in God, thereby—in my view—losing the war in order to win the battle for evolution. If you're prepared to compromise the war for the sake of the battle, then it's a sensible political strategy.

Throughout the ages, people resorted to that kind of political compromise. And maybe it would be a good thing for me to do as well. But as it happens, I think the war is more important. I actually do care about the existence or nonexistence of a supreme being. And therefore, I don't think I should say something which I believe to be false, which is that the question of whether God exists is a nonscientific question, and science and religion have no contact with each other, so we can all get along cozily and keep out those lunatic creationists.

Let's stay with the battle over evolution for a moment. Why do you think Darwinian evolution leads logically to atheism?
Well, I'm not sure it's a logical thing. I call it consciousness raising. I think the most powerful reason for believing in a supreme being is the argument for design. Living things in particular look complicated, look beautiful, look elegant, look as though they've been designed. We are all accustomed to thinking that if something *looks* designed, it *is* designed. Therefore, it's really no wonder that before Darwin came along, just about everybody was a theist. Darwin blew that argument out of the water. We now have a much more elegant and parsimonious explanation for the existence of life.

So the big reason for believing in God used to be the argument for biological design. Darwin destroyed that argument. He didn't destroy the parallel argument from cosmology—where did the universe come from? Where did the laws of physics come from? But he raised our consciousness to the power of science to explain things. And he made it unsafe for anyone in the future to resort automatically and uncritically to a designer just because they don't immediately have an explanation for something. So when people say, "I can't see how the universe could have come into being without God," be very careful, because you've had your fingers burned before over biology. That's the consciousness-raising sense in which, I think, Darwinism leads to atheism.

I want to turn to what you would call "the real war"—the war between supernaturalism and naturalism. A lot of religious people call you a reductionist and a materialist. They say you want to boil everything down to what can be measured and experimentally tested. "If you can't measure it, if you can't test it, it's not real."

The words "reductionist" and "materialist" are loaded. They have a negative connotation to many people. I'm a reductionist and a materialist in a much grander sense. When we try to explain the workings of something really complicated, like a human brain, we can be reductionist in the sense that we believe that the brain's behavior is to be explained by neurons, and the behavior of neurons is to be explained by molecules within the neurons, et cetera. Similarly, computers. They're made of integrated circuits. They're nothing but a whole lot of ones and noughts shuffling about. That's reductive in the sense that it seems to leave a lot unexplained. There is nothing else in computers apart from integrated circuits and resistors and transistors shuffling ones and noughts. Nevertheless, it's a highly sophisticated explanation for understanding how the computer does the remarkably complicated things it does. So don't use the word "reductive" in a sort of reducing sense. And ditto with "materialist."

But this seems to discount personal experience. It discounts the mystical experiences that people talk about—that oneness with something larger. Are some of these things just beyond the explanatory power of science?

As I've said, the brain is highly complicated. And one thing it does is construct remarkable software illusions and hallucinations. Every night of our lives, we dream and our brain concocts visions which are, at least until we wake up, highly convincing. Most of us have had experiences which are verging on hallucination. It shows the power of the brain to knock together illusions. If you're sufficiently susceptible and sufficiently indoctrinated in the folklore of a particular religion, it's not in the least surprising that people would hallucinate visions and hear small voices. I wouldn't be at all surprised if it happened to me.

It seems to me this is actually one of the key questions in the whole religion and science debate. What do you do with consciousness? I mean, do you really think the mind is totally reducible to neural networks and the electrochemical surges in the brain? Or might there be something else that goes beyond the physical mechanics of the brain?

Well, once again, let's not use the word "reducible" in a negative way. The sheer number of neurons in the brain, and the complication of the connections between the neurons is such that one doesn't want to use the word "reducible" in any kind of negative way. Consciousness is the biggest puzzle facing biology, neurobiology, computational studies, and evolutionary biology. It is a very, very big problem. I don't know the answer. Nobody knows the answer. I think one day they probably will know the answer. But even if science doesn't know the answer, I return to the question, what on Earth makes you think that religion will? Just because science so far has failed to explain something, such as consciousness, to say it follows that the facile, pathetic explanations which religion has produced somehow by default must win the argument is really quite ridiculous. Nobody has an explanation for consciousness. That should be a spur to work harder and try to understand it. Not to give up and just say, "Oh well, it must be a soul." That doesn't mean anything. It doesn't explain anything. You've said absolutely nothing when you've said that.

A lot of what we're talking about comes down to whether science has certain limits. The basic religious critique of your position is that science can only explain so much. And that's where mystery comes in. That's where consciousness comes in.

There are two ways of responding to mystery. The scientist's way is to see it as a challenge, something they've got to work on, we're really going to try to crack it. But there are others who revel in mystery, who think we were not meant to understand. There's something sacred about mystery which positively should not be tackled. Now, suppose science does have limits. What is the value in giving the label "religion" to those limits? If you simply want to define religion as the bits outside of what science can explain, then we're not really arguing. We're simply using a word, "God," for that which science can't explain. I don't have a problem with that except that it is just begging to be misunderstood. I do have a problem with saying God is a supernatural, creative, intelligent being. It's simply illogical to say science can't explain certain things; therefore, we have to be religious. To equate that kind of religiousness with belief in a personal, intelligent being, that's confusion. And it's pernicious confusion.

Simon Conway Morris

IF THERE IS ONE STRAND of evolutionary theory that sticks in the craw of nearly every religious believer, it's the idea that human beings are just a lucky accident in the evolutionary sweepstakes. How do you reconcile the belief that we're here for a purpose with the apparent randomness of evolution? But what if we aren't an accident? What if the evolution of humans—or some intelligent creature like us—was inevitable once life first appeared on Earth? That's the controversial argument made by Simon Conway Morris, a Cambridge University evolutionary biologist.

Conway Morris first came to public attention in Stephen Jay Gould's book *Wonderful Life*. One of Gould's heroes, Conway Morris was a young paleontologist who sifted through the Burgess Shale fossils to help uncover the remarkable story of the Cambrian explosion. Gould used these findings to argue that evolution is full of strange twists and turns. He believed that if you reran the tape of life, an entirely different set of creatures would emerge. But when Conway Morris wrote his own book about the Burgess Shale, *The Crucible of Creation*, he came to the opposite conclusion. He said evolution is actually constrained to move only in certain directions.

Conway Morris has spent years marshaling evidence for "evolutionary convergence." For instance, he and other scientists have isolated separate evolutionary histories that led to the development of the camera eye, which is found in species as diverse as mammals, squid, snails, and even some jellyfish. He can point to convergence in particular kinds of teeth and claws and even the farming techniques of ants and humans. When I visited his office in the Earth Sciences Building in Cambridge, I found piles of books and papers scattered all over the room and file drawers stacked right on his desk, filled with hundreds—if not thousands—of case studies of convergence. Conway Morris seems to be happiest when rummaging through the marvelous intricacies of various plants and animals—whether the canines of saber-tooth cats, the pollen production of flowers, or the tool-making abilities of New Caledonian crows.

In recent years, many biologists have come to accept evolutionary convergence—at least to some extent. Yes, the genetic mutations are random, but only certain mutations are then "selected" to survive in future generations. Where Conway Morris runs into trouble is his argument for the inevitability of human evolution. "That's romantic and mistaken," the philosopher of science Daniel Dennett told me. Many critics suspect that Conway Morris's scientific conclusions have been swayed by his Christian faith.

Conway Morris is surprisingly open about his own religious beliefs. I once heard him lecture to a group of journalists and—after a dazzling romp through evolutionary history—he announced, "I'm now going to commit intellectual suicide." He proceeded to claim that the shroud of Turin may, in fact, have been draped over the face of Jesus. That assertion stunned the journalists there, and yet I got the sense that Conway Morris enjoyed playing the role of provocateur.

We talked about his argument for human inevitability, his belief in miracles, and the limits of current scientific thinking.

■ ■ ■ ■

You've said that Darwin was right up to a point, but the science of evolution is incomplete. What is still unexplained?
First, let me say that no science is ever complete. My impression of physics is that the investigations could still be at an early stage. If it turns out that string theory is satisfactory and coherent in the way that general relativity is, it will open a whole new series of investigations. But evolution is widely regarded as a closed book. Even though the basic facts of evolution are not in dispute— certainly not by me or other evolutionary biologists—I think it's incomplete.

The majority of neo-Darwinists have emphasized the randomness of evolution and see its direction as almost open-ended. That I dispute very strongly. And there's unfinished business in all sorts of areas, like the origin of life and the nature of consciousness. I'm not saying these are impossible problems. I simply think they're exceedingly difficult problems. But the science we need to understand them goes considerably beyond the science we have available at the moment.

Are you suggesting that natural selection may not be the only process that explains evolution?

There's no dispute at all about the Darwinian mechanisms of selection, but I am less convinced that natural selection will explain how evolution operates on complex molecular structures. Nor are these ideas particularly contentious: Self-organization, for example, is evidently important. Remember also how these molecular structures are fantastically versatile. A particular molecule can often do dozens of different things. It's like a toolbox. It's analogous to a molecule acting as a bulldozer, as a tank, an airplane, a pile driver, a feather duster, and also as a cup of tea. But why so versatile?

And the way molecules interact is strongly constrained. So why are they constrained in that particular fashion? And there's a second question: How do they interact with each other? How do they interact within the cell? All those interactions are largely governed by processes that we call "self-organization." But self-organization is not an explanation; it's a description of the universe as we see it. Scientists are interested in explanations, not descriptions. Simply saying that evolution happens doesn't explain why we have the organismal complexity we see around us. And I'd go further. While this isn't fashionable at the moment, I would argue that the possible endpoints of evolution are much more constricted than is often thought to be the case.

So there are only so many ways that evolution can develop?

Yes, though many neo-Darwinians would say any endpoint is just as likely as any other endpoint. But if you want to swim in the ocean, you need certain things to do that, or if you want to fly, you need wings. This is very important when you consider, for instance, the search for extraterrestrial intelligence. There's a general feeling that if there's a sentient species out there, we could communicate with it. After all, why spend all that money building radio telescopes to see whether we can pick up signals? But from a neo-Darwinian perspective, you might wonder whether human evolution is an evolutionary fluke. I would differ from that point of view quite strongly.

If there is other intelligent life in the galaxy, you believe it will be similar to us?
Of course, that's a very big "if." But science depends on making hypotheses and finding general patterns. It's perfectly logical to look for extraterrestrial life. We know there are lots of planets out there, and the reason there might be something that's surprisingly similar to human intelligence is the phenomenon known as "evolutionary convergence."

Across the whole spectrum of biology, we see that only certain solutions to various biological problems are viable. Again and again, these solutions are arrived at. Perhaps the most famous example is the very intriguing similarity between the construction of the eye in our head, which first evolved in fish, and the eye of a squid or an octopus. Both are based on more or less the same design, what we call a camera eye. When one looks in detail, even at the construction of the lens, they are remarkably similar. Why is that so remarkable? After all, eyes have to see. And if you want to see very well, perhaps it's less surprising that the camera eye has evolved. And if that's true on this planet, where the camera eye has evolved perhaps as many as seven times, then surely it's a good guess it should happen elsewhere.

So ET will probably have a camera eye.
I think some ETs will have a camera eye, and other ETs will have eyes very similar to what insects have. We can do a fairly straightforward thought experiment: Let's equip humans with a compound eye—the sort of eye you find in insects, with not just a single lens but many lenses over the surface of the eye. We would need an enormous compound eye perched on the top of our head to work as effectively as the camera eye that we actually possess.

You said there may be seven different examples of the camera eye here on Earth, all arising from separate evolutionary histories. What are some other animals with camera eyes?

A number of mollusks, including various snails and the octopus, have independently developed a camera eye. But actually, the most interesting example is in a group of jellyfish called the box jellies, which have extremely toxic stings. Though these are primitive animals—they have a nervous system but not really a brain—these animals have camera eyes on their tentacles. There's been a lot of discussion about why these supposedly simple animals—the jellyfish—need such sophisticated optical equipment. It's quite a long story, but these jellyfish are as near as any jellyfish will get to becoming a fish. They are active hunters. They engage in courtship and they copulate.

Those animals which have evolved a camera eye tend to be hunters; they go after live prey. They also move quickly. And there's a tendency toward intelligence. There are many fascinating experiments on the intelligence of the octopus. They're very sophisticated animals.

I had no idea that the octopus is smart.

Oh, yes. They do all sorts of things. They memorize and learn things very readily. Experiments have shown that if one octopus sees another octopus doing something, it will learn from that octopus. A lot of animals don't have that degree of flexibility and sophistication. They even play and use tools.

What are some other examples of convergence?

Convergence is ubiquitous. Many different groups of plants have learned how to become trees. If you look at the way leaves capture sunlight—actually, not so surprising because leaves have certain prerequisites and environmental constraints—there's a strong degree of convergence in various kinds of leaves. My guess is that if you went to another planet and found extraterrestrials, not only would the intelligent ones have camera eyes, but there would be trees and forests. It suggests there's some predictability in the way evolution flows. It's not simply an open-ended game.

When we look at the tree of life, I'm also wondering whether all those branching points are predetermined in a certain way. We know there is a substrate of possibilities which is present long before an eye or a nervous system or a particular animal has actually appeared. This may point toward more general biological principles. I don't mind at all if I'm wrong, but I'm just beginning to wonder about the tree of life—as we go back in time, from terminal twig to slightly larger branch to trunk to the main trunk of the tree—whether a good part of what defines that shape is more or less inevitable.

You've pointed to agricultural technology as another convergent phenomenon, and you've talked about similarities between the farming techniques of humans and certain ants.

That's a fascinating example. We've found one group of ants in Central and South America that's learned to do agriculture independently. Squads of ants go out early in the morning. They cut leaves from the trees, which are dropped down to the ground where another party of ants is responsible for taking them back to the nest. These leaves are processed to form a sort of mulch. On this mulch, colonies of fungi convert the tough leaf material into sugars, which the young ants eat. The ants not only organize and collect this material; they also fertilize the fungus, and their weeding keeps this monoculture clean and tidy.

These ants also have filaments of bacteria around their bodies, which leak antibiotics, helping suppress pathogens which would otherwise devastate the ant farms. This is really fascinating, because one of the key challenges to human health is the ever-growing development of antibiotic resistance. This is an extremely serious problem. We know from the fossil record and molecular biology that this ant farming—which is a symbiotic relationship between fungi and ants—evolved millions of years ago. Scientists working in this area are increasingly impressed by the sheer sophistication of this ecological system. It's very complex, and the parallels with human agriculture are striking. But should we be surprised? How else are you going to grow crops? You need to keep the weeds out, you need to fertilize the crops, and you need to stop infestation by pests. That's agriculture. And of course not only the ants invented it; so did termites and beetles and even fish.

If we're looking for other examples of convergence, didn't the big cats evolve independently on different continents?

That's a fascinating story. The classic example is a comparison between the marsupials in Australia—animals which grow in a pouch—and the other group of mammals known as placentals, which include ourselves and hedgehogs and giraffes. These days, marsupials are confined largely but not entirely to Australia. But in the geological past, marsupials were spectacularly successful in South America. One of those marsupials evolved into a cat with huge stabbing canines. It was a saber-tooth cat but is related to the kangaroo. The more familiar saber-tooth cat, displayed most famously in the La Brea Tar Pits in Los Angeles, is related to the panther, the lion, and the house cat. Their skull and stabbing canines are remarkably similar, and yet there are differences. One is a marsupial, related to animals like the koala "bear," while the other is a placental related to us.

So predators are going to have certain similarities—maybe particular kinds of teeth and slashing claws.

Claws are convergent and teeth are convergent. We know they've evolved independently at least twice and maybe more times. Different sorts of teeth are convergent. For instance, teeth that crush shellfish are also highly convergent. But is this so surprising? One has to function in the real world. Yet in the professional literature, the adjectives used by biologists to describe these examples of convergence are "astonishing" or "remarkable" or "stunning." Why should we be stunned? This is the way the world works.

Your theory of evolution is most controversial when you get to human beings. Why do you think the evolution of a highly intelligent creature, such as *Homo sapiens*, was inevitable once life on Earth got started?

A great deal of our molecular make-up actually evolved long before there were animals, let alone vertebrates and mammals. The architecture of life has been made and is waiting to be reused in new contexts. Evolution is the cooption of previously evolved structures. If we look at the nervous system of animals, many of the molecules which are essential to the nervous system had already evolved in more primitive organisms. Then we get to advanced nervous systems with brains, and we see similar cognitive systems emerge. The most famous examples of convergence are between some of the birds—the crows and parrots—and ourselves.

What's turned out to be so fascinating is that the mental world of crows and parrots is astonishingly similar to the mental world of the great apes. Of course, we are apes that can do a few extra things. Yet we know the structure of the bird brain is really very different from the mammalian brain. If you dissect a bird brain, it's not similar at all. But despite these manifest differences, the same sort of mental world emerges. I think that's convergence. It suggests that you can get to the same solution with a very different route. That's what's so fascinating about evolution. It doesn't really matter where you start.

How do we know the mental world of these birds is similar to our own?
Many animals are good at mazes, but if you give them more difficult tests, they're completely stumped. But if you look at the behavior of the corvids, especially animals like the New Caledonian crow, they're very inventive about how to get hold of food. They're also very playful. Play is something we take for granted, but it involves a sense of curiosity. There's a one-to-one correspondence between the different categories of social play in mammals and in the most intelligent birds. The juveniles of kea parrots in New Zealand are famous for fooling around in delinquent gangs and trashing things. They clearly live in a rich mental world. Crows are incredibly good at remembering where they've left their food. They can remember hundreds, if not thousands, of sites in a forest where they've cached food. But more important, if they see they're being observed by a crow that might steal their food, they will recache that food when the thief has gone away. They can understand what's going on in the mind of another creature. The New Caledonian crow, which lives on an island in the Pacific, has tool-making abilities which are manifestly superior to anything that a chimpanzee can achieve.

Clearly, these are highly sophisticated animals, and we could also mention elephants, dolphins, and whales. But that still doesn't make the case that human evolution was inevitable.

The first thing to stress is that practically everything that makes us human is already present in a nascent form in other groups of animals. This is not to say that every species on the planet is trying to turn into humans, but the differences between ourselves and many other organisms is paper thin. They have cognitive capacities that are on the road to what is necessary for becoming fully human. So you have to ask, is that cognitive landscape likely to evolve in other animals? I think it's rather likely.

I'm not saying that crows, parrots, chimpanzees, or dolphins are the same as humans. There's now a complete gulf between us and the rest of biology. So the question is, why has it only happened to us—with one possible exception, the Neanderthals? You assume that humans must have had a process of gradual emergence. But the archaeological record doesn't really show that. We know that modern humans only appear about 200,000 years ago. But they didn't really do much for the first 100,000 years. Why not? They have the same brain size, but they seem culturally rather stagnant. I'm deeply puzzled about the origins of the things that make us completely human, such as our ability to use language and engage in rational discourse, our ability to employ our imagination. I'm not persuaded those things can simply be extrapolated from Darwinian processes.

But aren't human beings here by a massive stroke of luck? The asteroid that hit the Earth 65 million years ago wiped out the dinosaurs. If that asteroid had missed, wouldn't dinosaurs have continued to dominate the Earth, preventing large mammals from evolving, including humans?
I think that's absolutely correct. If the asteroid had sailed past harmlessly, then dinosaurs would be here today. But imagine that we've fast-forwarded our conversation by about 30 million years. I'm afraid to tell you the dinosaurs have disappeared. They've been hunted into extinction.

Who killed the dinosaurs?
One or another group of warm-blooded creatures. It could have been the birds, but more likely the mammals. The first thing to remember is that birds and mammals coexisted with dinosaurs, but the dinosaurs were in charge at that time. Most mammals were pretty small. Some were a reasonable

size—maybe the size of a dog. In the ocean, there were no killer whales or sperm whales because it was full of reptiles. In the sky, there were birds but not any bats. Even the birds were pushed to one side.

So the asteroid hits. Bang! Dinosaurs gone, big reptiles gone. Birds and mammals look at each other and say, "Well, this is a wonderful opportunity, let's evolve." So we get this dramatic evolutionary explosion, which is well documented in the fossil record and, indeed, here we are. Now, suppose that asteroid misses. It's a counterfactual history. What's going to happen? My view is that fortunately for us, but unfortunately for the dinosaurs, around 20 million years after the asteroid missed, the world starts to get surprisingly cold as we begin the great ice ages.

Dinosaurs are not effectively warm-blooded. They're warm-blooded in part because of size, but not in the way that birds and mammals are. In this counterfactual world, birds and mammals are more intelligent than reptiles, more socially adept, and convergently, they evolve proto-technologies. They are tool makers. So what will happen next? My sense is that sooner or later, one or another group of hunters will emerge. It doesn't have to be exactly the same history that we had on this planet, but the end result will be the same. When the hunting really gets going, all the big animals would disappear. Maybe they wouldn't all be speared to death by Clovis hunters, but with the changes in the environment and the mass killings of large vertebrates in this counterfactual world, it would have been a *Tyrannosaurus* going down under a hail of arrows rather than the mastodon in North America.

Isn't this all a rather large "what if"? And yet you seem to need this theory to argue for the inevitability of human evolution.
Well, you say this is science and that is theory. Of course, science depends on theory, and one can posit various things that could be expected to happen. The final test, of course, will be if we ever find an extraterrestrial planet which has a very similar set of arrangements.

Stephen Jay Gould celebrated your work on the Burgess Shale, but he was probably the best-known critic of your argument for evolutionary progress. He said if you reran the tape of evolution, the results would be totally

different. How could he come up with such a radically different position than yours?

Unfortunately, he died some years ago, so he's not here to discuss it with us. There is no doubt that everybody carries within them a whole series of assumptions about the world. I think at the heart of Gould's objection to progress was his fascination with human liberty. He was a fierce critic of sociobiology and genetic determinism. He felt if the genes "made us do it," then we become morally irresponsible; we become agents of molecules rather than agents of free will. Nonsense, of course, but the fact remains that no scientist can be completely neutral. We all bring a set of beliefs about the way the world is. We as scientists try to leave them at the office door, but whenever we go out there is metaphysics patiently waiting. I think Gould's ideology—that human freedom must be protected from Darwinian determinism—was praiseworthy but ultimately leading down a blind alley.

You are very open about your own Christian faith, and your theory has some obvious theological implications. It suggests there's some purpose to the evolutionary process—maybe even an endpoint. This supports the religious belief that humans have some inherent purpose. But it's much harder to reconcile evolution with religious belief if evolution is just a random process that could move in any direction.

Well, you could ask, is there purpose in the Big Bang? Or is there purpose in galaxies forming? Is there purpose in a sparrow? Once you start importing words like "purpose" or "design"—which have all sorts of agendas which I find too narrow and constricting—we're throwing away our imaginative powers.

Your critics say your theories are made to fit your religious beliefs. We must end up with human beings, which would seem to support a Christian view of the world.

Yes, those people say a theist is taking particular baggage with him. But all of us are taking intellectual baggage, even materialists. Materialism is a belief system, a metaphysics, which in my view doesn't take you very far. Any religion is ultimately trying to make sense of the world. If you look at people like

[Jacques] Monod or [Steven] Weinberg, underlying their "faith" is a sense that the world is completely meaningless. I'm very puzzled by this, because I don't see how a species which engages in philosophical discourse can talk about meaninglessness unless it knows what meaning is.

Now, one must be cautious and skeptical, but there are enough straws in the wind to suggest that the "visible" and "invisible" realities in the Christian tradition make sense in a wider theological context. If one starts with the assumption that the universe is very cannily constructed, but also is capable of indefinite investigation, then there might be aspects of reality which are familiar to philosophers and theologians that are not simply inventions of the human mind.

If you're a Christian, and you're serious about reconciling science and religion, do you have to assume that it was necessary for humans to evolve? Or can you be a good Christian and say, "Oh well, maybe human beings are just an evolutionary fluke"?

From a Christian viewpoint, the universe is utterly contingent. It needn't exist at all. It could be anything which God so chose. People who think religion is just a set of answers to keep you comfortable are sadly mistaken. It is an open-ended adventure. We don't know what the nature of the universe is. We don't know why we have our moral, intellectual, and poetic capacities. I know they have an evolutionary basis. But I think religious instincts and doctrines also tell us something real about the world. They're not simply fairy stories.

Can evolution tell us much about consciousness and how the human mind took shape?

I think our attempts to understand consciousness have failed completely and utterly. We just have no explanation for it at all. One problem is the apparent separation between body and mind. I see no conceivable way how we can understand how matter makes mind, even though paradoxically we are embodied minds. I suspect that if we have access to mind through our brains and our nervous systems, then you could regard the brain as more like an antenna. It's embedded in mind substance, and that's why we connect. That has interesting ramifications. Where does our imagination come from? Why do some ideas turn out to be incredibly fruitful? Why do dreams actually work for some people? The materialist argument has been useful and has taken us a long way, not least in revealing the extraordinary complexity of the brain, but please don't imagine it's going to take us down the whole road.

If the brain is like an antenna, are you suggesting that it can somehow pick up signals or information that's outside our skulls?

I am, but please remember I'm using metaphors and analogies associated with technology. From this point of view it is no accident that people claim the brain is a computer. Whatever it is, it's not a computer. But we're all stuck with the words we have when we're grasping for deeper explanations. We can look at philosophical traditions of reality. The most familiar is Plato, who says there are real things and we're just reflections of those things. In the Christian tradition, you have circles of reality which are difficult to access, and yet certain people apparently know about them. Of course, the materialists will say these are just dollops of molecular fantasy. But they ring true to us, and we also know that some people engage with invisible realities which turn out to be extremely harmful. The medical evidence is that they are very damaged. My interest is to keep an open mind. Why should it all be in our brain?

The materialist philosopher Daniel Dennett has described you as a "mind creationist." He says you take evolution right up to the human brain and then you stop.

Using the word "creationist" is perhaps his attempt to put me close to intelligent design, which I'm not at all. We don't have any satisfactory explanation for consciousness. Simply to label someone a "mind creationist" is to reduce my arguments to a facile level. Science is by necessity a reductive enterprise. It has to be as objective as possible. But we live in a world that's full of value and meaning and beauty. My guess, or hunch, is that our mind is not completely in our brain. That's not a scientific statement. But the universe is a funny place in terms of its laws of physics and its whole construction. Could there actually be other dimensions to our existence?

This seems to be one of the key questions in the science and religion debate. It's hard to say the mind is capable of contacting other dimensions if it's nothing more than the neurochemistry of the brain.

I certainly think it is. But it may be that what we now think of as science—which is an investigation of the known world—is cripplingly narrow. There are lots of people who have very unorthodox ideas which are almost impossible to test. That's the difficulty with trying to explain consciousness. I don't think anybody really knows how to get a grip on it. If somebody dies, their brain stops and we have every reason to think they have no understanding of any world, this or others. Correct? Well, for a materialist there is no alternative. But near-death experiences and similar experiences are well documented and difficult to explain away. Remember that if you are a materialist these things simply must not be true. Do I see a closure of mind, just like the enemies of Galileo? So let's keep an open mind. And I don't think more MRI scans or injections of particular drugs will unlock the seat of consciousness.

Even though the great ancient civilizations didn't have the technology that we have, they weren't stupid by any stretch of the imagination. They had methods of inquiring about the world. They had ideas on how to arrive at moral decisions. There are depths of mystery which are inaccessible to the science we now understand.

Do you believe in a God who intervenes in the natural world?

Yes. In the Christian tradition, this raises the vexed question of miracles. I'm not a theologian, but there are attested examples which appear to be miraculous. Indeed, the Catholic Church bases part of its identification of a saint on the basis of attested miracles, which are subject to rigorous scrutiny. You don't have to accept them. It's more important to step back and remember that when Jesus performed a miracle, as often as not he said, "Don't tell anybody." He wasn't a wonder worker or a magician. He wasn't doing it to show off. He was merely doing it to heal the world, which was grievously broken.

Yet miracles would seem to defy the laws of nature.

First of all, who decides what are the laws of nature? Second, the laws of nature are based on local observations. We all know the standard materialist arguments. After all, your child has cancer and you pray and your child dies. But we know other cases where prayer has worked—or at least it's offered—and the child has recovered. Nobody can possibly establish whether there's a causal connection. With regard to the New Testament narratives, unlike many fashionable Christians, I regard the so-called nature miracles as correct. I think they actually did happen. And I'm surprised there aren't more of them.

By "nature miracles" are you talking about healing miracles? Or the stories about Jesus and the Virgin Birth?

Yes, any one of those, like walking on water. I can see all the materialists saying, "He doesn't really believe that. How pathetic!" But if the person who made the universe shows up, he's in charge, right? So if he says to a storm, "Shut up!"—of course it's going to shut up. These famous nature miracles are generally regarded as pure myth, invented by credulous peasants. Well, it might have been, but on the other hand, if a creator turns up in his own creation, what on Earth do you think is going to happen?

When you reread the Gospels in particular, I think they suddenly become alive in a very interesting new way. I see an internal coherence in these narratives. Of course, the Resurrection is the miracle to end all miracles. If that happened, which I believe it did—I believe the tomb was empty—then all the other miracles are peanuts. I realize these statements will appall some people. But I'm not the only one to believe in them.

Do you see a clear dividing line between science and religion? Is science the thing you do in your lab, while religion is what you do in other parts of your life?

For me, it has to be. Scientists have to retain an objective view of the world. They have to know they can always be proved wrong. But if you don't want to be a scientist, you can be a poet. If you don't want to be a poet and you want to spend a good deal of time talking with God, then you become a mystic. This world allows poets and scientists and mystics to coexist. I think there's a divide between what science is proclaiming and what faith is proclaiming because each side is unwilling to listen to the other. Believe it or not, they are involved in a common adventure.

Ronald Numbers

DESPITE MASSIVE SCIENTIFIC CORROBORATION for evolution, roughly half of all Americans believe that God created humans within the past 10,000 years. Many others believe the "irreducible complexity" argument of the intelligent design movement. This widespread refusal to accept evolution can drive scientists into a fury. I have heard biologists call anti-evolutionists "idiots," "lunatics," and worse. The question remains: How do we explain the stubborn resistance to Darwinism?

Ronald Numbers, a University of Wisconsin historian, is in a unique position to offer some answers. His 1992 book *The Creationists*, which was recently reissued in an expanded edition, is probably the definitive history of antievolutionism. Numbers is an eminent figure in the history of science and religion—a past president of both the History of Science Society and the American Society of Church History, and a recipient of the George Sarton Medal for lifetime achievement in the history of science. What is most refreshing about him is the remarkable personal history he brings to this subject. He grew up in a family of Seventh-Day Adventists and, until graduate school, was a dyed-in-the-wool creationist. When he lost his religious faith, he wrote a book questioning the foundations of Adventism, which created a huge rift in his family. Perhaps because of his background, Numbers is one of the few scholars in the battle over evolution who remain widely respected by both evolutionists and creationists. In fact, he was once recruited by both sides to serve as an expert witness in a Louisiana trial on evolution. (He went with the ACLU.)

Numbers says much of what we think about antievolutionism is wrong. For one thing, it's hardly a monolithic movement. There are, in fact, fierce battles between creationists of different stripes. "Creation scientists" who believe in a literal reading of the Bible have, in turn, little in common with the leaders of intelligent design. Numbers also dismisses the whole idea of warfare between science and religion going back to the scientific revolution. He says this is a modern myth that serves both Christian fundamentalists and secular scientists.

I talked with Numbers about the competing brands of creationism, his quarrel with atheism and his breaking with faith, and why some famous scientists—like Galileo—hardly deserve the label "scientific martyr."

■ ■ ■ ■

Given the overwhelming scientific support for evolution, how do you explain the curious fact that so many Americans don't believe it?
I don't think there's a single explanation. To many Americans, it just seems so improbable that single-celled animals could have evolved into humans. Even monkeys evolving into humans seems highly unlikely. For many people, it also conflicts with the Bible, which they take to be God's revealed word, and there's no wiggle room for them. And you have particular religious leaders who've condemned it. I think there's something else that I hate to mention but probably is a serious contributing factor. I don't think evolution has been taught well in the United States. Most students do not learn about the overwhelming evidence for evolution.

At the university level or the high school level?
Grade school, high school, and university. There are very few general education courses on evolution for the nonspecialist. It's almost assumed that people will believe in evolution if they've made it that far. So I think we've done a very poor job of bringing together the evidence and presenting it to our students.

There's a stereotype that creationists just aren't that smart. I mean, how can you ignore the steady accumulation of scientific evidence for evolution? Is this a question of intelligence or education?
Not fundamentally. There is a slight skewing of antievolutionists toward lower levels of education. But it's not huge. One recent poll showed that a

quarter of college graduates in America reject evolution. So it's not education itself that's doing this. There are really dumb creationists and there are really dumb evolutionists. Of the 10 founders of the Creation Research Society, five of them earned doctorates in the biological sciences from major universities. Another had a Ph.D. from Berkeley in biochemistry. Another had a Ph.D. from the University of Minnesota. These were not dumb, uneducated people. They rejected evolution for religious and, they would say, scientific reasons.

But that's so hard to understand. If you get a graduate degree in the biological sciences, how can you still allow religion to trump science?
They don't see it that way. They see religion as informing their scientific choices. I think it's extremely hard for human beings to see the world as others see it. I have a hard time seeing the world as Muslim fundamentalists see it. And yet there are many very smart Muslims out there who have a totally different cosmology and theology from what I have. I think one of the goals of education is to help students, and perhaps help ourselves, to see the world the way others see it so we don't just judge and say, "They're just too stupid to know better."

My guess is that the most persuasive arguments for evolution are not going to come through scientific reasoning. They're going to come from scientists, and from theologians and other people of faith, who say you can believe in God and still accept evolution, that there's nothing incompatible about the two. Do you agree?
To a large extent, I do. But I think the influence of those middle-ground people is limited. Conservatives don't trust them. They think they've already sold out to modernism and liberalism. And a lot of the more radical scientists spurn them as well. Richard Dawkins, for example, would argue that evolution is inherently atheistic. That's exactly what the fundamentalists are saying. They agree on that. So you have these people in the middle saying, "No, no. It's not atheistic for me. I believe in God and maybe in Jesus Christ. And in evolution." Having these loud voices on either side of them really tends to restrict the influence that they might otherwise have.

If you're going to persuade devout Christians to accept evolution, don't you also have to show that you can't read the Bible literally, especially the story of Genesis?

Good luck! They do read it literally. Six thousand years, six 24-hour days, a worldwide flood at the time of Noah that buried the fossils, people that lived over 900 years before the flood. There are millions of people who don't seem to have much trouble reading it literally.

What about those creation scientists with Ph.D.s at the Creation Research Society? That's what is hard to understand.

Well, most people who reject evolution do not see themselves as being antiscientific in any way. They love science. They love what science has produced. It's allowed the conservative Christians to go on the airwaves, to fly to mission fields. They're not against science at all. But they don't believe evolution is real science. So they're able to criticize one of the primary theories of modern science and yet not adopt an antiscientific attitude. A lot of critics find that just absolutely amazing.

And it's a rhetorical game that's been played fairly successfully for a long time. In the latter part of the nineteenth century, when Mary Baker Eddy came up with her system that denied the existence of a material world—denying the existence of sickness and death, which flew in the face of everything that late-nineteenth-century science was teaching—what did she call it? "Christian science." The founder of chiropractic thought that he had found the only true scientific view of healing. The creationists around 1970 took the view that's most at odds with modern science and called it "creation science." They love science! And they want to partake in the cultural authority that still comes to science.

Given your field of study, you have a particularly interesting personal history. You grew up in a family of Seventh-Day Adventists.

That's correct. All my male relatives were ministers of one kind or another.

All? Going how far back?

Both my grandfathers. My maternal grandfather was president of the international church. My father and all my uncles on both sides worked for the church. My brother-in-law is a minister.

Did you go to Adventist schools?

First grade through college. I graduated from Southern Missionary College in Tennessee.

And what did you think about life's origins as you were growing up?

I was never exposed to anything other than what we now call "young Earth creationism." Creation science came out of Seventh-Day Adventism. My father was a believer, all my teachers were believers, all my friends believed in that. I can remember as a college student—I majored in math and physics—there was a visiting professor from the University of Chicago lecturing on carbon-14 dating, and he was talking about scores of thousands of years. And my friends and I just looked at each other, wincing and smiling, saying he just didn't know the truth.

But at some point, your ideas obviously changed. What caused you to question the creationist account?

I wish I knew. There are a few moments that proved crucial for me. I went to Berkeley in the 1960s as a graduate student in history and learned to read critically. That had a profound influence on me. I was also exposed to critiques of young Earth creationism. The thing that stands out in my memory as being decisive was hearing a lecture about the fossil forest of Yellowstone, given by a creationist who'd just been out there to visit. He found that of the 30 successive layers you needed—assuming the most rapid rates of decomposition of lava into soil and the most rapid rates of growth for the trees that came back in that area—you needed at least 20,000 to 30,000 years. The only alternative the creationists had to offer was that during the year of Noah's flood, these whole stands of forest trees came floating in, one on top of another, until you had about 30 stacked up. And that truly seemed incredible to me. Just trying to visualize what that had been like during the year of Noah's flood made me smile.

Did your beliefs come crashing down at that moment?

Well, the night after I heard that, I stayed up till very, very late with a fellow Adventist graduate student, wrestling with the implications of it. Before dawn, we both decided the evidence was too strong. This was a crucial night for me because I realized I was abandoning the authority of the prophet who founded Adventism, and the authority of Genesis.

You went on to write a book about Ellen White, the founder of the Seventh-Day Adventists. Didn't that prove to be quite controversial?

It did. I wrote about her as a historian would, without invoking supernatural explanations. That bothered a lot of people, because according to traditional Adventism, she was chosen of God, who would take her into visions, where she would see events past, present, and future. Once, God actually took her back to witness the creation. And she saw that creation occurred in six literal 24-hour days. Which made it impossible for most Adventists to play around with symbolic interpretations of Genesis. I also found in my research that she had been copying some of her so-called testimonies, which were supposed to be coming directly from God. So it did create something of a stir.

That must have created trouble for you in your own family of Adventists.

It did. And it created trouble for my father, who was a minister. Some church ministers were very harsh with him. Here I was, about 30 or so. They were telling him he had no right being a minister if he couldn't control his son. So he took early retirement.

Because of your book?

Yes. He was thoroughly humiliated by this.

Did he try to talk you out of the book?

Oh, yes. We had hours and hours of argument. He had a limited number of explanations for why I would be saying this about the prophetess. One was that I was lying. But he knew me too well, so the only explanation left for him was that somehow Satan had gained control of my mind. And what I was writing reflected the power of Satan. For a number of years, he could not bear to be seen in public with me.

Did you ever heal that rift?

We did. Some information came out a number of years later that he read before he died. It showed that the early ministerial leaders of the church had some of these qualms and decided to bury it. So he regretted that the church had not dealt with this issue a hundred years earlier and come clean. Before he died, he said, "I understand you now. And I understand what you said about Ellen White is probably true. But if I fully accept the implications of what you're saying, I'd have to give up all my religious belief." And I said, "Dad, I don't want you to. It's too important for you."

What are your religious beliefs now?

I don't have any.

Are you an atheist?

I don't think so. I think that's a belief—that there's no god. I really wanted to have religious beliefs for a long time. I miss not having the certainty of religious knowledge that I grew up with. But after a number of years of trying to resolve these issues, I decided they're not resolvable. So I think the term "agnostic" would be best for me.

You mentioned that Seventh-Day Adventism actually played a crucial role in the history of creationism. Didn't an early Adventist lay out the whole idea of "flood geology"?

Exactly. George McCready Price, a disciple of Ellen White, came along in the early twentieth century and made Noah's flood the key actor in the history of life on Earth. He tried to show that the conventional interpretations of the geological column were fallacious, and that, in fact, the entire geological column could have been deposited in about one year. And that became the centerpiece of what he called "the new catastrophism."

Then, in about 1970, that view—flood geology—was renamed "creation science" or "scientific creationism." Two fundamentalists—a theologian named John Whitcomb Jr. and a hydraulic engineer named Henry Morris—took Price's flood geology, reworked it a little bit, and published it as *The Genesis Flood*. Notice that the seminal books in the history of creationism have focused on geology and the flood, not so much on biology. And as a result of what Whitcomb and Morris did, Price's views exploded among fundamentalists and other conservative Christians.

But why did this particular version of creationism catch on? Why did Noah's flood somehow resolve all the contradictions in the fossil record?

Your question is all the more difficult to answer because fundamentalists had two perfectly orthodox interpretations of Genesis 1 that would have allowed them to accept all of the paleontological evidence. One was that the days of Genesis represented vast geological epochs, or even cosmic epochs. William Jennings Bryan accepted that. The founder of the World's Christian Fundamentals Association accepted that.

So in that account, you could have the Earth going back billions of years.

Time was no problem. Another view, very popular among fundamentalists, was called the gap theory. After the original creation in the beginning, when God created the heavens and the Earth, Moses—the author of Genesis— skipped in silence a vast period of Earth history before coming to the Edenic creation in six days, associated with Adam and Eve. Those fundamentalists and Pentecostals could slip the entire geological column into that period between the original creation and the much, much later "Edenic restoration." You had these perfectly good interpretations of Genesis available to fundamentalists. So why would they accept this radical, reactionary theory that everything was created only about 6,000 or 7,000 years ago?

I'm willing to bet you have some explanation. Why did flood geology suddenly explode in popularity in the 1960s?

The biggest explanation, I think, is that for more than 100 years, Christians had been reinterpreting God's sacred word—the Bible—in the light of new scientific discoveries. And people like Whitcomb and Morris, the authors of *The Genesis Flood*, struck a really sensitive chord when they said, "It's time to quit interpreting God in the light of science, and start with God's revealed word and then see if there's any model of Earth history that will fit with that."

Otherwise, science keeps chipping away at religion.

Exactly. It never ends. It always changes and it means you'll have to be constantly reinterpreting God. It wasn't so much that they invested in the Genesis account as that many of them were concerned about the last book of the Bible. Revelation foretold the end of the world. And they would argue, how can we expect Christians to believe in the prophecies of Revelation, about end times, when we symbolically interpret Genesis, and interpret it away? So if you want people to take Revelation seriously, you have to get them to take Genesis really seriously.

More recently, we've had the intelligent design movement. I know some people see this as a new version of creationism, stripping away all the talk about God and religion so you can teach it in the schools. Is that true?

There's a little bit of evidence to support that. But I think that both demographically and intellectually, it doesn't hold a lot of water. The intelligent design leaders are people, by and large, who do not believe in young Earth creationism.

So they would accept the Earth being four and a half billion years old.

That's not an issue with most of them. They want to create a big tent for all antievolutionists, even non-Christians. Whitcomb and Morris and the Creation Research Society wanted to create a tightly knit group of people who all subscribed to flood geology. The intelligent design leaders say it's premature to insist on a particular interpretation of Genesis. This approach has really irritated many of the young Earth creationists, who feel they're being told by these intellectual leaders of intelligent design, "You're just a divisive group dedicated to a particular interpretation of Scripture." They are. But they've been very successful. And they're not about to abandon their crusade to get people to accept scientific creationism in favor of some mushy intelligent design.

The intelligent design leaders insist that they are doing science. Michael Behe has said that the scientific discovery of "irreducible complexity" should rank in the annals of the history of science alongside the discoveries of Newton and Lavoisier and Einstein. They're after something much bigger than a natural theology. They want to change one of the most fundamental ground rules for practicing science. Around 1800, the practitioners of science reached a consensus that whatever they proposed would have to be natural.

Not supernatural. You can never resort to a supernatural explanation in science.

Exactly. To be scientific meant to be natural. But it said nothing about the religious beliefs of these people. Evangelical Christians believed that; liberal Christians believed that; secularists believed that's the way we're going to do science. And it worked out beautifully. But the leaders of the intelligent design movement, beginning with the Berkeley lawyer Philip Johnson, have wanted to resacralize science. They want to ditch the commitment to naturalism and allow for supernatural explanations. That's the most radical revolution I can imagine in doing science. And many Christians who are scientists don't want to do that.

Now, one thing I find curious is your own position in this debate. Your book *The Creationists* is generally acknowledged to be *the* history of creationism. You've also been very up front about your own lack of religious belief. Yet as far as I can tell, you seem to be held in high regard by both the creationists and by scientists, which—I have to say—is a neat trick. How have you managed this?

Unlike many people, I haven't gone out of my way to attack or ridicule critics of evolution. I know some of the people I've written about. They're good people. I know it's not because they're stupid that they are creationists. I'm talking about all my family, too, who are still creationists. So that easy explanation that so many anticreationists use—that they're just illiterate hillbillies—doesn't have any appeal to me, although I'm quite happy to admit that there are some really stupid creationists.

Can you put the current battles over evolution in some historical context? If we take this history back to the scientific revolution—back to Newton and Galileo—was there a war between science and religion then?

There were conflicts at times. But there was no inevitable war. Just think about it. Most of the contributors to the so-called scientific revolution were believers. They were theists. They didn't see any inherent conflict between what they were doing and their religious beliefs.

These were the giants—Newton, Galileo, Boyle, Kepler. Weren't they all devout Christians?

Well, Newton was a little lax at times, though he was certainly a theist. Boyle was a good, sound Christian. I think Galileo was a true believer in the Church. And Copernicus was a canon in the Catholic Church. Kepler was a deep believer in God. So yeah, these people were believers. Occasionally, there were problems—for instance, between Galileo and the pope. But Galileo had gone out of his way to insult the pope, who had previously supported him. He put the pope's favorite argument against heliocentrism into the mouth of the character Simplicio—the simple-minded person.

So Galileo wasn't really arrested because of his science. It was because he was a lousy diplomat?

Yeah, he was a terrible diplomat, thumbing his nose at the most powerful person who critiqued him. Also, Galileo was not as badly treated as many people suggest. When he was summoned down to Rome by the Inquisition, he lived in the Tuscan palace. And then when he was asked to move into the Vatican, to the palace of the Inquisition, one of the officials in the Inquisition vacated his three-room apartment so that the distinguished guest, Galileo, could have a nice apartment. And they allowed him to have his meals catered by the chef at the Tuscan embassy. Ultimately, he was under house arrest in his villa outside of Florence.

Is the whole notion, then, that Galileo faced possible execution because of his scientific statements just baloney?

It was highly unlikely. In fact, I don't know of a single pioneer in science who lost his life for his scientific beliefs.

Well, what about the sixteenth-century philosopher and cosmologist Giordano Bruno? I've always heard that he was burned at the stake because of his Copernican view of the universe.

No, it was for his theological heresies, not for his Copernicanism. He happened to be a Copernican, but that's not what got him into trouble. No, the bitterest arguments have taken place *within* religious groups. If you want to hear bitter argument, listen to some old-age fundamentalists argue with young Earth creationists. Then you're talking about warfare.

If science and religion aren't really historical enemies, why do so many people think they are?

Because it serves the needs of two different groups. Scientists who are beleaguered today by creationists and opponents of stem cell research like to dismiss religion as something that has been an eternal impediment to the progress of science. And the conservatives—whether they're creationists or intelligent design theorists—probably represent a majority in our society. But they also love to present themselves as martyrs. They're being oppressed by the secularists of the world. The secularists may only amount to about 10 percent of the American society, but of course they do control many of the papers and the radio stations and TV stations of the country. So clearly these ideas serve some intellectual need of the parties involved, or they wouldn't persist, especially in the face of so much historical evidence to the contrary.

My sense is that you don't much like the stridency of certain atheists. The most obvious examples would be Richard Dawkins and Daniel Dennett.

Right. I don't know what the figures are right now, but I bet half of the scientists in America believe in some type of God. So I think Dawkins and Dennett are in a minority of evolutionists in saying that evolution is atheistic. I also think it does a terrible disservice to public policy in the United States.

So even if they believe that, you're saying politically it's a real mistake for them to link atheism to evolution.

Yes. Because in the United States, our public schools are supposed to be religiously neutral. If evolution is in fact inherently atheistic, we probably shouldn't be teaching it in the schools. And that makes it very difficult when you have some prominent people like Dawkins, who's a well-credentialed biologist, saying, "It really is atheistic." He could undercut—not because he wants to—but he could undercut the ability for American schools to teach evolution.

Dawkins himself acknowledges that politically, this is not the smartest thing to do. But he says there is a higher principle at stake, and it's really the war between supernaturalism and naturalism. He says that's the real fight he's waging.

But you have to be careful. In the United States, the 90 percent who are theists far outnumber the 10 percent who are nontheists. So you want to remember that you are a minority, and that you need to get along, so some compromise might be in order. I'm not suggesting that he should compromise his own views. But by arguing not only that the implications of evolution for him are atheistic, but that evolution is inherently atheistic is a risky thing.

So far, the rejection of evolution seems to be a predominantly Christian movement. Do we see much of this in other religious traditions?

We are now. It was mostly a Christian tradition, although to a certain extent the reason we didn't see this in other religious cultures is because it was so dormant. Most modern Muslims weren't accepting evolution, but they weren't coming out in opposition to it. Most ultra-Orthodox Jews didn't accept evolution, but they didn't see any reason to say anything about scientific evolution. Today—especially in the last decade or two—we're seeing antievolutionism erupt in these non-Christian cultures. It's very big in the Muslim culture. The center for that is in Turkey, and the leader goes by the pen name Harun Yahya. His work circulates in millions of copies. They're translated into virtually every language spoken by Muslims.

Are we going to see this war between evolutionism and creationism continue for years to come?

I probably shouldn't even try to answer that question. Historians generally shouldn't try to be prophets. But it doesn't seem to be declining in any way right now. I think the creation scientists are still extremely strong. Some people say the intelligent design movement has eclipsed the creation scientists. But I think that's judging strength by press coverage. And the press will cover it only when it's exciting, when there's a legislative battle or a court case. And I'm shocked by how much publicity the intelligent design movement has gotten in 15 years. They have a very good public relations machinery. So you have a handful of people in Seattle at the Discovery Institute and a few million dollars a year to play with, and they've convinced *Time, Newsweek,* and others that the whole scientific community is divided over intelligent design. It's amazing!

Alan Wallace

THE DEBATE BETWEEN SCIENCE and religion typically gets stuck on the troublesome question of God's existence. How do you reconcile an all-powerful God with the mechanistic slog of evolution? Can a rationalist do anything but sneer at the Bible's miracles? But what if another religion—a nontheistic one—offered a way out of this impasse? That's the promise that some people hold out for Buddhism. The Dalai Lama is deeply invested in reconciling science and spirituality. He meets regularly with Western scientists, looking for links between Buddhism and the latest research in physics and neuroscience. In his book *The Universe in a Single Atom*, he wrote, "If scientific analysis were conclusively to demonstrate certain claims in Buddhism to be false, then we must accept the findings of science and abandon those claims."

B. Alan Wallace may be the American Buddhist most committed to finding connections between Buddhism and science. A former Buddhist monk who went on to get a doctorate in religious studies at Stanford University, he once studied under the Dalai Lama and has acted as one of the Tibetan leader's translators. Wallace, now president of the Santa Barbara Institute for Consciousness Studies, has written and edited many books, often challenging the conventions of modern science. "The sacred object of its reverence, awe and devotion is not God or spiritual enlightenment but the material universe," he writes. He accuses prominent scientists like E. O. Wilson and Richard Dawkins of practicing "a modern kind of nature religion."

In his book *Contemplative Science: Where Buddhism and Neuroscience Converge*, Wallace takes on the loaded subject of consciousness. He argues that the long tradition of Buddhist meditation, with its rigorous investigation of the mind, has in effect pioneered a science of consciousness, and it has much to teach Western scientists. "Subjectivity is the central taboo of scientific materialism," he writes. He considers the Buddhist examination of interior mental states far preferable to what he calls the Western "idolatry of the brain." And he says the modern obsession with brain chemistry has created a false sense of well-being: "It is natural then to view psychopharmaceutical and psychotropic drugs as primary sources of happiness and relief from suffering." Wallace also chastises cognitive psychologists and neuroscientists for assuming the mind is merely the product of the physical mechanics of the brain. He talks openly about ideas that most scientists would consider laughable, including reincarnation and a transcendent consciousness.

In conversation, Wallace is a fast talker who laughs easily and often gets carried away with his enthusiasm. We talked about the Buddhist theory of consciousness, his critique of both science and Christianity, and why he thinks reincarnation should be studied by scientists.

■ ■ ■ ■

Why do you think Buddhism has an important perspective to add to the science and religion debate?
Buddhism has a lot to add for a number of reasons. Some are simply historical. Especially since the time of Galileo, there has been a sense of unease, if not outright hot war, between religion and science in the West. And Buddhism is coming in as a complete outsider. It's not theistic, as is Christianity. At the same time, it's not just science, as is physics or biology. And there's another reason why Buddhism may bring a fresh perspective. While there's no question that Buddhism has very religious elements to it—with monks and temples, rituals and prayers—it does have a broad range of empirical methods for investigating the nature of the mind, for raising hypotheses and putting them to the test.

There's a common assumption that science and religion are entirely separate domains. Science covers the empirical realm of facts and theories about the observable world, while religion deals with ultimate meaning and moral value. But you don't accept that dichotomy, do you?

Not at all. In fact, most religious people don't. This has been brought up by Stephen Jay Gould with his whole notion of "nonoverlapping magisteria." But it's never been true. All of the great pioneers of the scientific revolution—Copernicus, Galileo, Kepler, Newton, and on into the nineteenth century with Gregor Mendel—they were all Christians. And their whole approach to science was deeply influenced by Christianity. Religion, whether we like it or not, is making many truth claims about the natural world as well as the transcendent world. And now that science is homing in on the nature of the mind and questions of free will, it is definitely invading the turf that used to belong to religion and philosophy.

Many people would acknowledge that Buddhism has some profound insights into the human mind—why we get depressed, what makes us happy, and how we become slaves to our attachments. But what does this have to do with science?

In Buddhism, the very root of suffering and all our mental distress—what Buddhists call mental afflictions—is ignorance. The path to liberation, or enlightenment, is knowledge. It's knowing reality as it is. So despite many differences in methodology, both science and Buddhism are after knowledge of the natural world. But what defines the natural world? In modern science, the natural world is often equated with the physical world, and mental phenomena and subjective experiences are regarded as emergent phenomena or simply functions of the brain. But there are many other domains of reality that the physical instruments of science have not yet been able to detect.

But science is as much about method as anything. The scientific method posits hypotheses and theories that can be tested. Is that something Buddhism does as well?

Not in the same way. I wouldn't want to overplay the case that Buddhism has always been a science, with clear hypotheses and complete skepticism.

It's too much of a religion, and so there's a lot of vested interest in the Buddhist community not to challenge the statements made by the Buddha and other great patriarchs in the Buddhist tradition. So there are some fundamental differences. At the same time, science is not just science. This very notion that the mind must simply be an emergent property of the brain—consisting only of physical phenomena and nothing more—is not a testable hypothesis. Science is based upon a very profound metaphysical foundation. Can you test the statement that there is nothing else going on apart from physical phenomena and their emergent properties? The answer is no.

You're saying we don't know for sure that the physical functions of the brain—the neural circuits, the electrochemical surges—are what produce our rich inner lives, what we call the mind?
Cognitive science has plenty of hypotheses that are testable. For instance, is Alzheimer's related to a particular malfunctioning of the brain? More and more, scientists are able to identify the parts and functions of the brain that are necessary to generate specific mental states. So these are scientific issues. But now let's tap into what the philosopher David Chalmers has called "the hard problem"—the relationship between the physical brain and consciousness. What is it about the brain—this mass of chemicals and electromagnetic fields—that enables the brain to generate any state of subjective experience? If your sole access to the mind is by way of physical phenomena, then you have no way of testing whether all dimensions of the mind are necessarily contingent upon the brain.

But that is certainly the paradigm of the vast majority of neuroscientists and psychologists. The mind is nothing more than the brain, and what happens in the mind is strictly because of the physical mechanics of the brain. I'm sure most of these scientists would say it's absurd to talk about the mind functioning independently of the brain.
Well, when you have no possible means of investigating the mind as it might operate independently of the brain, then to even raise it as an issue is indeed absurd. But there is one avenue of inquiry that's been largely left out or simply repudiated. Right now, you and I have an ability to monitor our own mental states. Can we generate a mental image of an apple? Can we remember our

mother's face? Can we recite the opening lines of the Gettysburg Address or some favorite poem? Are these mental images that you generate nothing other than brain states or parts of the brain? At this point, those are not even scientific questions because nobody knows how to tackle them.

You have called for a new field of study, what you call "contemplative science." What would that involve?

Contemplative science must live up to the rigorous standards that neuroscience, cognitive psychology, chemistry, and physics have set for us. They've set the bar very high. So I'm a great admirer of the rigor and skepticism of science at its best. But William James, who's one of my intellectual heroes, suggested we have a triadic approach. We should study the mind by way of behavior and brain studies, but, first and foremost, he said we should study the mind by observing mental phenomena directly. But what he didn't have, and neither did any of his contemporaries, was a rigorous methodology.

Is that what Buddhism offers—a rigorous methodology?

Yes. I'm not saying we should fuse religion with science. Rather, we should select very specific methodologies from Buddhism and other contemplative traditions where the ability to monitor the mind has been honed over thousands of years—beginning with the training of attention and then using sophisticated methods for investigating the nature of the mind, feelings, and the very nature of consciousness itself during the waking state, the dream state, even during deep sleep. Now, because of the great advances in transportation and communication, we have easy access to the Taoist tradition of China, the Sufi tradition of the Near East, the Buddhist tradition of Tibet and Southeast Asia. I'm convinced this would add much greater depth and breadth to the types of questions that are raised in modern cognitive science.

In science, you have a hypothesis that's tested, and it can be disproved. Does that happen in Buddhism?

On its home turf, frequently not. But I'm also waiting for a neuroscientist to tell me how the hypothesis that mental states are nothing more than neural states will be repudiated. I don't see that as a testable hypothesis. So there's a fair amount of dogma, not in science per se but in the minds of scientists. Likewise, there's plenty of dogma in the minds of Buddhists. But Buddhism at its best—and we go right back to the teachings of the Buddha himself—encourages a spirit of skepticism. He said, "Do not take my statements to be true simply out of reverence for me. But rather, put them to the test." Well, if you do that, you should be able to repudiate them, as well as confirm them.

Well, let me ask you about that. I know there is a tradition, particularly among advanced contemplatives, that you have your meditative experience, and then you talk about it, you analyze it, and your peers critique it. Does that really happen? When someone comes out of meditation, would someone else say, "Sorry. You didn't do it right"?

Absolutely. You know, Buddhism, like any other tradition, is subject to degeneration. So if you and I headed off to India or Nepal or Tibet, we'd find plenty of Buddhist meditators who are simply going through rote ritual, who are just trying to come up with the right answers at the end of the book. But when Buddhism is really thriving, it's exactly what you described. You go into a three-year retreat, where you are meditating 8 to 12 hours a day. You're training the mind. You're investigating the nature of the mind. But you're probably not doing that in entire isolation. You're in consultation with a mentor who's going to review your experience and help you deepen your experience. You'll be questioning your insights. So your relationship with your mentor is analogous to working on your Ph.D. with a mentor. If at any point your research becomes flaky or not up to snuff, the mentor is there to say, "No, that's a dead end. This is not good research." This happens frequently in the Buddhist contemplative tradition when it's really robust and healthy.

Has that happened to you? You've meditated for decades. And you were a Buddhist monk for 14 years. Did you have your meditative practice analyzed and critiqued?

Definitely.

I can imagine that might be kind of humiliating.

(*Laughs*) No. Take the first long retreat I did, in 1980. I was a monk at the time. I'd just spent the last 10 years in very rigorous theoretical and practical training in India and in a monastery in Switzerland. And then all I wanted to do was go to the lab—basically, go into a meditation hut and spend 8, 10, 12 hours a day meditating. Well, I had the tremendously good fortune to have the Dalai Lama as my personal mentor. So he guided me in the meditation. I would meet with him every few weeks. I would discuss the practice and he'd give me feedback. I was living in a little hut in the mountains above Dharamsala, India. I went into a five-month solitary retreat. Somebody brought me food once a week. I was meditating 10 hours a day. I was honing my attention skills. And I would consult with the Dalai Lama. I would consult with other yogis up there on the hill about technique and problems that were arising. They would draw from their decades of experience to help me. And I started to adapt some of these methods for myself as a Westerner who grew up in America and Europe, rather than as a nomad out at 14,000 feet up on the Tibetan plateau.

Did you have profound mystical experiences? Did you have moments of what might be called enlightenment?

Well, the word "enlightenment" has been used in so many different ways, I won't tread on that minefield. Eighteenth-century Europe itself went through an enlightenment, but I'm not sure that would be an enlightenment in my category. So for me to make any claims about enlightenment would be counterproductive. Did I find any transformation of consciousness? Did I find attention skills honed? Did I experience states of consciousness that I'd never experienced before such sustained meditative training? The answer is yes, yes, yes. But what a mature meditator is even more concerned with than those epiphanies—those moments of revelation or breakthrough—is the overall impact on the quality of your life, your way of engaging with other people, and dealing with adversity. Is it helpful? Does it give you a clearer sense of reality? If it doesn't, then I say meditation is merely a hobby. If it does, then meditation can be something very central to developing greater mental health and clear engagement with reality itself.

I've heard that your father was actually a Protestant theologian. It does raise the question of why you became a Buddhist. Why has Buddhism resonated with you in a way that Christianity has not?

Well, it's a personal issue. You're quite right. My father was—and is—a Christian theologian. We have a loving and very trusting relationship. The fact that he is a Christian theologian definitely had a profound impact on the course my life has taken. As I was growing up, from the age of 13, I had a very clear sense that I wanted to dedicate my life to science. And so I immersed myself in chemistry, biology, physics, and calculus. At the same time, my religious background had made a very deep impact on my life. But what really struck me very painfully—I would say existentially—was the profound incompatibility between science and the whole worldview of Christianity, with God being the creator, responding to prayer, and human identity being that of an immortal soul. Basically, everything was God-saturated in this Judeo-Christian view. On the other hand, in the scientific worldview I was simply a body, an animal. There was no creator. There was no ethics in nature. It was just Darwin. It was a great big machine. And I looked at these two worldviews and said, "Wow, these are incompatible."

So I basically went AWOL from Western civilization for 14 years. I picked up one book on Buddhism when I was 20. It was like a starving man picking up some fragrance of hot baked bread. So I spent a year studying the Tibetan language in Germany, where I was spending a year abroad. And then I bought myself, literally and metaphorically, a one-way ticket to India. I wanted to go live with Tibetans and explore as deeply as I could this Buddhist worldview. It's not just a religion. It's not theistic. It doesn't posit the existence of God as standing outside of creation, governing it, ruling it, punishing the wicked, and rewarding the virtuous. It doesn't have any of that. Nor is it materialistic, flattening my very existence to being an epiphenomenon of my brain.

You've suggested that there might be certain functions of the mind, certain aspects of consciousness, that don't have a material foundation.

Yes.

Advanced contemplatives in the Buddhist tradition have talked about tapping into something called the "substrate consciousness." What is that?

Just for a clarification of terms, I've demarcated three whole dimensions of consciousness. There's the psyche. It's the human mind—the functioning of memory, attention, emotions, and so forth. The psyche is contingent upon the brain, the nervous system, and our various sensory faculties. It starts sometime at or following conception, certainly during gestation, and it ends at death. So the psyche has pretty clear bookends. This is what cognitive neuroscientists and psychologists study. They don't study anything more. And they quite reasonably assume that that's all there is to it. But as long as you study the mind only by way of brain states and behavior, you're never going to know whether there's any other dimension because of the limitations of your own methodologies. So here's a hypothesis: The psyche does not emerge from the brain. Mental phenomena do not actually emerge from neuronal configurations. Nobody's ever seen that they do.

So your hypothesis is just the reverse from what all the neuroscientists think.

Precisely. The psyche is not emerging from the brain, conditioned by the environment. The human psyche is in fact emerging from an individual continuum of consciousness that is conjoined with the brain during the development of the fetus. It can be very hampered if the brain malfunctions or becomes damaged.

But you're saying there are also two other aspects of consciousness?

Yeah. All I'm presenting here is the Buddhist hypothesis. There's another dimension of consciousness, which is called the substrate consciousness. This is not mystical. It's not transcendent in the sense of being divine. The human psyche is emerging from an ongoing continuum of consciousness—the substrate consciousness—which kind of looks like a soul. But in the Buddhist view, it is more like an ongoing vacuum state of consciousness. Or here's a good metaphor: Just as we speak of a stem cell, which is not differentiated until it comes into the liver and becomes a liver cell, or into bone marrow and becomes a bone marrow cell, the substrate consciousness is stem consciousness. And at death, the human psyche dissolves back into this continuum.

So this consciousness is not made of any stuff. It's not matter. Is it just unattached and floating through the universe?
Well, this raises such interesting questions about the nature of matter. In the nineteenth century, you could think of matter as something good and chunky out there. You could count on it as having location and specific momentum and mass and all of that. Frankly, I think the backdrop of this whole conversation has to be twenty-first-century physics, not nineteenth-century physics. And virtually all of neuroscience and all of psychology is based on nineteenth-century physics, which is about as up to date as the horse and buggy.

So not everything in the universe can be reducible to matter, to particles?
According to quantum field theory, string theory, and quantum cosmology—cutting-edge fields of twenty-first-century physics—matter itself is not reducible to matter. And Richard Feynman, the great Nobel laureate in physics, commented very emphatically, "We don't know what energy is." He said it's not stuff out there that has a specific location. It's more like a mathematical abstraction. So matter has been reduced to formations of space. Energy is configurations of space. Space itself is rather mysterious. And so when I introduce this theme of a substrate consciousness, it's not something ethereal that's opposed to matter. Matter is about as ethereal as anything gets. But could there be this continuum of substrate consciousness that's not contingent upon molecules? From the Buddhist perspective, yes. But again, this frankly sounds like one more system of belief.

I have to say, you could put a religious spin on all of this. What you're describing as substrate consciousness sounds a lot like how people talk about God. There is some kind of divine presence that's outside the material world but somehow intervenes in our material lives.
I think we're jumping the gun there. In the Buddhist perspective, the substrate consciousness is individual. It's not some great collective unconscious like

Jung talked about. In the Buddhist view, it's an individual continuum of consciousness that carries on from lifetime to lifetime. That's not God. Beyond that is this whole third dimension, the deepest dimension, called "primordial consciousness." This has certain commonalities with Christian mystical notions of God beyond the trinity. It has a thoroughly and deeply transcendent quality to it. And that's way beyond the pale of scientific inquiry. But when I speak of substrate consciousness, I think it would simply be a mistake to say that's God. If you want to relate this to something in Western religions, you might say it's the immortal soul. Christianity really has nothing to say about the existence of your continuum of consciousness prior to your conception. There's nothing in the Bible that says, where was Steve Paulson 70 years ago? Where did your stream of consciousness, your identity, your soul, come from? But Buddhism has a lot to say about this.

Here in the West, we have on the table three large hypotheses about the nature of human consciousness. One of these looks really good from a scientific perspective. Your consciousness is a product of the brain. Damage the brain and your consciousness evaporates into nothing. Now what's the experiment by which you repudiate that hypothesis? Well, all the mental states you're studying are by way of the brain, so the answer is nada. So it's not scientific and it's not testable, at least not yet. We have another major hypothesis. You die and your soul carries on to heaven or hell in the Protestant tradition. You go there and it's forever. Or in the Roman Catholic tradition, you have another couple of options—limbo and purgatory. But these are all one-way tickets. You can't say, "I didn't like it in purgatory" and then come back. My point here is the Christian hypothesis is not testable scientifically. It may be true, but it's not a scientific hypothesis.

Of course, the Tibetan Buddhist tradition has reincarnation. Is that testable scientifically?

Well, here's the hypothesis. Your psyche emerged sometime while you were in your mother's womb. It's continuing to evolve, and eventually it's going to implode back into the substrate, carry on as a disembodied continuum of consciousness and then reincarnate. There's the theory in a nutshell. Is that one testable? My short answer is yes, I think this is a testable hypothesis, and in principle it really should be able to be repudiated. But we're also looking for positive evidence.

There are two types of studies being done at the University of Virginia. One is by Bruce Greyson. He's got a very good track record of doing rigorous, objective scientific studies of alleged—I'm choosing my words carefully here—alleged out-of-body experiences and near-death experiences of patients undergoing surgery. Does it ever happen that a person, while being under general anesthetic, has an out-of-body experience and can actually perceive something, as they hover above, that only the surgeons see? That's an empirically testable question. And Greyson is studying this scientifically.

So basically, the premise here is that consciousness can exist outside the body. I've heard that Greyson has started these tests but so far hasn't come up with any results.

Quite so. As you can imagine, the National Science Foundation is not exactly jumping over itself to fund this type of research. Nor is the NIH [National Institutes of Health]. This is outside the paradigm. They're not interested in providing funding for things that challenge the foundations of materialism. So basically, it's like asking the Catholic Church to pay for research to show that Jesus never lived.

Okay, that's one test for out-of-body experiences. What about reincarnation?

Well, lo and behold, at the same university—they have some chutzpah over there—the University of Virginia, the late Ian Stevenson worked in the psych department. He wasn't a Buddhist, he wasn't a Hindu, and he didn't believe in reincarnation. Forty years ago he heard anecdotes of children maintaining that this wasn't their first life and giving detailed accounts of their alleged memories of past life experiences. So he started studying it. On a shoestring budget, he and a team of researchers did this for about 40 years. And about halfway through, he wrote a book called *Twenty Cases Suggestive of Reincarnation*. He scanned thousands of accounts of children giving these accounts, throwing out most of them because they're either false or the child could have heard about it from parents, relatives, television, and so forth. He then selected 20 cases where the accounts given by the child wound up being true when they were subjected to objective corroboration. He couldn't see any way the child could have known this information. But he also said in that book, "I don't believe in reincarnation. But I don't know what else to do with these 20 cases because I can't see any other way to explain them."

And then he did another 20 years of research and wrote another book, *Where Biology and Reincarnation Intersect.* It showed the empirical findings of more cases of children giving these very detailed accounts of past life experiences. And usually they were not glorified, like "I was Cleopatra" or Einstein or somebody spectacular. No, it was like, "I was a philanderer, and one of the husbands of the wives I had sex with shot me dead because I cuckolded him." So that's not very glamorous, but that was the recollection of one of these children. This is empirical evidence. It should be scrutinized rigorously but not thrown out dogmatically.

This raises some interesting questions about Buddhism. Is Buddhism a religion or is it something else? Because there are some people in the West who say we should strip Buddhism of any vestiges of the religious or the transcendental. For instance, Stephen Batchelor, in his book *Buddhism without Beliefs,* writes, "The Buddha was not a mystic. His awakening was not a shattering insight into a transcendental truth that revealed to him the mysteries of God. He did not claim to have had an experience that granted him privileged, esoteric knowledge of how the universe ticks." Is Stephen Batchelor right?

(*Laughs*) I've known Stephen Batchelor for almost 35 years. We were monks together for years, both in India and in Switzerland. To come up with this picture of the Buddha, you have to bring out a carving knife and chop off great sections of the most authentic accounts we have of the Buddha's own teachings. You simply have to ignore and pretend he never said an enormous number of things he did say. I think Stephen, my dear friend, has recast the Buddha in his own image as an English skeptic who was raised in an agnostic background, who really doesn't believe in anything nonphysical.

So we should forget trying to strip Buddhism of its transcendentalism. You haven't quite come out and said it, but you're suggesting we should stop saying Buddhism is not a religion.

Well, we have to be very cautious when we take these Western categories—religion, science, philosophy—which are deeply and inextricably embedded in our Judeo-Christian and Greco-Roman heritage. But I have to add a footnote to our conversation about reincarnation research. The Buddhists have been looking at this critically and empirically for 2,500 years. They're not waiting with baited breath to see what the people at the University of Virginia come up with. They, unlike psychologists and neuroscientists, have been exploring mental phenomena directly. And they have specific strategies for going into a deep meditative state, directing your attention backward beyond the scope of this lifetime, directing it back to past lifetimes, and coming up with memories. So you have a template here.

This could be studied, together with skeptics. Train very advanced contemplatives to tap into this substrate consciousness—this storehouse of memories from past lives, if in fact it exists—and do this in conjunction with neuroscientists and psychologists. If I had unlimited funds, I'd say this is one of the most important questions we can ask. Make this a 20-year research project, well funded, with all the skepticism of science. Make sure you have some hardcore atheists involved, but ones who are open-minded and not just knee-jerk dogmatists. And then put it to the test. In 20 years, I think you could come up with something that could repudiate or validate a startling, truly astonishing hypothesis that there is such a substrate consciousness.

Daniel Dennett

DANIEL DENNETT, A TUFTS UNIVERSITY philosopher, is all over the science and religion debate. No other scholar has written such a diverse collection of books that directly tackle the key controversies. You want a closely argued defense of evolution? Dennett lays it out in *Darwin's Dangerous Idea*. What about the knotty mind–brain problem? Check out Dennett's *Consciousness Explained*. How about the mysterious origins of our religious impulses? *Breaking the Spell* is your ticket. Dennett is a voracious scholar and also the rare philosopher who has had a real impact on public thinking.

He is also supremely confident in his own ability to sort out these age-old questions. Critics say his claim to have explained how the mind works is grossly premature; I've even heard one wag refer to his book as *Consciousness Extinguished*. When I suggested that scientists may never unlock the mysteries of the mind, Dennett replied, "There are lots of puzzles, but there aren't any mysteries." He seems convinced that science will answer the hardest questions out there, even the mind–body problem.

Dennett's particular specialty is the philosophy of mind, which is strongly influenced by his understanding of evolution. He is also keenly interested in efforts by computer designers to build intelligent machines, and he has become the go-to philosopher for scientists working on artificial intelligence. Not surprisingly, he has sparred with philosophers who don't accept the mind-as-computer model, such as John Searle and Jerry Fodor.

Dennett wants to demystify certain ideas that have been with us for centuries, especially religious concepts like the disembodied mind, the designer God, and the soul. One of America's best-known atheists, he calls himself a "bright" to describe his naturalistic worldview. In fact, he has suggested that people who believe in mysticism and the supernatural should be referred to as "supers" (which, incidentally, is also the epithet that the villain in *The Incredibles* pins on the movie's superheroes). Although he isn't as overtly hostile to religion as Richard Dawkins or Sam Harris, Dennett told me that religious belief could be "a bad habit that's infectious," like the common cold.

I spoke with Dennett about a wide range of ideas—from the origins of religion to the inherent radicalism of Darwinism.

■ ■ ■ ■

The debate over evolution tends to get bogged down in questions about the creation stories in Genesis. But once we get past the Bible, evolution still poses serious problems for people looking for some underlying purpose to human existence. Has evolution changed the way we talk about meaning and purpose?

I suppose it has. We used to think that we could only have purpose if we inherited it from something bigger and greater, such as God. In that sense, we're God's playthings or God's children. I call that the "trickle-down theory" of purpose. But evolution by natural selection is a process that has no purpose at all, and yet it systematically generates things that do have purpose. Initially, it's just the process of staying alive and reproducing. But when you get to humans, we can reconsider and adjust that purpose in ways that are not dependent on our biological purpose. We're the species that invented birth control. The genetic imperative—to have more grandchildren than anybody else—is an imperative that's obeyed by every other species on the planet, but not us.

So the human project is to keep redefining what our meaning and purpose is?

Yes, that's a familiar lesson that goes back directly to Darwin and continues through Nietzsche and the existentialists. We make our own purposes. We don't inherit our purposes from our ancestors or from God.

The response you'll get from religious people—and even some scientists— is that there's an inexorable drive in the evolutionary process toward greater complexity, which inevitably leads to consciousness. What do you make of this argument?

I think that's romantic and mistaken. There is a sense in which complexity does arise in evolution: from no complexity there's only one direction to go, and that process has created one language-using, conscious species. But we may extinguish ourselves in the near future and then it will be back to square one, back to bacteria. The process will happen again, but it might not go as far as consciousness. There's no guarantee that as evolution unrolls over the eons, there will be the kind of consciousness we have. That's an illusion.

The paleontologist Simon Conway Morris believes that the evolution of human beings—or some other highly intelligent creature—was inevitable. He says our intelligence has given our species clear evolutionary advantages, so it would be surprising if humanlike creatures did not evolve.

He's just wrong to say this is inevitable. Is the evolution of marsupials inevitable? If we went to another planet like Earth, would marsupials have to be on it? I don't think humanoid intelligence is any more inevitable than marsupials. But he's right to say that the evolution of our intelligence has given us an astonishing superiority over other species. The late Paul MacCready pointed out that just 10,000 years ago—a mere eyeblink in biological history—human beings, plus their livestock and pets, accounted for less than 1 percent of the total biomass, by weight, of all animals. Now we're 98 percent. We've engulfed the planet with our cattle, our pets, and ourselves. That's a stunning fitness difference over the last 10,000 years. What happens in the next 10,000 years is not so obvious.

There are obvious religious implications to this question, and it's worth pointing out that Simon Conway Morris is a committed Christian. Let me put the question bluntly: Do you think the case for Christianity collapses if the evolution of humans is not inevitable?

It all depends on what you mean by "collapse." When you take a cosmological view and realize that the Earth is one tiny planet in the midst of a solar system, in the midst of a galaxy, in the midst of other galaxies, the idea that this whole great universe was designed just for us to show up strikes me as bizarrely self-involved, one of the most stunningly narcissistic visions that I've ever encountered.

In your book *Darwin's Dangerous Idea,* you say evolution is like a universal acid—a radical idea with far-reaching consequences. What do you mean?

Some of my classmates and I invented the idea of a universal acid. If an acid could eat through anything, what could you keep it in? You couldn't keep it in glass because it could eat through glass just as it could eat through a tin can. Then it occurred to me that Darwinism is an idea that eats through everything. That's both scary and wonderful. The Darwinian idea of natural selection really does turn everything upside down. Before Darwin, we had the idea that it takes a big fancy smart thing to make a less intelligent thing. You never see a pot making a potter, or a horseshoe making a blacksmith. That's our model of creation.

Then Darwin comes along and says we can turn the process upside down. Natural selection has no intelligence, no foresight. It just mechanically sifts and sorts, sifts and sorts. It's just a brute mechanical process. Yet we can have absolutely stupendous creation and brilliant designs emerging from a process that has no intelligence or purpose at all. That's a very radical idea.

Can a Darwinian in good conscience believe in God? Or has evolution killed God?

You can certainly believe in God if you find a way to give God a slightly different role. Some Darwinians manage by compartmentalizing their imagination: They believe in something like the traditional Christian God, even though they no longer think God plays the traditional role of making all creatures great and small. That job is done by evolution. And some people maintain that evolution itself is a phenomenon that had to be designed by God the designer. This idea goes back to Darwin's day when some of his first disciples, like Asa Gray at Harvard, thought that God simply creates the process of natural selection and lets it do the rest of the work.

Didn't Darwin himself have a nuanced answer to this question? He called himself an agnostic and clearly had lots of problems with religious superstition. But when he was asked if evolution meant you could no longer believe in a personal God, he said no, that was not the necessary conclusion. In some of his letters, he suggested that science and religion were two different realms of understanding.

One always has to remember that Darwin loved his wife, Emma, very dearly and she was quite devout. He constantly worried about how she would respond to the implications of his work. And he didn't want to upset people and their traditional beliefs. Was he some kind of believer? That's a biographical question that we can't answer. But I don't think it's important. Do you?

I do think it's important. Given Darwin's central role in the debate about evolution and creationism, it seems that what he really thought about religion does matter.

Well, that's the difference between science and religion. Darwin was the founder. But it's not the beginning of a religion, it's the beginning of a science. Darwin was completely backward about some things, and we don't have any trouble saying he was wrong. Those things are calmly replaced as the science proceeds. He was just an ordinary human being who made a lot of mistakes. What he actually thought about religion is of historical interest, but that's all. Today, we can find biologists who are religious. Kenneth Miller at Brown and Francisco Ayala at University of California at Irvine are two famous evolutionary biologists who are deeply religious. They're famous, in part, because they're so rare.

Your book *Breaking the Spell* examines the origins of religion. What exactly is the spell you want to break?

It's the idea that religion is so special that we mustn't look too closely at it. There are actually two spells. There's the spell that religion itself casts. I don't know that I want to break that—probably not. But in order to find out, I have to encourage people to break the spell that says, "Thou shalt not study religion as a natural phenomenon."

You're saying there's a taboo against subjecting religion to serious analysis?

Yes. Some people will say, "I don't see this taboo at all. People have been studying religion for centuries." True, they've been studying its doctrines and its history, but they haven't been studying it as a biological or psychological phenomenon. I think we should study it scientifically as a supplement to the historical scholarship.

Why do we need a scientific study of religion?

Because there isn't any more influential or important phenomenon on the globe in the twenty-first century. Every major problem we face in the world interacts in one way or another with religion. In all the major religions, and in many sects, there's a fringe that veers into terrorism or fanaticism. These are toxic. We don't understand what happens when religions go bad, as they sometimes do. Actually, people in favor of preserving religion should be just as interested in this as I am. We also don't understand the conditions under which religions get healthier and stronger.

Aren't the toxic effects of religion mainly a matter of extremists taking over and spouting Scripture to justify their violent actions? Isn't it fairly simple?

I don't think it is. First of all, who are the extremists? And which religions are they going to take over? Why aren't there any extremists trying to take over the Church of England? Why aren't there any extremists trying to take over Jainism?

Some critics would say your project is more than just subjecting religion to the rigors of scientific analysis. Don't you want to show that God is just a construction of the human mind?

I myself am an atheist, but that's not my purpose. It doesn't matter if other people don't share my atheism, as long as they share politically reasonable attitudes about other things. But I do get concerned when they impose truly irrational creeds that affect public policy. For instance, we run a serious public health risk because people don't understand the evolution of viruses and other pathogens. We're at the edge of the antibiotic age. The antibiotic age may be coming to a close if we don't keep pace with the pathogens that have evolved invulnerability to some of our best antibiotics.

As far as we know, every culture has had some system of religious belief. This suggests that humans are hardwired to believe in a transcendent reality. Is it also evidence that a transcendent reality really exists?

Well, the term "hardwired" is too simple. I'm sure there are genetically based adaptations of the human nervous system that make us susceptible to religious beliefs. We're certainly not hardwired to believe in any particular god or gods. But I think we have hardwired tendencies, which lead to belief in invisible agents. Eventually, what happens is that particularly robust and fascinating invisible agents are accepted by various communities of belief. Monotheism is then a much later and more sophisticated development.

Why did our ancient ancestors tens of thousands of years ago become religious?

There's an instinct we share with most mammals, which you can see in your dog's reactions. When something puzzling or strange happens, he wonders not just what happened but who's there. He's looking for an agent. So when the snow falls off your roof and lands with a thud outside the window, the dog jumps up and growls. He's wondering who the intruder is. The dog then goes back to sleep, but humans don't stop there. They ponder it and before they know it, they've conjured up a talking tree or forest god or gremlin. Only the most gripping and unforgettable of these invisible agents survive in the brains of our ancestors. So you can be sure that whatever gods are believed in, they're not going to be lame or boring.

But isn't it striking that all cultures believe in some transcendent reality?

Is it surprising? We have a built-in curiosity that favors finding agents, and these spirits are always invisible. Sometimes people claim to have seen them, but generally they are hidden. Why aren't there religions with visible agents? It seems obvious. All those sprites and goblins and little micro-gods are figments of imagination driven by this instinct to find agency. That doesn't establish that these beliefs are useful, just that they can exist. It could be like a bad habit that's infectious, which spreads because people copy each other. It may not do any good at all. It spreads because it can. After all, every human group also has the common cold. What's it for? It's not for anything.

Are you suggesting that religion is a bad habit?
That's one possibility that has to be taken seriously. Those who are sure it's a wonderful habit must not take it for granted because it's ubiquitous. What survives does so because it can survive. Lots of things spread. Every time you meet someone, you pass some germs their way and they pass some germs your way, and they spread because they can. There are good ideas, bad ideas, and neutral ideas. Some of them are very infectious and some aren't.

When you examine religion through this historical and sociological lens, why are some religious traditions more durable than others?
That's the right question to ask, but it's hard to get good data on this. Right now, there are a dozen or so major religions, but thousands of minor ones. Religions are born every day. But we don't know much about the hundreds of thousands of religions that flourished and then died without a trace. If we just look at the organized religions, we're seeing the survivors of a very rigorous competition for places in people's heads. They attract and hold people's allegiances over long periods of time.

Religion can also be incredibly demanding. For the true religious seeker, there's a constant struggle with doubt and even with God's existence.
People want their lives to have meaning. It's all too easy to see lives around us that are pointless. If it wasn't obvious enough, the media bombard us with examples of lives that are either thrilling or terrible. Whether people are glamorous or outrageous, everybody wants a life that tells not just an interesting story but an important story.

You're remarkably magnanimous. This doesn't sound like the critique of religion that we usually hear from outspoken atheists.

I think religion is very important and does a tremendous amount of good. If you ask me, would you like to see religion abolished, I'd say I don't know what I'd replace it with. Many problems facing the world are precisely the sort of problems that religions have done a great deal to help with. There is no force on the planet that equals religion's capacity for self-sacrifice and everyone pitching in for common ends, whether we're talking about ending apartheid in South Africa or the civil rights movement in the United States. Religion has not only done a tremendous amount of moral good work; it's done it better than any other institution.

But the price that religions pay for this is considerable. Why can't a secular organization—like Oxfam, Common Cause, or the American Civil Liberties Union—achieve the same ends? One reason is that those secular groups won't be comfortable with something that's ubiquitous in religion: at a certain point, encouraging people to stop thinking and simply take on faith that this is the right course of action. Don't question it because it comes from the highest authority. It's the capacity of religions to persuade people to turn off their critical faculties that worries me more than anything else.

Did you grow up in a religious family?

I went to Sunday school. I learned a great many Bible verses and lots of hymns. I know the rituals and the liturgy. I know Christian symbolism. But it was not a devout upbringing. It was not a big thing for me to walk away from.

What denomination was your family?

Congregational. I call it "liberal suburban Protestantism." I was fascinated by religion as a child. I had some friends who were Christian Scientists, so I read Mary Baker Eddy's *Key to the Scriptures*. I went to their meetings and saw some remarkable recoveries from illnesses and injuries. But in the end, I didn't believe in it. Once I was comfortable as an atheist, religion didn't play a big role for me, though I continue to love many of the rituals and especially the music.

Some atheists want to reclaim a sense of spirituality. They say the problem with most atheistic thinking is that it leaves no space for awe and wonder. Do you think life has a sacred dimension? And do you have experiences of rapture and wonder?

I think we all have sacred values. I have sacred values: love, truth, beauty, democracy, and freedom. These are values to die for. And absolutely, I have experiences of awe and wonder. Some of them are with music—for instance, with "The St. Matthew Passion" by Bach—and with many other great pieces of music, both religious and secular. But also with great mathematical and scientific ideas. Appreciating the stupendous complexity of the life on this planet is to me not just a worthy alternative to religious awe; it's deeper and more detailed. Because you don't have to squint and fog your eyes, you can study it with utter intensity. And it just gets more wonderful the more you study it. It's completely awesome.

Why is evolution the hot spot in the science and religion debate? Why doesn't quantum physics or artificial intelligence inspire this kind of controversy?

I think artificial intelligence would inspire very much the same anger, but it's just not well enough known and it hasn't made the dramatic progress that evolutionary biology has made. But it's part of the recognition that our species, *Homo sapiens*, is a product of evolution. Our brains are material organs. There's no such thing as an immortal soul as a separate immaterial entity. That's a fragile myth that science can't support.

So if you accept natural selection, the soul goes out the window because there's no way to account for the evolution of the soul?

Absolutely. Or let me put it slightly differently. An Italian journalist interviewed me about my work on consciousness and the paper ran a wonderful headline: "Yes, we have a soul, but it's made of lots of tiny robots." That's brilliant. That's exactly my position. We do have a soul. Human beings are different from all other species. We are the moral animal. We have minds that make us morally responsible in a way that no dog or chimpanzee or dolphin is. We have a kind of moral free will that no other creature does. But we can explain it as a perfectly natural phenomenon. One species on this planet has evolved a dominion and responsibility because our cognitive powers are so much greater than any other species'. We're the ones who can make the difference.

You wrote a book called *Consciousness Explained*. But it seems to me that we actually know very little about how the mind works. The connection between the brain and the mind is still largely a mystery. Do you really think the study of neural networks and electrochemical surges in the brain will fully explain everything that happens in the mind?

There are lots of puzzles, but there aren't any mysteries. There are plenty of very hard problems out there, but I don't think consciousness is a mystery, any more than reproduction is a mystery. If we go back just 200 years, reproduction was really mysterious. Preformationism was actually a serious contender. That was the idea of something like Chinese boxes: Inside a sperm, there was a little tiny person, and if it was a man, inside that tiny little man's testes, there were even tinier sperm. Today, that looks like a hilarious theory. It's hard to imagine that people took it seriously. They did because they couldn't think of anything better. Now, when you understand how DNA replicates, it's so complicated, it's breathtaking. There simply isn't any mystery about reproduction anymore. And the same thing is happening with consciousness.

But it seems like there are all kinds of things that science will never be able to explain. For instance, the precise nature of how we love someone else. I'm not talking about the sex drive, but the mystery of love. Or why we have certain dreams, which aren't even rooted in the physical world. If you dissect the brain and look at all the neural connections, do you think science will ever be able to explain these things?

Sure. In what sense do you mean explaining? Let's build up to it, because science doesn't do all this in one fell swoop. There are modest inroads. Would you find it unimaginable that science might, in the next 15 or 20 years, be able to read people's brains while they sleep and then write down what they're dreaming?

Actually, I don't think that will happen.

Well, hang on to your hat, because that's coming.

You're saying science will be able to figure this out without any self-reporting by the dreamer?

No, we'll use waking reports by dreamers to calibrate the instruments and understand how to decode the neural signals.

That's my point. If you don't actually ask the person what they're dreaming, will you ever be able to decipher the dreams?

Let's build up to it. We ask the person what they're dreaming for a hundred nights and we build up a nice library. We translate the relevant brain states for that person and then later, we'll be able to say, "Jones is having that dream about the old car. And look, he's falling over a cliff." And we wake him up and that's what he reports. If you think that's beyond the reach of science, I think you're wrong.

But that's just correlation. You're just looking at what Jones has dreamed and you're going to match the brain images to some future dream. That still doesn't explain how the brain actually generates that particular dream.

We have to do that, too, but we're making good progress. We now have more theories about why we dream than we have the data to sort them out. It's not that we're stumped for theories. Right now, we have too many theories. But those will get winnowed down in due course. Eventually, we'll be able to see how the brain conjures up certain themes in dreams in response to a particular disturbance within a person. We can't do that now. Might we do that in the future? Certainly. That still won't explain all the mystery. This is going to be an incremental process. But we'll be able to understand how the brain represents information and why the brain gets distracted, why it gets obsessed, why some ideas have more staying power than others. As you say, it isn't all sex drive or fear. It's going to be much more complicated than that.

What about the spiritual or mystical experiences that so many people report? How do you explain the feelings of connection with a transcendent being, or the rapture of oneness with the universe?

I don't know how to explain them yet. But in the near future, I'm sure that neuroscience will be able to explain the rapturous states that people go into.

There's a speculative theory suggesting that our capacity to be enraptured or swept up into religious ecstasy is related to our capacity to be hypnotized. And our capacity to be hypnotized has a clear biological foundation in early shamanic healing rituals. Before there were any doctors or hospitals, there were healers and shamans who developed rituals that had a very potent effect on people. They developed those rituals by trial and error over many thousands of years, and they found all the right buttons to push. If you look at the rituals of shamans around the world, you find they can reliably induce trance-like states in many people.

For many conditions, a hypnotic state is genuinely healing. It reduces pain, it's a reliable anesthetic, it even has a curative effect. It's a placebo effect. What shamans hit on was how to induce placebo effects with rituals. For instance, if you can ease the pain and suffering of childbirth with a ritual, you've got a very potent biological tool. And women who were not susceptible to it would be likely to die in childbirth.

We certainly know a lot about how different parts of the brain are activated, but will we ever be able to go down to the neuronal level to understand why certain thoughts pop into our heads?

I think we will. I don't see any reason to think that's impossible. Nobody has to understand it all the way down to the quantum effects in the proteins inside the cells. But those will be understood. The cell interactions will be understood. The cell assembly interactions will be understood. And finally, we'll understand the architecture of the brain's consciousness.

How long do you think that will take?

I really don't think the job will be completed in my lifetime, even if I live to be 100. But in my grandchildren's lifetime, sure.

Your critics call you a scientific reductionist. And they have a word to describe this way of thinking: "scientism." Are you trying to explain all of life through the lens of science?

"Scientism" is a completely undefined term. It just means science you don't like. There's no way of responding to the claim that I'm overly fond of science without getting down to details. Just exactly which application of science is beyond the pale? I don't think science has answers to all questions. I never say it does. I'm a philosopher. I'm not really a scientist.

What are some important questions that are beyond the scope of science?

What should we do? All the ethical questions are outside of science. They're the province of philosophy and particularly the province of a political process, where we try to get everybody to sit down and talk about what we ought to do. Science isn't about what we ought to do. Science can tell you how we got to where we are in our moral thinking—how our moral attitudes evolved, both biologically and culturally. But once science has done that, we have to sit down and figure out what we ought to do.

Ken Wilber

KEN WILBER MAY BE THE MOST important living philosopher you've never heard of. He has written dozens of books, but you would be hard-pressed to find his name in a mainstream magazine. Still, Wilber has a passionate—almost cultlike—following in certain circles, as well as some famous fans. Bill Clinton and Al Gore have praised his books. Deepak Chopra calls him "one of the most important pioneers in the field of consciousness." The Wachowski brothers asked him, along with Cornel West, to record the commentary for the DVDs of their *Matrix* trilogy.

A remarkable autodidact, Wilber's books range across entire fields of knowledge, from quantum physics to developmental psychology to the history of religion. He's steeped in the world's esoteric traditions, such as Mahayana Buddhism, Vedantic Hinduism, Sufism, and Christian mysticism. He also practices what he preaches, sometimes meditating for hours at a stretch. His "integral philosophy," along with the Integral Institute he founded, holds out the promise that we can understand mystical experience without lapsing into New Age mush.

Though he is often described as a New Age thinker, Wilber ridicules the notion that our minds can shape physical reality, and he's dismissive of New Age books and films like *The Tao of Physics* and *What the Bleep Do We Know?* But he's also out to show that "transrational" states of consciousness are real, and he has dubbed the scientific materialists who doubt it "flatlanders."

Wilber's hierarchy of spiritual development—and the not-so-subtle suggestion that he himself has reached advanced stages of enlightenment—has also sparked a backlash. Some critics consider him an arrogant know-it-all, too smart for his own good. His dense style of writing, which is often laced with charts and diagrams, can come off as bloodless and hyperrational.

In conversation, I found Wilber to be chatty and amiable, even laughing when he described a recent brush with death. He's a fast talker who leaps from one big idea to the next. And they are *big* ideas—God and "Big Self" and why science can only tell us so much about what's real.

■ ■ ■ ■

You've written that there's a philosophical cold war between science and religion. Do you see them as fundamentally in conflict?

Personally, I don't. But it depends entirely on what you mean by science and what you mean by religion. There are at least two main types of religion. One is dependent upon a belief in a mythic or magic dogma. That is certainly what most people mean by religion. Science has pretty thoroughly dismantled the mythic religions. But virtually all the great religions themselves recognize the difference between "exoteric" or outer religion, and "esoteric" or inner religion. Inner religion tends to be more contemplative and mystical and experiential, and less cognitive and conceptual. Science is actually very sympathetic with the contemplative traditions in terms of its methodology.

When you refer to mythic religions, are you talking about the kinds of stories we read in the Bible?

Or any of the world's great religions. I mean, Lao Tsu is 900 years old when he was born. According to the Hindus, the Earth is resting on a serpent, which is resting on an elephant, which is resting on a turtle. Those kinds of mythic approaches aren't wrong. They're just a stage of development. Look at [the Swiss philosopher] Jean Gebser's structural stages of development. They go from archaic to magic to mythic to rational to pluralistic to integral and higher. Magic and mythic are actual stages. They're not wrong any more than saying "five years old" is wrong. It's just five years old. We expect there to be higher stages. There was a time when the magic and mythic approaches years ago were evolution's leading edge of development. So we can't belittle them.

Where do you think the scientific worldview falls short when dealing with religion?

Conventional science has correctly dismantled the prerational myths, but it goes too far in dismantling the trans-rational. The mythic and magic approaches tend to be prerational and preverbal, but the meditative or contemplative practices tend to be trans-rational. They completely accept rationality and science. But they point out that there are deeper modes of awareness, which are scientific in their own way.

What do you mean by trans-rational?

People at these higher stages of spiritual development report "a nondual awareness," a type of awareness that transcends the dichotomy between subject and object. The mystical state is often beyond words. It is transrational because you have access to rationality but it's temporarily suspended. A six-month-old infant, for instance, is in a prerational state, whereas the mystic is in a trans-rational state. Unfortunately, "pre-" and "trans-" get confused. So some theorists say the infant is in a mystical state.

Are you saying people with a rationalist orientation just can't make these distinctions?

I'm saying that when people look at mystical states, they often confuse them with prerational states. People like Sigmund Freud take trans-rational, oceanic states of oneness and reduce them to infantile states of unity. The infant is one with the breast in what looks like a nondual union. But it's not trans-rational. It's prerational and preverbal.

Why has the scientific worldview completely dismissed this trans-personal dimension? For most intellectuals around the world, the secular scientific paradigm has triumphed.

It's understandable. Historically, if you look at these broad stages, the magical era tended to be 50,000 years ago, the mythic era emerged around 5,000 B.C.E., and the rational era—secular humanism—emerged in the Renaissance and

Enlightenment. The Enlightenment was an attempt to liberate myth and base truth claims on evidence, not just dogma. But when science threw out the church, they threw out the baby with the bathwater.

You can't prove a higher stage to someone who's not at it. If you go to somebody at the mythic stage and try to prove to them something from the rational, scientific stage, it won't work. You go to a fundamentalist who doesn't believe in evolution, who believes the Earth was created in six days, and you say, "What about the fossil record?" "Oh yes, the fossil record; God created that on the fifth day." You can't use any of the evidence from a higher stage and prove it to a lower stage. So someone who's at the rational stage has a very hard time seeing these trans-rational, trans-personal stages. The rational scientist looks at all the prerational stuff as nonsense—fairies and ghosts and goblins—and lumps it together with the trans-rational stuff and says, "That's nonrational. I don't want anything to do with it."

So where does God fit into this picture? And do you believe in God?
God is a perfect example of how these two types of religion treat ultimate reality. You asked, "Do you believe in God?" In exoteric religion, it's a matter of belief. Do you believe in the kind of God who rewards and punishes and will sit with you in some eternal heaven? But in the esoteric form of religion, God is a direct experience. Most contemplatives would call it "godhead." It's so different from the mythic conceptions of God—the old man in the sky with a gray beard. The word "God" is much more misleading than it is accurate. So there's a whole series of terms that are used instead by the esoteric traditions— super consciousness, Big Mind, Big Self. This ultimate reality is a direct union that is felt or recognized in a state of enlightenment or liberation. It's what the Sufis call the "supreme identity"—the identity of the interior soul with the ultimate ground of being in a direct experiential state.

It does raise the question of whether God—or ultimate reality—has some independent existence, or whether this is just a mental state that our minds can conjure up.
That's right. One way we try to find out is by doing cross-cultural studies of individuals who've had the experience of the supreme identity and see if it

shows similar characteristics. The most similar characteristic is it doesn't have characteristics. It's radically undefinable, radically free, radically empty. This formless ground of being is found in virtually all esoteric religions around the world. For the final test, take scientists with a Ph.D. who are studying brain patterns and put them in a contemplative state of the supreme identity and ask them whether they think that state is real or just a brain state. Nine out of 10 will say they think it's real. They think this experience discloses a reality that's independent of the human organism.

Do you see this ultimate reality as some sort of being or intelligence out there?

Well, if you look cross-culturally, what you'll find is that spirit or godhead can be looked at either through first-person, second-person, or third-person perspectives. The third-person perspective is to see spirit as a grand "it." In other words, a vast web of life. Gaia in this third-person view is the sum total of everything that exists. A second-person way of looking sees spirit as a "thou," as an actual intelligence that is present and is something you can, in a sense, have a conversation with, keeping in mind the ultimately unknowable nature of godhead. Many of the contemplative traditions go further and say you can approach spirit as a first person. So that spirit is "I." Or that would be Big Self.

This means "I am God."

That's right. This first-person perspective is an experience of pure "I-am-ness," behind your relative ego. Discovering your Big Self comes directly in the contemplative state of nondual awareness. This means subject and object are one. It's not that you're looking at the mountain when you're going on a nature walk. You *are* the mountain. You're not listening to the river anymore. You *are* the river.

You are a longtime meditator. You've written about having sustained experiences of this nondual awareness. What does it feel like?

(*Laughs*) It's very simple. It's something that's already present in one's awareness, but it's so simple and so obvious that it's not noticed. Zen refers to it as the "such-ness" of reality. [The Christian mystic] Meister Eckhart called it "thus-ness." These states of consciousness are temporary, peak experiences.

There's no bliss. Rather, it's an absence of any constriction, including feelings of bliss. The feeling is vast openness and freedom and lightness. You don't have a sense that I'm in here and the world is out there.

You were actually a budding scientist at one point, a graduate student in biochemistry. Why did you give up the scientific track to study these spiritual matters?

I had a scientific orientation. I think I was a born scientist. In fact, I was one of those kids with the early science labs—you know, all the frogs you cut up, the explosions in the basement. I went to Duke University in the medical track. And then I decided I wanted to do something more creative, so I switched to biochemistry at Nebraska. But as I moved into young adulthood, mere rationality didn't really seem to be answering the questions that were arising in that stage of my life: Why am I here? What's it all about? What's the nature of reality?

What changed for you?

I realized that exterior science wasn't working. So I turned to Zen Buddhism. To me it was very scientific. It's a practice, an actual experiment. And if you do this experiment, you'll have some sort of experience, and you'll get some data. William James defined data as an experience. Then you check your direct experience with other people to make sure you didn't goof up. Some sort of consensual evidence is required. There are several schools of thinking about how to evaluate scientific evidence. One of the most famous is Karl Popper's, where you try to disprove it. So this process is exactly what I was doing in Zen Buddhism. You have to train your mind. And frankly, this mind-training was more difficult than anything I did in graduate school.

What about Karl Popper's objection: If you can't disprove something, then it's not science. Can you disprove the effects of meditation? How far can you take this scientific analogy when you're talking about a contemplative practice?

Pretty far, I think. These meditative disciplines have been passed down for hundreds of years, sometimes thousands of years. Much like judo, there are actual techniques that you can learn and pass on. In Zen, you have the practice of *zazen*. You have to sit and count your breath for up to an hour and concentrate on an object for at least five minutes without losing track. The average American adult can do it for 18 seconds. Then you have the data, what's called *satori*. Once you train your mind and look into your interior, you investigate the actual nature and structure of your interior consciousness. And if you do this intensely enough, you'll get a profound "a ha!" experience, a profound awakening. And that satori is then checked with others who've done this practice.

But I doubt many scientists would accept this as proof of science because ultimately, people are left to describe their own experiences. You can't measure this with any conventional scientific instruments.

You move in the realm of phenomenology. And you either accept phenomenology or you don't. This also applies to psychoanalysis. You get the same complaints that it's not real science, that you can't prove it. Well, fine, but then you can't prove any interior experience you're having. You can't prove you're loving your wife, you can't prove you're happy. Forget all of that, it's not real. If that's the mind-set you have, nobody's going to convince you otherwise. It really comes down to whether there are interior sciences. These interior sciences use the same principles as the exterior sciences. If you define science as based on sensory experience, then these interior endeavors are not science. But if you define science as based on experience, then these interior ones are.

What about brain-imaging studies? Various neuroscientists are hooking up Buddhist monks and Christian nuns to brain-scanning technology, and they see changes in brain activity during meditation or prayer. But can they really tell us anything fundamental about the nature of consciousness?

Yes and no. What's starting to show up are significant and unique fingerprints of these meditative states on the brain. That's been demonstrated with people who do a type of meditation that's said to increase compassion—imagining someone else who's in pain and breathing in their pain, creating a feeling of oneness with that person. These people start showing distinctive gamma wave patterns. These gamma waves show up almost no place else. But let me tell you what it doesn't prove. The claim that it's a higher mental state can only be made if you're looking at it from the inside. We say that waking is more real than dreaming. But brain waves won't tell you that. The brain waves are just different. You can't say one is more real than the other.

This raises a fundamental question about the whole mind–brain problem. Virtually all neuroscientists say the mind is nothing more than a three-pound mass of firing neurons and electrochemical surges in the brain. Why do you think this view is wrong?
It reduces everything. And you can make no distinctions of value. There's no such thing as love is better than hate, or a moral impulse is better than an immoral impulse. All those value distinctions are erased.

But is that scientific view wrong?
At this point, you enter the philosophy of science, and the argument is endless. Is there nothing but physical stuff in the universe? Or is there some sort of interiority? We're not talking about ghosts and goblins and souls and all that kind of stuff. Just, is there interiority? Is there an inside to the universe? And if there is interiority, then that is where consciousness resides. You can't see it, but it's real. This is the claim that phenomenology makes.

For example, you and I are attempting to reach mutual understanding right now. And we say, "A ha, I understand what you're saying." But you can't point to that understanding. Where does it exist? But if you take a phenomenology of our interior states, then you look at them as being real in themselves. And that's where values lie and meaning lies. If you try to reduce those to matter, you not only lose all those distinctions, but you can't even make the claim that some are right and some are wrong.

But somewhere down the road—50 years from now, 500 years from now— once neuroscience becomes much more advanced, will scientists be able to pinpoint where these values and thoughts come from?
I'm saying we'll never understand it. The materialists keep issuing promissory notes. They always promise they're going to do it tomorrow. But interior and

exterior arise together. You can't reduce one to the other. They're both real. Deal with it.

You're saying there's no way we can map what's happening in our brains— the neuronal activity, the synaptic connections—to explain what's going on in our inner experience.

That's right. All you can do is map certain correlations. You can say that when a person's thinking logically, certain parts of the brain light up. But you can't determine what the person is thinking. More important, you can't reproduce the reality of the person thinking because that's a first-person experience. This first-person reality can't be reduced to third-person material entities. What that means is that consciousness can't be reduced to matter. You can't give a material explanation of how the experience of consciousness arises.

Let's talk about evolution. It seems to me that the great religious traditions really don't know what to do with the evolution of the human brain. At some point in our evolutionary history—maybe 50,000 or 100,000 years ago—the brain developed a new level of complexity that produced language and conceptual thought; basically, the human beings we are today. Is our consciousness rooted in the material matter in our brains?

An integral approach maintains that an increase in the complexity of matter is accompanied by an increase in the degree of consciousness. The greater the one, the greater the other. So if we look at complexity in evolution, it goes from atoms to molecules to cells to early organisms to organisms with a reptilian brainstem to organisms with a mammalian limbic system to organisms with a triune brain. We find major leaps in consciousness with each of those levels of complexity.

But can you even talk about consciousness before you reach a certain level of evolution? I mean, bacteria don't have consciousness. Plants don't have consciousness.

Well, I don't talk about consciousness. I talk about interiority. What you see is that as soon as you have a cell, it starts to respond to the environment in ways that can't be predicted. If you're just looking at material stuff—like a planet that doesn't have life on it—a physicist can tell you where that planet is going to be, barring other forces, 1,000 years from now. But that physicist can't tell you where my dog is going to be two seconds from now. There is a degree of nondetermined interiority. It's simply there. You can't dismiss it.

What do you think of the New Age writers who see a link between mysticism and the weirdness of quantum physics? There have been popular books like *The Tao of Physics* and *The Dancing Wu Li Masters,* as well as the hit film *What the Bleep Do We Know?* They point out that reality at the quantum level is inherently probabilistic. They say that the act of observing a quantum phenomenon plays a critical role in actually creating that phenomenon. The lesson they draw is that consciousness itself can shape physical reality.

They are confused. Even people like Deepak Chopra say this. These are good people; I know them. But when they say consciousness can act to create matter, whose consciousness? Yours or mine? They never get to that. It's a very narcissistic view.

But the real problem is what's called "the measurement problem." And 95 percent of scientists do not think the measurement problem involves consciousness. It simply involves the fact that you can't tell where an electron is until you measure it. It's very different from saying it doesn't exist until you measure it. That's entirely different from saying human consciousness causes matter to come into existence. We have abundant evidence that the entire material universe existed before human beings evolved. So the whole notion that human consciousness is required—it retroactively creates the universe—is a much harder myth to believe than myths about God being a white-haired gentleman pulling strings up in the sky.

But you seem to have a dualistic view of how to look at reality. There's the material stuff and then there's this interior stuff, and the two have nothing to do with each other.

Well, that's simply a metaphorical way that I talk about it. Spirit is not some other item sitting over here, separate from the material world. It's the actual reality of each and every thing that's arising. The ocean and its waves are typically used as an example to describe this. The ocean is not something different from the waves. It's the wetness of all waves. So it's not a dualistic stance at all.

You've written that many of the great twentieth-century physicists— Einstein, Bohr, Planck, Heisenberg—were actually mystics, even though none of them thought science had any connection to religion.

I wouldn't say it quite that strongly. What happened is they investigated the physical realm so intensely looking for answers, and when they didn't find these answers, they became metaphysical. I collected the writings of the 13 major founders of quantum mechanics. They were saying physics has been used since time immemorial to both prove and disprove God. Both views are fundamentally misguided. These physicists became deep mystics not because of physics but because of the limitations of physics.

So understanding that physics can only go so far—that there are many things it can't explain—is ultimately a mystical position?

That's correct. These are brilliant writings. They're really quite extraordinary. Not many people realize that Erwin Schrödinger, the founder of quantum mechanics, had a deep satori experience. He found that the position that most matched his own was Vedantic Hinduism—that pure awareness is aware of all objects but cannot itself become an object. It's the way into the door of realizing ultimate reality. Werner Heisenberg had similar experiences. And Sir Arthur Eddington was probably the most eloquent of the lot. All of them basically said that science neither proves nor disproves emptiness.

You've said Buddhism is probably the esoteric tradition that's influenced you the most. But you also criticize what you call "Boomeritis Buddhism." What is this?

What we found in the 1960s was that there was an overinfluence of feelings. Anti-intellectualism was rampant, and it continues to be rampant in a lot of meditative and alternative spiritualities. There's a tendency to explain the trans-rational states in terms that are really preverbal. So instead of a Big Self, you're just experiencing a big ego. For heaven's sake, this generation was known as the "me generation."

So the irony is that Buddhism is supposed to be a practice where you get rid of your self, but it sometimes becomes all about yourself.

Exactly. If you're caught in Boomeritis, you pay attention only to sensory experience. Mental experience is thrown out the door, and so is spiritual experience. It ends up being, inadvertently, all about yourself and your own feelings.

There's an assumption that master contemplatives, people who can reach exalted states of enlightenment, are wonderful human beings, that goodness radiates from them. Do you think that's true?

Nothing's ever quite that simple. There are different kinds of intelligence, and they develop at different rates. If your moral development reaches up into the trans-personal levels, then you tend to be St. Teresa. But some, like Picasso, have their cognitive development very high but their moral development is in the bloody basement. We think someone is enlightened in every aspect of their lives, but that's rarely the case.

You have many admirers. You also have critics. One objection is that you are too full of yourself. The science writer John Horgan, in his book *Rational Mysticism*, said the vibe he got from you was, "I'm enlightened. You're not." How do you respond to this charge of arrogance, the sense that you've unlocked the secrets of the universe and no one else has?

A lot of people see me as much more humble. I continue to change because I'm open to new ideas and I'm very open to criticism. Basically, I've taken the answers that have been given by the great sages, saints, and philosophers and have worked them into this integral framework. If that vibe comes across as arrogant, then John would get that feeling. Of course, he was trying to do the same thing, so I would have brushed up against his own egoistic projections. But some people do agree with him and feel that my support for this integral framework comes across as arrogant.

All I've done is provide a map. We're always updating it, always revising it, based on criticism and feedback and new evidence. You see those maps that Columbus and the early explorers drew of North and South America, where Florida is the size of Greenland. That's how our maps are. What's surprising to me is the number of savvy people who've expressed support for my work.

About a year ago, you nearly died from a grand mal seizure, which triggered more seizures. From what I heard, you were on life-support systems. You almost bit off your tongue. Weren't you unconscious for several days?

I did have 12 grand mal seizures in one evening. I was rushed to the ER comatose. I was in a coma for four days. During that time, I had electric paddles put on my heart three times. I was on dialysis because my kidneys had failed. I developed pneumonia. Ken Wilber was unconscious, but Big Mind was conscious. Ken Wilber came to on the fourth day.

Are you saying some part of you was aware of what was going on, even though you were unconscious?

Yes. This is a very common experience of longtime meditators. There is an awareness during waking, dreaming, and deep sleep states.

I'm having trouble understanding this. Some part of you was aware of the people moving around you?

There was a dim awareness of the room. It did include people moving in and out of the room and people sitting by the table. It did include certain procedures being done. But there wasn't a Ken Wilber as a subject relating to things that were happening. There was no separate self. Ken Wilber, if he were conscious, presumably would be upset or would be happy when the heart started beating again. But there were none of those reactions because there was just this Big Mind awareness, this nondual awareness.

The way you talk about this, it doesn't sound like such a bad experience! I would've thought this would be horrible.

(*Laughs*) Exactly. When you listen to more conventional near-death experiences, they don't sound so bad either. In any event, I was told that I would take quite a while to recover. But I walked out of the hospital two days later, with everything normal. So I put that down in part to my own spiritual practice and the rejuvenating capacity that this awareness has.

Does the prospect of dying frighten you?

Not really. What comes up is just thoughts of how much work in the world there is still to do. And with this recent experience—letting me know that Big Mind is what there is—that fundamental fear of dying has basically left. Still, when someone asks if I have a fear of dying, I find myself hesitating. What goes through my mind is positive stuff—friends that I would lose and work that needs to be done.

Robert Wright

ROBERT WRIGHT HAS CARVED OUT a distinct niche in American journalism. While his essays range freely across the political landscape—from foreign policy to technology—his meaty, book-length forays into evolutionary psychology and the sweep of history have set him apart. His latest book goes after even bigger game: God Almighty.

Actually, *The Evolution of God* never grapples with the most basic religious question—the existence of God. Instead, it charts the twists and turns of how God's personality kept changing over the centuries—specifically, how the rough-and-tumble politics of the ancient Middle East shaped the Abrahamic religions. The book is filled with richly observed details about the Bible and the Quran, though Wright wears his learning lightly as he guides us through several thousand years of religious history.

There's something to offend just about everyone in this book. Wright recounts in harrowing detail how the early Israelites, who had been conquered and humiliated by the Babylonians, invoked Yahweh to wreak vengeance on their enemies. This is no God for the faint of heart! He's no gentler on Christianity. Wright's Jesus is not the prophet of peace and love but a sometimes mean-spirited apocalyptic preacher obsessed with the approaching end times. Islam's founder, Muhammad, comes across as much a warrior as a prophet, bent on annihilating his enemies when they cross him. Despite all this religious mayhem, the book also shows a gentler side of the Abrahamic religions, especially when they manage to find common cause with their heathen neighbors and rival monotheists.

At first, *The Evolution of God* reads like another atheistic tract exposing the seamier side of religion. But then I came to Wright's account of the "moral imagination" and his surprising conclusion: He may not believe in God, but he thinks humanity is marching—however wobbly—toward moral truth.

In our interview, we talked about the bloody history of monotheism, what a mature religion would look like, and Wright's own spiritual awakening at a meditation retreat.

■ ■ ■ ■

At the very beginning of your book, you describe yourself as a materialist. This raises an interesting question: Can a materialist really explain the history of religion?

I tend to explain things in terms of material causes. So when I see God changing moods, as He does a lot in the Bible and the Quran, I ask, "What was going on politically or economically that might explain why the people who wrote this Scripture were inclined to depict God as being in a bad mood or a good mood?" Sometimes God is advocating horrific things, like annihilating nearby peoples, or sometimes He's very compassionate and loving. So I wanted to figure out why the mood fluctuates. I do think the answers lie in the facts on the ground. And that's what I mean by being a materialist.

What do you mean by the "facts on the ground"?

My basic premise is that when a religious group sees itself as having something to gain through peaceful interaction with another group of people, including a different religion, it will find a basis for tolerance in its Scriptures and religion. When groups see each other as being in a non–zero-sum relationship—there's a possibility of a win-win outcome if they play their cards right, or a lose-lose outcome if they don't—then they tend to warm up to one another. By contrast, if people see themselves in a zero-sum relationship with another group of people—they can only win if the other group loses—that brings out the intolerance and the dark side of religion. You see that in the world today. A lot of Palestinians and Israelis think they're playing a win-lose game. They think their interests are opposed and inversely correlated. In the long run, I think they're wrong. They're either both going to win or both going to lose.

You're saying these attitudes keep fluctuating back and forth over the history of religion. It's not just a gradual movement from less tolerance to more tolerance.

There hasn't been any smooth progression toward tolerance in any of the religions. If you look at the way human beings treated each other 10,000 years ago, it was not uncommon for members of one hunter-gatherer tribe to consider strangers as subhuman and worthy of death. I try to show that all the Abrahamic religions—Judaism, Christianity, and Islam—are capable of making great moral progress by extending compassion across national and ethnic and religious bounds. But there has not been any kind of smooth progression.

Do you think all religions share certain core principles?

Not many. People in the modern world, certainly in America, think of religion as being largely about prescribing moral behavior. But religion wasn't originally about that at all. To judge by hunter-gatherer religions, religion was not fundamentally about morality before the invention of agriculture. It was trying to figure out why bad things happen and increasing the frequency with which good things happen. Why do you sometimes get earthquakes, storms, disease, and get slaughtered? But then sometimes you get nice weather, abundant game, and you get to do the slaughtering. Those were the religious questions in the beginning.

And bad things happened because the gods were against you or certain spirits had it out for you?

Yes, you had done something to offend a god or spirit. However, it was not originally a moral lapse. That's an idea you see increasingly as societies get more complex. When you have a small group of hunter-gatherers, a robust moral system is not a big challenge. Everyone knows everybody, so it's hard to conceal anything you steal. If you mess with somebody too much, there will be payback. Moral regulation is not a big problem in a simple society. But as society got more complex with the invention of agriculture and writing, morality did become a challenge. Religion filled that gap.

But it's easier to explain why bad things happen in these older religions. You can attribute it to an angry spirit. It's harder to explain evil if there's an all-powerful, all-loving God.

The problem of evil is a product of modern religion. If you believe in an omnipotent and infinitely good God, then evil is a problem. If God is really good—and can do anything He or She wants—why do innocent people suffer? If you've got a religion in which the gods are not especially good in the first place, or they're not omnipotent, then evil is not a problem.

Why did monotheism first develop?

My explanation for Abrahamic monotheism is different from the standard one. I believe it emerged later than most people think—in the sixth century B.C.E., when Israelite elites were exiled by the Babylonians who conquered them. The spirit of monotheism was originally a lot less sunny and benign than people claim. Morally, it got better, but at its birth, monotheism was fundamentally about retribution.

Israel was a small nation in a bad neighborhood that got kicked around. This culminated in the exile, which was humiliating. It dispossessed the Israelites. It's not crazy to compare the mind-set of the Israelites then to the mind-set of today's Palestinians, who feel humiliated and dispossessed. This kind of mind-set brings out the belligerence in a religion. You see that in the Book of Isaiah, thought to be written by so-called Second Isaiah. These are the earliest Scriptures in the Bible that are clearly monotheistic. You get the sense that monotheism is about punishing the various nations that have persecuted Israel.

So you see a connection between the political power of a people and the god they believed in?

In ancient times, there was always a close association between politics and gods. The victor of a war was always the nation whose god beat the other god. But the specific political dynamic that monotheism reflected at its birth was Israel's desire to punish other nations by denying the very existence of their gods and also envisioning a day when Israel's god, Yahweh, would actually subjugate those nations.

Does Yahweh become a tool for Israelite kings to consolidate power?

You see that especially with King Josiah. Israel was polytheistic for a lot longer than most people think. A lot of things factored into its movement toward monotheism. One was a king who wanted to eliminate domestic political rivals. Those political rivals would have claimed access to various gods other than Yahweh, so King Josiah wanted to eliminate them. He killed some of them and also made it illegal to worship their gods. That gets you to the brink of monotheism. I think the exile pushes you over. You have a very belligerent, exclusive monotheism, whose very purpose is to exclude other nations from this privileged circle of God's most favored people.

King Josiah comes off rather badly in your book. He's hugely influential in the development of monotheism, but also a brutal tyrant who tried to wipe out people with competing religious beliefs.

He was an authoritarian. By the standards of the day, maybe not an unusually harsh one. Politics were pretty rough and tumble in those days. He was a nationalist, populist authoritarian—maybe a little bit like Hugo Chávez. It was a rejection of cosmopolitanism and internationalism. By our standards, King Josiah was a bad guy. He kills a bunch of priests who had the misfortune of not focusing their devotion exclusively on Yahweh. He cleans out the temple.

For people who claim that Israel was monotheistic from the get-go and its flirtations with polytheism were rare aberrations, it's interesting that the Jerusalem temple, according to the Bible's account, had all these other gods being worshiped in it. Asherah was in the temple. She seemed to be a consort or wife of Yahweh. And there were vessels devoted to Baal, the reviled Canaanite god. So Israel was fundamentally polytheistic at this point. Then King Josiah goes on a rampage as he tries to consolidate his own power by wiping out the other gods.

However, after the exile, monotheism evolves into something much more laudable and inclusive. Now the exiles have returned to Jerusalem and Israel is in a secure neighborhood. It's part of the Persian empire, and so are its neighbors. So you see a much sunnier side of God, with expressions of tolerance and compassion toward other nations. This shows that monotheism isn't intrinsically good or bad. It depends on the circumstances in which it finds itself.

This gets pretty confusing for today's religious believer. There's a vengeful God in some of these early books of the Old Testament—a God who at times says you need to wipe out people with different religious beliefs. But within this same sacred text, you can also read about a very compassionate God.

You're right, the contrasts are extreme. At one point in the Hebrew Bible, God is saying, "I want you to annihilate nearby peoples who worship the wrong gods." He says do not leave anything alive that breathes—not livestock, women, or children. Then other times you have Israelites not only tolerating a neighbor who worships another god but using that other god to validate their desire for tolerance. So they'll say to the Ammonites, "Look, you've got your god, Chemosh. He gave you your land. We've got our god, Yahweh, who gave us our land. Can't we just get along?"

You see this kind of vacillation in the Bible and also in the Quran. In both cases, it's a question of whether people think they can gain through peaceful interaction with other people. I think that's also the challenge in the modern world. Barack Obama gets this. So long as Israeli settlements are expanding, you're not going to convince Palestinians that they're playing anything other than a zero-sum game with the Israelis. Obama understands that it's partly a question of perception. Muslims who feel disrespected—whether or not they really are—will fuel religious extremism.

Let's skip ahead to the next great monotheistic religion. Why did Christianity take root?

The doctrines we associate with Christianity probably took root a little later than most people think. There's reason to doubt that Jesus is actually the source of the stuff we consider most laudable in Christianity: universal, trans-national, trans-ethnic love. I think that is a product of people like the Apostle Paul, who—after the crucifixion—carried the Jesus movement into the Roman empire. Paul wanted to build a network of churches. He was a true believer, but he went about this in a very pragmatic, businesslike way. In many ways, the church served as a networking service. That was part of its appeal. The network of Christian churches made it easier for merchants to travel from city to city in the Roman empire and do business.

Paul also made some good strategic choices. There were followers of Jesus who dictated that any non-Jews who became part of the Jesus movement had to be circumcised. Adult men had to be circumcised to join the church. This was before modern anesthesia, so you can see this would be a disincentive. Paul said no, and they don't have to follow the dietary laws either. They also developed an attractive doctrine of an afterlife. The Roman empire was in a way waiting for a church to dominate it. The more Christians there were, the more valuable it was to join that network. When Christianity reached critical mass, then its dominance of the Roman empire became almost inevitable.

So later Christians, Paul among others, really institutionalized Christianity. What about the historical Jesus? What do we know about him?
It's popular to say he said the good stuff and not the less good stuff. I think it's the opposite.

He's typically seen as the great prophet of peace and love.
Yeah. But the fact is, the Sermon on the Mount, which is a beautiful thing, does not appear in Mark, which was the first written gospel. And these views are not attributed to Jesus in the letters of Paul, which are the earliest post-crucifixion documents we have. You see Paul develop a doctrine of universal love, but he's not, by and large, attributing this stuff to Jesus. So, too, with "love your enemies." Paul says something like love your enemies, but he doesn't say Jesus said it. It's only in later gospels that this stuff gets attributed to Jesus. This will seem dispiriting to some people to hear that Jesus wasn't the great guy we thought he was. But to me, it's actually more inspiring to think that the doctrines of transnational, transethnic love were products of a multinational, imperial platform. Throughout human history, as social organization grows beyond ethnic bounds, it comes to encompass diverse ethnicities and nations. And if it develops doctrines that bring us closer to moral truth, like universal love, that is encouraging. I think you see it in all three religions.

If Jesus was not the prophet of love and tolerance that he's commonly thought to be, what kind of person was he?

I think he was your typical Jewish apocalyptic preacher. I'm not the first to say that. Bart Ehrman makes these kinds of arguments, and it goes back to Albert Schweitzer. Jesus was preaching that the kingdom of God was about to come. He didn't mean in heaven. He meant God's going to come down and straighten things out on this Earth. And he had the biases that you'd expect a Jewish apocalyptic preacher to have. He doesn't seem to have been all that enthusiastic about non-Jews. There's one episode where a woman who's not from Israel wants him to use his healing powers on her daughter. He's pretty mean and basically says, no, we don't serve dogs here. He compares her to a dog. In the later gospels, that conversation unfolds so you can interpret it as a lesson in the value of faith. But in the earliest treatment, in Mark, it's an ugly story. It's only because she accepts her inferior status that Jesus says, okay, I will heal your daughter.

But wasn't Jesus revolutionary because he made no distinctions between social classes? The poor were just as worthy as the rich.
It's certainly plausible that his following included poor people. But I don't think it extended beyond ethnic bounds. And I don't think it was that original. In the Hebrew Bible, you see a number of prophets who were crying out for justice on behalf of the poor. So it wasn't new that someone would have a constituency that includes the dispossessed. It's good. I'm sure in many ways Jesus was a laudable person. But I think more good things are attributed to him than really bear weight.

So you are distinguishing between Jesus and Christ—Jesus the flesh-and-blood historical figure as opposed to how he was later represented as Christ, the son of God.
That's right. There's no evidence that Jesus thought he should be equated with God. He may have thought he was a messiah, but "messiah" in those days didn't mean what it's come to mean to Christians. It meant a powerful figure who leads his people to victory, perhaps a successful revolt against the Romans. But Christ as we think of Christ—the son of God—that's something that emerges in the later gospels and reaches its climax in John,

which is the last of the four gospels to be written. So the story of what Jesus represents in theology did not take shape during his lifetime.

Do you see Islam as essentially an offshoot of the Judeo-Christian tradition or as something fundamentally new?

Muhammad was trying to create a synthetic religion, drawing on the existing traditions of Judaism and Christianity. He says very nice things in the Quran about Christians and Jesus, though he can't quite accept the idea that Jesus was the son of God. He also made great overtures toward Jews. He established a fast that was essentially Yom Kippur. The ban on eating pork probably comes as a reflection of Judaism. There's every indication that he hoped to play a successful non–zero-sum game with Christians and Jews and draw them into a larger religion. He insisted that his God was their God. But it didn't work out. Apparently, not that many Jews bought into his mission.

In the standard telling, once Muhammad was ruling the city of Medina and he'd become a statesman as well as a prophet, some Jewish tribes betrayed him and were collaborating with the enemy. So there was a very violent falling-out. And he expelled Jewish tribes and in one case killed the adult males. But there's no doubt that the origins of Islam are rooted in the existing traditions of Christianity and Judaism.

You make the point that the Quran is a different kind of sacred text than the Bible. It was probably written over the course of two decades, whereas the stories collected in the Bible were written over centuries. That's why the Bible is such a diverse document.

We think of the Bible as a book, but in ancient times it would have been thought of as a library. There were books written by lots of different people, including a lot of cosmopolitan elites. You also see elements of Greek philosophy. The Quran is just one guy talking. In the Muslim view, he's mediating the word of God. He's not especially cosmopolitan. He is, according to Islamic tradition, illiterate. So it's not surprising that the Quran didn't have the intellectual diversity and, in some cases, the philosophical depth that you find in the Bible.

I do think he was actually a very modern thinker. Muhammad's argument for why you should be devoted exclusively to this one God is very modern.

Do you think it has been harder for today's Muslims to take liberal interpretations of the Quran because it's linked so directly to Muhammad, while the Bible isn't so closely associated with Moses or Jesus?

Yes, and because Muhammad spent a certain amount of his career as a politician and a military leader. There are parts of the Quran that are a military manual, which advocate killing the enemy. Of course, the Bible has these things too, but they're a smaller portion of the overall Bible. But when you look at that part of the Quran, it's much more subtle than a lot of people think.

Take the famous verse "Kill the infidels wherever you find them." Actually, it's a mistranslation. It's "Kill the polytheists." So it probably wouldn't include Christians and Jews. If you look at the verse in context, it seems that he exempts those polytheists who are on the side of the Muslims in this particular war. So all that passage says is: "Kill the people who are enemies in this war." It's not fundamentally about religion. In this case and others, it complies with my basic argument: When people see themselves in a non–zero-sum relationship with other people, they will be tolerant of them and of their religion. Muhammad probably exemplifies that better than any single figure in ancient Abrahamic history.

Your book focuses on the Abrahamic religions. But aren't Eastern religions like Buddhism and Hinduism actually more open to the idea that other religions can also be the path to truth and salvation?

Yes, it's not uncommon in Asia for somebody to be a little bit of a Buddhist and a little bit of a Taoist. It's certainly possible for religion to be nonexclusive. Parts of Buddhism are exemplary. In some ways it was the earliest religion to recognize the fundamental problem of being human. The challenge is to change the already-existing character of a religion. The world is not full of Buddhists. And even Buddhist monks have gone on rampages. There is no religion that is always a religion of peace. But in Buddhism, you're seeing some very interesting developments. The Western, quasi-secular Buddhism is an interesting adaptation to a scientific age because it makes relatively few claims about the supernatural.

You have written a secular history of how religion has been used by various political movements to consolidate power. But you're ignoring the power of personal spiritual experience—what some people would call revelation. Can you really explain religion without acknowledging the importance of actual religious experience?

I do think religious experience has played an important part in religion. I think the Apostle Paul felt genuinely inspired. I myself have had profound experiences that could be characterized as religious. I certainly had some when I was young and a believing Christian. And I've had some since then. I did a one-week silent meditation retreat and had very profound experiences.

What kinds of experiences?

As the week wore on, the walls between me and other people and the rest of reality broke down a little. I became much less judgmental. I remember at one point looking at a weed and thinking, "I can't believe I've been killing weeds, because they're as pretty as anything else. Who put this label on weeds?" And that's just a metaphor for what was changing in my consciousness. It was completely profound by the end of the week. Of course, a week later it wore off and I was a jerk again. But I think it was a movement toward moral truth. The truth is that I'm not special, and you're not special.

That is the key adaptation that religions have to make in the modern world— to make people appreciate the moral value of people in circumstances very different from their own. That is a move toward moral truth. It's a fascinating feature of the world we live in that as technology expands the realm of social organization, its coherence and integrity depend on moral progress.

There is another way to understand religion. Certain influential people have intense and profound spiritual experiences, which are later codified and turned into systems of belief for their followers. Do you accept this distinction between spiritual experience and organized religion?

I'm against the idea that there was a golden age of spiritual experience, but then at some point organized religion corrupted everything. I try to show that shamans are as political as anyone and were as self-serving as modern religious leaders. At the same time, there are valid spiritual experiences. I've had them.

But you don't acknowledge that there's anything transcendent about spiritual experience—any communication with a deeper, alternative reality.
No, I do think the experience I had at that meditation retreat was transcendent. It removed me from the ordinary trappings of mundane consciousness. There is a moral axis to the universe. If we don't make moral progress, chaos ensues. If only in that sense, we are tethered to a moral axis. It raises legitimate questions as to whether the whole system was in fact set up by some being, something you could call a divinity.

It's really interesting to hear you say there's moral truth. That's not the kind of thing we usually hear from someone who calls himself a materialist.
Maybe not, but materialism has gotten a bad name. You can be a materialist and still believe that some larger purpose is unfolding through the history of life on this planet. And you can think of the source of that purpose—however hard it is to conceive of that source—in favorable terms. You can use the term "divine" if you want. I do believe there's evidence of some larger purpose unfolding; you'd think religious people would like that. On the other hand, I take a very skeptical view of the claims to special revelation that religions make. You would think my account of religious history would be to the liking of atheists and agnostics.

So we can believe there's an underlying moral truth without believing in God.
The phrase that philosophers use is "moral realism." Do you think morality is in some sense a real thing out there? It's a very elusive question. What I feel sure of is that there's a moral axis to the universe, a moral order, without believing in God.

Are you also saying we can be religious without believing in God?
By some definitions, yes. It's hard to find a definition of religion that encompasses everything we call religion. The definition I like comes from William James. He said, "Religious belief consists of the belief that there is an unseen order and that our supreme good lies in harmoniously adjusting to that order."

In that sense, you can be religious without believing in God. In that sense, I'm religious. On the God question, I'm not sure. But I can call myself religious and have a fully scientific worldview.

You write, "Religion needs to mature more if the world is going to survive in good shape—and for that matter, if religion is going to hold the respect of intellectually critical people." How does it need to mature?
You can't believe the Earth was created 6,000 years ago. There's a whole list of things that are not compatible with modern science.

That's obvious. But some people would also say the idea of a personal God does not square with the scientific worldview today.
It's not a logical impossibility that there's a personal God out there. It's not even quite impossible that God intervenes when the scientists are not measuring stuff, when nobody's watching. But if you're going to have a religion that's broadly reconcilable with a scientific worldview and going to win acceptance among intellectual elites, then it's not going to involve an interventionist God. There are certainly people who find tremendous reassurance and guidance from religions that don't involve a god of any kind, and here I'm thinking about secular Buddhism.

Or you have a Christian theologian like Paul Tillich who tried to get away from an anthropomorphic God. He talked about God as "the ground of being."
Of course, he got accused of sugarcoating what was in fact something like agnosticism or atheism. It's easier to get reassurance by thinking that there's some powerful being looking out for you than for something called "the ground of being." But for my money, if you're interested in hanging on to some kind of religious worldview that's viable in the modern world, you have to make that effort. I haven't tried to work out any detailed program here. It's something I'd like to think about in the future.

At the end of your book, you say the great divide in modern thinking is between people who think there is some divine source of meaning—a

higher purpose in the universe—and those people who don't. Is this different than the usual dichotomy between believers and atheists?

It's a little different. I'm trying to get members of the different Abrahamic religions to realize that if they want to have an enemy, there's a bigger one than each other. I don't want them to declare jihad on atheists, but it might be good for them to realize, in the modern intellectual battle, they all have something in common: not only a specific Abrahamic God, but belief in a transcendent source of meaning. And I'd like to add that there are a lot of other people who don't subscribe to your notion of God, maybe not to any notion of God, who do believe in a transcendent source of meaning and a larger purpose that's unfolding.

As opposed to the Nobel Prize–winning physicist Steven Weinberg, who famously said, "The more the universe seems comprehensible, the more it also seems pointless."

I think he's wrong. But it's not surprising. Physicists don't think much about the animate world. So he probably hasn't given a lot of thought to the human condition and the direction of human history. But I'd say even the realm of physics—just the weirdness of quantum physics—should instill in all of us a little humility. It should make us aware that human consciousness, designed by natural selection to do really mundane things, is clearly not capable of grasping some ultimate things that are probably out there.

Elaine Pagels

AS EVERY CHRISTIAN CHILD KNOWS, Judas was the disciple who betrayed Jesus, selling his life for 30 pieces of silver. If there's an archvillain in the story of Jesus, it's Judas Iscariot. Or is it? The recently discovered Gospel of Judas suggests that Judas was, in fact, the favorite disciple, the only one Jesus trusted to carry out his final command to hand him over to the Romans.

Rumors about the gospel have circulated for centuries. Early church fathers had called it a "very dangerous, blasphemous, horrendous gospel," according to historian Elaine Pagels. We now know that the manuscript was passed around the shadowy world of antiquities dealers, at one point sitting in a safe-deposit box in a small town in New York for 17 years. Pagels was once asked by a dealer in Cleveland to examine it, but he only showed her the last few pages, which revealed little more than the title page. She assumed there was nothing of significance. Finally, the manuscript was acquired by the National Geographic Society, which hired Pagels as a consultant.

More than any other scholar, Pagels has brought the lost texts of early Christianity to public attention. A Princeton University historian of religion, she wrote the 1979 best-seller *The Gnostic Gospels*—the book that launched the popular fascination with the Nag Hammadi manuscripts found by Egyptian peasants in 1945. That book, which won both the National Book Award and the National Book Critics Circle Award, was later chosen by the Modern Library as one of the 100 best books of the twentieth century. Pagels went on to write a series of acclaimed books about early Christianity and, along the way, recounted her own personal tragedies—her young son's death after a long illness and, just a year later, her first husband's death in a hiking accident. It's no surprise that she has felt compelled to wrestle with some of religion's most challenging subjects, like how to make sense of suffering and evil.

For much of her career, Pagels has straddled two worlds—the academic and the popular. She's often the go-to expert when a magazine needs a comment on the latest theory about Mary Magdalene or some other bit of revisionist Christian history. Her standing among the scholars who study early Christianity is more complicated. Conservative scholars tend to dismiss the Gnostic texts as a footnote in Christian history, hardly worth all the hype that's been generated by *The Da Vinci Code* and other racy stories. Not surprisingly, these scholars have questioned Pagels's interpretations of early Christian texts.

With Harvard historian Karen L. King, Pagels wrote the book *Reading Judas: The Gospel of Judas and the Shaping of Christianity*. The authors argue that this recently discovered gospel offers a new understanding of the death of Jesus. I spoke with Pagels about the bitter quarrels among early Christians, why it's a bad idea to read the Bible literally, and the importance of this recent discovery.

■ ■ ■ ■

When was the Gospel of Judas written?
As far as we can tell, probably at the end of the first or early second century.

So it's clearly not written by Judas himself, or even dictated by Judas.
That's right. And most New Testament scholars would say the gospels in the New Testament—all of them attributed to disciples or followers of disciples—were probably not written by the people whose names are on them. If you say, "the Gospel according to Matthew," you might not be pretending to be Matthew if you wrote it. You might be saying, "This is the gospel the way Matthew taught it, and he was my teacher." So these are certain followers of Jesus who collected and transmitted his teaching.

Does this Gospel of Judas reveal something new about early Christianity?
Yes, the Gospel of Judas really has been a surprise in many ways. For one thing, there's no other text that suggests that Judas Iscariot was an intimate, trusted disciple, one to whom Jesus revealed the secrets of the kingdom, and that conversely, the other disciples were misunderstanding what he meant by the gospel. So that's quite startling.

It's shocking to suggest that Judas wasn't just one of the disciples but was actually the favorite disciple of Jesus.
That's right. And also the idea that he handed over Jesus to be arrested at the orders of Jesus himself. This wasn't a betrayal at all. In fact, it was obedience to a command or request that Jesus had made.

But how do we reconcile this with all the other stories we've ever heard about Judas? He's the symbol of treachery and betrayal.
Well, he has become the symbol of treachery and betrayal. But once you start to look at the gospels one by one, you realize that followers of Jesus were trying to understand what had happened after he was arrested and killed. They knew Judas had handed him over to the people who arrested him. The earliest gospel, Mark, says Judas handed him over, but it doesn't give any motive at all. The people who wrote after Mark—Matthew's and Luke's gospels—apparently felt that what was wrong with the Gospel of Mark was that there was no motive. So Matthew adds a motive. Matthew says Judas went to the chief priests, who were Jesus' enemies, and said, "What will you give me if I hand him over to you?" And they agree on a certain sum of money. So in Matthew's view, the motive was greed. In Luke's gospel, it's entirely different. It says the power of evil took over Judas. Satan entered into him.

I think Luke is struggling with the question: If Jesus is the son of God, how could he be taken by a mere trick, by a human being? And Luke is trying to show that all evil power was concentrated in Judas. So they are very different stories. However, other gospels, like John's, suggest that Jesus not only anticipated what was going to happen but initiated it. The Gospel of John says that he told Judas to go out and do what he had to do, which Jesus knew was to betray him. So the Gospel of Judas just takes the suggestion one step further. Jesus not only knew what was going to happen but initiated the action.

There's something else that's striking about the Gospel of Judas. Judas is very angry, and he's especially angry at the other disciples.

Yes, that's where we realized that it's not just a story about Jesus and the disciples. It's a story about this follower of Jesus—the Christian who's writing this story, maybe 60 years after the death of Jesus. Even using the name of Judas is a slap in the face to the tradition. You realize that whoever wrote it was a very angry person. And we were asking, what's going on here? Why is he so angry? And we discovered that it's very dangerous to be a follower of Jesus in the generations after his death. You know, they say his disciple Peter was crucified upside down. And Paul was probably beheaded by the Romans. James was lynched by a crowd, and so were Stephen and other followers. So leaders of this movement were in great danger. And other Christians were also in danger of being arrested and killed because they followed Jesus. The question for many of them was, what do you do if you're arrested?

To acknowledge that you were a Christian would probably kill you.

Exactly. All you had to do is say "no." Or you can try to escape or bribe the people persecuting you. And many did. The only answer that most Christians agreed was right was to say, "Yes, I'm a Christian." You defy them and you go heroically into the lions. So we've always thought of Christianity as a religion that glorifies martyrdom. Now we realize that we've had that impression because the people who weren't in favor of martyrdom had their writings buried and burned and trashed and ridiculed. And they were called cowards and heretics.

So the Gospel of Judas is a kind of protest literature. It's challenging leaders of the church. Here the leaders are personified as disciples who are encouraging people to get killed, to "die for God," as they called martyrdom. This gospel is challenging them and saying that when you encourage young people to die for God, you're really complicit in murder.

Are there also theological issues at stake? This gets at the meaning of suffering and the nature of evil as well.

It does. This was at a time when all followers of Jesus were struggling with the question, why did Jesus die? What does it all mean? In the New Testament, the gospels say he died as a sacrifice. Paul says Christ, our Passover lamb, was sacrificed for us. Why? Well, to save us from sin.

But this author is saying, wait a minute. If you think God wants his son to be tortured and killed before he'll forgive people their sins, what kind of God do you have in mind? Is this the God who didn't want animals to be sacrificed in the temple anymore? So this author's asking, isn't God a loving father? Isn't that what Jesus taught? Why are we saying that God requires his son to die for the sins of the world? So it's a challenge to the whole idea of atonement, and the idea that Christians—when they worship—eat bread and drink wine as if it were the body and blood of Christ. This person sees that whole thing as a celebration of violence.

You can see why some early Christians would have attacked this gospel. This is very threatening to other Christian accounts of why Jesus died.

It contradicts everything we know about Christianity. But there's a lot we don't know about Christianity. There are different ways of understanding the death of Jesus that have been buried and suppressed. This author suggests that God does not require sacrifice to forgive sin, and that the message of Jesus is that we come from God and we go back to God, that we all live in God. It's not about bloody sacrifice for forgiveness of sins. It suggests that Jesus's death demonstrates that, essentially and spiritually, we're not our bodies. Even when our bodies die, we go to live in God.

Does this raise questions about how we should think about the Resurrection? In orthodox Christian accounts, this is considered a resurrection of the flesh.

That's right. The idea that Jesus rose in the flesh is very important for a lot of Christians. And certainly for the martyrs. When people were going to get themselves killed, some of them were asked, do you believe that you're going to be raised from the dead in your body? And many of them said, "Yes, of course we do. That's why we're doing this." So those promises of bodily resurrection and heavenly rewards were very important for many Christians.

Some of the things we're talking about would seem to have great resonance in the Islamic world. Do you see any parallels between this Christian history and what we're seeing among Muslim martyrs today?

I do. The author of the Gospel of Judas wasn't against martyrdom, and he didn't ever insult the martyrs. He said it's one thing to die for God if you have to do that. But it's another thing to say that's what God wants, that this is a glorification of God. I think he would have spoken in the way that an imam might today, saying those who encourage young people to go out and supposedly die for God as martyrs are complicit in murder. The question of the uses of violence is very much at the heart of the Gospel of Judas. If you have to die as a martyr, you do because you don't deny Christ. But you don't go around encouraging people to do it as though they would get higher rewards in heaven.

Can you put the Gospel of Judas in perspective, alongside some of the other Gnostic texts that have come to light in recent decades—the Gospel of Thomas, the Gospel of Mary Magdalene? Do these really change our understanding of early Christianity?

Before, we had a puzzle with just a few pieces. Now we have many more pieces. We begin to see that in the early Christian movement, people discussed and struggled with all the issues that we now think of as normative Christianity— like, what does the death of Jesus mean? There wasn't one kind of understanding of Jesus in the early Christian movement. Actually, there were many.

In recent years, there's been a huge debate over what to make of the Gnostic Gospels. And plenty of Christian scholars and theologians say there's good reason they were not admitted into the Christian canon. They say the Bible presents the most reliable story of Jesus based on eyewitness accounts. For instance, Ben Witherington has written, "The four canonical gospels have stood the test of time and other apocryphal gospels and texts have not. . . . This is because the canonical gospels are

our earliest gospels and have actual historical substance, while the later gospels have none."

Well, Witherington has a particular point of view to prove. I would say it's very hard to date these other texts. Some of them are as early as the gospels of the New Testament, like the Gospel of John. But what's different is the emphasis. Let me give you an example. The Gospel of Thomas says that all who recognize that they come from God are also children of God, instead of teaching that Jesus is the only son of God through whom one must be saved. It's a teaching that is akin to what the Quakers and some other Christian groups teach, including some Greek and Russian Orthodox groups. The divine is to be found in everyone, and we can discover, at some level, that we're like Christ. It's not a complete contradiction, but it is somewhat different.

But aren't there crucial doctrinal issues at stake in terms of what it means to be a Christian? For instance, was Jesus the son of God? Was the return of Jesus an actual resurrection of the flesh?

In the fourth century, the Council of Nicaea established certain doctrines about what it means to be orthodox: belief in one God, maker of heaven and Earth, and one Jesus Christ, His only son and Lord. So Jesus Christ is the only one who brings salvation to the whole world. There are, of course, Christians who believe in Jesus but also wonder whether people can't find God in other religions—if they're Jews or Muslims or Buddhists and so forth. There's nothing Jesus himself said that contradicts that, as far as I can see. But fourth-century Christian orthodoxy did set out the doctrines you're talking about.

Some people say the historical study of early Christianity really doesn't matter to a person's faith. Being a Christian means you believe in certain things, like the Resurrection, like the Virgin Birth. These are matters of faith, not historical research. You can choose not to believe those things, but then you're not part of the Christian creed. How do you respond to that argument?

Well, it's absolutely true that the Virgin Birth and the Resurrection can't be verified historically. On the other hand, if you start to look at it historically, you find out that there are plenty of people who call themselves Christians who see those very things differently. There have been Christians from the beginning—St. Paul is one of them—who say the Resurrection is not a matter of this kind of body. Paul talks about the Resurrection as a matter of being transformed. Yes, it's about the body, he said, but it's more like a body of the stars or the moon or the sun—a body of light. So there are many ways that people have understood themselves to be Christians.

This has huge implications for so many people today, especially those who simply can't accept these kinds of miracles. It does raise the question of whether you can be a Christian if you don't believe any of the Bible's supernatural stories.

I don't think you have to discard all the supernatural stories. The Bible is really about what is beyond the natural. But there are other ways of understanding. For example, the Gospel of Philip, which some people called a heretical text, actually says Jesus had human parents as you and I do. His parents were Mary and Joseph. But when he was born of the spirit, he became the son of the Heavenly Father and the Holy Spirit. In Syriac and Hebrew, the spirit is spoken of in feminine forms, so metaphorically, one could speak of her as a divine mother, just as one speaks of God as a divine father. So there are Christians who didn't reject the Virgin Birth, but said wait a minute, why would you take it literally? Why don't you take it as an image for spiritual reality?

You have spent decades studying early Christian history. Do you consider yourself a Christian?

Yes, I do. And the reason I can is that I understand that there are countless people who've been Christians for 2,000 years, in many different ways. It's not a matter of one version—you must believe this exactly the way I tell it to you. Christian theologians have always said that the truth of God is beyond our understanding. And so we speak in metaphors. Paul said we see through a glass darkly.

I've heard that you didn't grow up in a religious family.

Well, it was a Protestant family, nominally. We went to church, but my father had rejected the Bible for Darwin. He decided the Bible was a bunch of old fables and that evolution was right. So I was brought up to think the Bible was just kind of irrelevant. I grew up and became deeply and passionately interested in it and went to a church and was born again. I was 14 or 15. It was quite wonderful, and I loved what I found there.

Even though your father was a confirmed atheist.
It did shock him, yes. Of course, that's one way adolescents like to shock their parents. I didn't do it for that reason, but it had that effect. The power and the passion of that kind of evangelical Christianity was very real for me. And it was a discovery of something very important—a spiritual dimension in life that I was not able to ignore. On the other hand, after a year of living in that church, one of my friends in high school was killed in an automobile accident. The people at the church asked, was he born again? And I said, no, he wasn't. And they said, well, then he's in hell. And I thought to myself, "I don't believe that." That doesn't match up with what I'd heard about God. So at that point, I decided I had to find out for myself what I could about the early Christian movement, what I believe about it, and what is being said in the name of Jesus that I found not true.

That's fascinating. Basically, it was because you couldn't buy into that fundamentalist version of Christianity that you launched your career as a historian of Christianity.
That's the truth, yes.

Well, this does raise the question of what we mean by God and what we mean by transcendence, and whether there is a transcendent reality out there. Is that discussion of transcendence meaningful to you?
Oh, certainly it is. If we don't understand how important spiritual life is to people, I don't think we're going to understand human beings or the twenty-first century. There are many people who said religion is essentially over now, and everyone will become rational. They don't understand that the way humans are has a lot to do with religious experience.

**Your late husband, the eminent physicist Heinz Pagels, wrote very elo-
quently about the mysteries of science. Did he influence your thinking
about this intersection between science and religion?**

Oh yes, he was deeply interested in philosophy and religion and science,
and understood how profound and complicated those issues are. When
you're dealing with science, for example, you're dealing all the time with
metaphors. So to assume that religious language isn't metaphor doesn't
make sense to me.

**There's a big debate right now over whether religion and science are two
totally different domains, as Stephen Jay Gould once said, or whether they
overlap. Where do you come down on that?**

That's a very tough question. I think religion and science both have a lot to do
with understanding and imagination, but they certainly explore the world in
very different ways. For example, when the eminent physicist Steven Weinberg
wrote in his book *The First Three Minutes*, "The more we know about the
universe, the more we know it's pointless and meaningless," my late husband
said, "That doesn't make any sense." Einstein thought the more we knew about
the universe, the more we knew about the divine intelligence. There are many
ways to make inferences from physics. And inferences like that are not scientific at all; they're philosophic.

**Of course, there's still a huge debate about whether Einstein was religious
or not. The atheists want to claim him for their camp, but religious people
say he was actually quite open to religious ideas.**

Part of the problem is that Einstein used the language about God as a metaphor. When he said, "God does not play dice with the universe," he meant the
universe is not put together in an accidental way. It does show a kind of intelligent process in it. Einstein was speaking about God in the way that physicists
would—aware that language like that is always going to be metaphorical,
speaking beyond our understanding. But many people took him literally and
said he's a religious man. Scientists said he was just using language
carelessly.

Isn't that part of the problem that we get into when we talk about metaphor and the religious imagination? If you don't take Scripture literally, how do you take it?

You can take Scripture seriously without taking it literally. If you speak about the Resurrection of Christ, all we know historically is that after Jesus died, his followers became convinced that he was alive again. Now, what does that mean? They told many stories. Some of them said, "I saw him with my own eyes, I touched him, he actually ate food, he was not a ghost." That's in Luke's gospel. And others said, "I saw him for a moment and then he faded"—the way many people say they've seen people they knew who died. What I'm saying is there are many ways that people who believe in the Resurrection speak about Christ being alive after his death without meaning that his body got out of the grave and walked.

It sounds like you're saying that it's perfectly possible to take the Bible very seriously, to be a Christian, and yet not to believe in the supernatural miracles that so many people simply cannot accept.

Well, that may be. I don't dismiss all supernatural miracles, like a healing that can't be explained. Those do happen sometimes.

You've been studying these texts for decades. Has your scholarly work deepened your own faith?

Yes. And the scholarly work is part of the spiritual quest. Opening ourselves to exploring as much as we can about this can be, in fact, an act of faith. At Princeton, there's a course in the study of the New Testament that some evangelical students were warned not to take. They called it "Faith Busters 101." And some of them come just to flex their muscles and see if they can sit there and stand it while somebody teaches them about how the gospels were written. But what they usually discover is that learning about those things doesn't change the fundamental questions about faith.

Does faith necessarily involve some leap into mystery, into something that can't be explained?

I think it does. Earlier this year, I was asked to do an interview with somebody who had written a book to demonstrate that Jesus had been raised bodily from the dead. And they expected me to say that was impossible. But I can't say it's impossible. From a historical point of view, there's no way you can comment on that. It's just not susceptible to that kind of analysis. So there's a lot that history can't answer and that science can't answer. I mean, there's a lot about all of our lives that we have no rational understanding of. And so faith comes into our relationships with the people we love, and our relationship to our life and our death.

There seems to be a rather vigorous movement among scientists to try to explain the origins of religion. I'm struck by how often these theories come from atheists. And I think the underlying impulse is to demystify the divine. But can religion really be explained from the outside, by people who are not themselves religious?

Probably not. For example, suppose you found the basic brain chemistry that explains religious perceptions. In fact, there are neurologists in New York trying very hard to understand precisely that. And you find that when people who've clinically died say they've had a near-death experience, they've gone into a brilliant light and then they've come back from some place. This is the flashes of light on the brain as it expires. Well, it may be. And it may not be. Is this a trick that our brain plays on us? Or is this intimations of some other kind of reality? I don't think science is going to answer that question.

Isn't there an inherent limitation to any of those brain-imaging studies? Because there's the whole question of are we just imagining this? Or is there really some contact with the divine?

Exactly. For example, there's a study at New York University about epilepsy. We know that epileptics often have an experience of seeing an aura. They can have an epileptic convulsion and they have a kind of vision. It was understood in ancient times to be demonic possession. So if people then say, "Epilepsy has a certain relationship to electrical activity in the brain, and that's what precipitates these experiences," does that mean that they are not real? I don't think that answers the question.

What do you make of the recent claim by the atheist Richard Dawkins that the existence of God is itself a scientific question? If you accept the idea that God intervenes in the physical world, don't there have to be physical mechanisms for that to happen? Therefore, doesn't this become a question for science?

Well, Dawkins loves to play village atheist. He's such a rationalist that the God that he's debunking is not one that most of the people I study would recognize. I mean, is there some great big person up there who made the universe out of dirt? Probably not.

Are you saying that part of the problem here is the notion of a personal God? Has that become an old-fashioned view of religion?

I'm not so sure of that. I think the sense of actual contact with God is one that many people have experienced. But I guess it's a question of what kind of God one has in mind.

So when you think about the God that you believe in, how would you describe that God?

Well, I've learned from the texts I work on that there really aren't words to describe God. You spoke earlier about a transcendent reality. I think it's certainly true that these are not just fictions that we arbitrarily invent.

Certainly many people talk about God as an ineffable presence. But if you try to explain what transcendence is, can you put that into words and explain what it means?

People have put it into words, but the words are usually metaphors or poems or hymns. Even the word "God" is a metaphor, or "the son of God," or "Father." They're all simply images for some other order of reality.

There's one aspect of the Bible that's especially troubling. What do you make of the many passages that condone violence? Killing infidels seems to be what God wants.

You mean in the Hebrew Bible?

Yes, I'm particularly thinking about the Hebrew Bible.

Well, yes. When you read the discussion of holy war in the Hebrew Bible, it's violent, definitely. This was a war god, identified with a particular tribe, with particular kinds of religious war. Christians often don't read that now. But when I talk with Jewish leaders, they say, yes, we remember that very well because we remember the Crusades. And the Muslims, of course, say the same. They say, why are you talking to us about violence? Christians have done violence in the name of Christ for nearly 2,000 years.

So how should we read those passages that are so violent?

That gets us back to the question: Can you read the Bible seriously without reading it literally? There are parts of the New Testament which encourage slaves to remain slaves. Do we take that literally? Those were fighting words during the Civil War when some Christians said slavery was part of God's plan and some people should live and die as slaves. I think few would agree with that now. But it was a position that one could seriously take on the basis of many biblical passages.

You're saying that we have to understand context.

I think we do. You were saying that some people believe faith has nothing to do with history. The fact is, somebody wrote those texts. They wrote them in a world in which slavery was taken for granted. That's a different world. So if we don't understand that, well, it says, "Slaves obey your masters, for this is right."

Nidhal Guessoum

IN 2007, MALAYSIA'S FIRST ASTRONAUT blasted off into space with a Russian crew. The news of a Muslim astronaut was cause for celebration in the Islamic world. But some unusual questions popped up before the launch. How will he face Mecca during his five daily prayers while the ship is whizzing around the Earth? How can he hold the prayer position in zero gravity? Such concerns may sound absurd to us, but the Malaysian space chief took them quite seriously. In fact, a team of Muslim scholars and scientists spent more than a year drawing up an Islamic code of conduct for space travel.

This story illustrates the obstacles that face scientists in Muslim countries. Although it is always risky to draw generalizations about Islam—Turkey, after all, is far more secular than Saudi Arabia—even conservative Muslims admit that the Islamic world lags far behind the West in science and technology. This is a big problem for Muslims who envy the economic and military power of the United States.

What's so striking about the Muslim predicament is that the Islamic world was once the unrivaled center of science and philosophy. During Europe's Dark Ages, Baghdad, Cairo, and other Middle Eastern cities were the key repositories of ancient Greek and Roman science. Muslim scholars themselves made breakthroughs in medicine, optics, and mathematics. So what happened? Did strict Islamic orthodoxy crush the spirit of scientific inquiry? Why did Christian Europe, for so long a backwater of science, later launch the scientific revolution? What about our own time: Can a devout Muslim be a good scientist when he's told that every word in the Quran is the literal word of God?

Nidhal Guessoum is in a unique position to examine these questions. He is an Algerian-born astrophysicist who teaches at American University in the United Arab Emirates. He's also an observant Muslim steeped in the contentious debate over science and religion. Unlike the vast majority of Muslims, he doesn't believe in miracles, but he takes the teachings of the Quran seriously and has worked out his own understanding of the sacred Scriptures.

For a scientist in the heart of the Arab world, Guessoum is unusually willing to poke his nose into matters that could cause him trouble. He recently surveyed students and professors at his university—a diverse group of Muslims and non-Muslims—to determine their attitudes about evolution. He found widespread acceptance of evolution among non-Muslims but much greater skepticism among Muslims of all educational levels, whether first-year students or longtime faculty members. Guessoum says Muslim culture is "largely creationist." Unlike American culture, where creationism is mostly confined to a religious subculture, hostility to evolution is common among educated elites throughout the Islamic world.

I sat down with Guessoum for a frank discussion about the difficulties of reconciling science with Islam, the disturbing influence of Turkish creationist Harun Yahya, and what we might learn from Islamic history.

■ ■ ■ ■

Many Muslims look back to the golden age of Islam, especially the tenth and eleventh centuries, and find evidence that Islam is not only compatible with science but has special insights into the scientific process. How do you look back on this history?
The history does show that there can be great harmony and that a rational civilization can come out of the Islamic worldview. There were very liberal and very conservative theologies that emerged from Islam, sometimes clashing with each other. The whole mystical Sufi tradition also emerged, but sometimes it had to retreat and hide before reemerging.

We know that Muslim scholars played a crucial role in passing on the insights of the ancient Greeks to the modern world. Did they also develop new fields of science?

At first they digested the Greek heritage, as well as the Indian and Babylonian traditions. Then people realized that this knowledge from the Greeks was not set in stone. They found errors and absolutely wrong ideas. Whole fields needed to be invented form scratch, such as algebra and the science of optics. Medicine and astronomy were also greatly pushed forward.

Who were the great figures in this golden age of Islamic science?

One of the first great figures is al-Khwarizmi, who transformed and created new fields of science. He gave us two extraordinarily important words: "algebra" and "algorithm." You have to remember that solving equations in those times was done by words, not symbols. He described the method of how you go about it. So the whole field of algebra was invented by al-Khwarizmi. Another great scientist slightly later, in the tenth and eleventh centuries, is Ibn al-Haytham, who started out in Iraq and moved to Egypt. He's the father of modern optics. Ibn al-Haytham is the first person to describe how vision functions. He realized that rays of light travel straight and at a finite speed, meaning the speed of light is not infinite.

Another great figure is (Ibn Sina) Avicenna, who is famous in the West for being a great physician, though he should be known more as a philosopher. He wrote a book called *The Canon of Medicine*, which remained in use in Europe until the sixteenth or seventeenth century. He had a long exchange of letters with a lesser-known figure, al-Biruni, who lived in what is today Afghanistan. Al-Biruni was a great rationalist who described himself as a scientist. He says to Avicenna, "The difference between you and me is that you're a philosopher and I'm a scientist." In fact, al-Biruni described himself as a mathematical scientist.

That distinction really hadn't been made before. At that time, philosophers were the scientists.

That's why it's so significant. Al-Biruni realized that there are different methodologies. He said philosophers, like mathematicians, are deductionists. They lay out hypotheses and then extract further truths from them, whereas scientists are inductionists. They observe facts and then generalize to obtain some law or principle to explain how nature functions.

I've heard that you have a special fondness for another great philosopher from that time, Averroes of Andalucia. Can you tell me about him?
Averroes (Ibn Rushd) had a multifaceted education. Early on, he was found to be a very bright young man. In fact, as a teenager, Averroes was called the finest mind in Spain. So his father, who was a great scholar of Islamic law, brought in many tutors to teach him philosophy, Islamic law and theology, medicine, as well as astronomy and mathematics. He excelled at almost all of them, and his books are still read today. He also became a famous physician—the physician of the court. What makes Averroes important is that he realized that there's no conflict between any of these subjects. You don't have to choose one over the other. He developed the model of "harmony" between philosophy and religion, which I have adopted for my own views on science and Islam.

What you're describing is a remarkable period of intellectual flourishing. The Islamic world was the center of the scientific world for several centuries, from the ninth through the twelfth centuries.
At least.

So what happened? Just a few centuries later, the scientific revolution took off in Europe instead of the Muslim world.
Indeed, it's the great mystery. Scholars are still trying to figure out what happened. There were several factors, but the decline of Islamic civilization was so much more striking because it coincided with Europe's huge Renaissance and scientific revolution that began in the fifteenth and sixteenth centuries. I think prosperity was one factor that led to the rise of Europe and the decline of the Islamic world. Money always plays a role in science.

When you don't have a lot of money, science, philosophy, and art no longer look like reasonable activities to fund. Also, most of the scientific work in Europe was in Italy and England, with some in France and Germany, so there was a limited area. But the Islamic world was huge. It stretched from Morocco to Uzbekistan and perhaps all the way to China. So it was very hard to keep a continuous civilization going when exchanges and interactions were so hard. But more important, there were very few universities in the Muslim world where people came to study. There were some centers of learning, such as Baghdad, Cairo, and Córdoba in Spain. A few students would come to study, but there was no such thing as the university as we know it. The whole tradition of intellectual debate started to dwindle in the Arab and Islamic world.

So far, your explanations have nothing to do with religion. It's striking that the scientific revolution took off in Europe when the Christian church still had enormous influence. But was there something about Islam itself that led to the decline of scientific culture?
Maybe some versions of Islam contributed to this decline. But we can't say it was about Islam, just like we can't say it was about Christianity. Some people today argue that modern science emerged because Christianity and Judaism had an idea of order in the universe. These people believe that religion actually led to the emergence of modern science. And for centuries, the Islamic world, led by Muslim rulers, developed science to the utmost. But the versions of Islam that impose strict readings of Scripture made it very hard. If any religion, including Islam, denies the spirit of free inquiry, people can't investigate and write what they want to write. That's the end of science.

Isn't this especially a problem when there's too much deference to authority figures, whether it's your imam or your parent?
Or the Book, with a capital B. "X said, therefore, end of discussion." There can be too much adherence to authority in Muslim culture. This stifles creativity and the development of science and philosophy. Conservatives are always afraid of open-ended inquiry.

Let's skip ahead to our own time. How would you assess the state of science in the Islamic world today?
It's abysmal by all kinds of measures: how many books and publications are written or translated in the Muslim world, how many patents come from Muslim inventors, how Muslim students are performing in the international

arena. By all these measures, the Muslim world is way, way down. Surveys by the UN Development Program and the World Bank place the Muslim world somewhere below sub-Saharan Africa.

This is a huge percentage of the world's population.
We're talking about roughly one-fifth of the world's population—1.2 billion people out of 6 billion. These 20 percent produce slightly more than 1 percent of the intellectual production of the world. This is heartbreaking. This is crushing. But that's the situation right now.

How do you explain this?
There are several factors. Some people point to the fact that most of the Muslim world was under colonial rule for a long time. When the rate of literacy during the colonial period was less than 10 percent, how can you expect anybody to do science or produce books? But I don't regard this as the prime factor, because 99 percent of the Muslim world has been out of colonial rule for the last half-century. We can blame colonialism for only so much.

We now have the money and the capability. There are huge resources in the Muslim world, but we need freedom of inquiry so people can investigate, debate, and exchange views. It's not a coincidence that democracy and freedom are equally dismal in the Muslim world.

Do you see this mainly as a political issue rather than a religious issue?
Religion also plays a role, but that's not the main factor that has left the Muslim world in such a sorry state. So how does religion factor into this? The culture of authority, which is Islamic culture today, is dominated by religious figures. The religious dimensions of society are crushing and stifling inquiry, and we have had too many people who were declared heretics. For example, you may know the case in Cairo of Nasr Hamid Abu Zayd, who was up for promotion at his university. The committee looked at the books he'd written and said, "Wait a minute. We can't allow this." Then somebody took him to court and the court declared him a heretic. Once you're declared a heretic, your wife is automatically divorced from you because a Muslim woman is not allowed to be married to a non-Muslim man. And now, anybody can kill you because of the law of apostasy.

What did he write that was considered so offensive?

He's a philologist. He was analyzing the Quran and said there was some evolution of the meaning of the Quran, which points to a human element in the
writing of the Quran. And people said, "You can't even think that. You can't
go in that direction."

**This raises a loaded question about how to read the Quran. Unlike the
Bible in Christian cultures, isn't the Quran seen as the literal word of
God?**

Absolutely. Of course, there are some Christians who say the Bible is the word
of God, but most people understand that Scriptures in other religions were
written by humans, maybe with divine inspiration, so they carried the thoughts
and understandings of their time. But in Islam, everybody is required to believe
that every word in the Quran was revealed by God. So there was no rewriting.
Muhammad didn't compose it and teach it to his followers. No, it's letter to
letter, word by word, the revelation of God.

**Doesn't that make it hard to read the Quran metaphorically rather than
literally?**

Some people argue that. If it was revealed by God, how can you say God really
spoke in metaphors and analogies? But other people, including myself, argue
the exact opposite. We believe that the Quran was not revealed just for a
specific people at a certain time, but was revealed for all people at all times.
It's a book of guidance, not a book of specific prescriptions. If that's the case,
then there's no way that the Quran can be understood literally and still be
applicable to many people, in many different places, in many different
centuries.

**Yet it would be easy to draw scientific conclusions from the Quran, because
it has many references to the natural world. For example, it says God created Adam out of clay. What do you make of those pronouncements?**

In my view, God must have made the Quran flexible to understand because
He knew people would have different intellects, different social upbringings,
different languages, different geographies. If you're a literalist, you're going to

say God created Adam as a human being, so there was no evolution. Case closed. But there are many examples in the Quran which can only be understood metaphorically. So this must be one of them. I argue that the particular verses dealing with natural phenomena are not to be understood literally because the Quran isn't supposed to be a book of science.

But isn't this cherry-picking? You don't want to interpret that literally because you're a scientist, whereas the other passages are not talking about the natural world. Aren't you saying it's fine to take that other stuff at face value?

I didn't say it's okay to take anything at face value. I'm against literalism as a rule of thumb. Always keep in mind that there may be different views and different meanings. I argue for a multilevel reading of the Quran. In fact, my hero, Averroes, said exactly this. He said certain verses are a little convoluted and only the most knowledgeable among you will understand all of it. But Averroes said many parts of the Quran must be simple enough to be understood by the layman. Otherwise, is this just a book for philosophers? Of course not. But for those of us who are able to look deeper, it's incumbent on us to try to see whether we're getting the real meaning or whether we're just being lazy and looking at the surface. So if people are simple-minded, okay, go for the literal meaning. We can't expect you to do more than that. But anybody who can avoid the literal meaning should do so.

There's still the thorny issue of revelation. Is the Quran the literal word of God or did humans write it?

The whole idea of revelation is complex. What does it mean that a scripture was revealed? Ninety-nine percent of Muslims—if not 99.99 percent—will say the angel Gabriel came and dictated some sentences to Muhammad and that's revelation. But that's not an acceptable description to me. No, revelation was probably some kind of inspiration. Muhammad had reached a certain spiritual level. If you read about the history of Muhammad, you will find that before he started receiving revelation, he had spent many years, for extended periods of time—sometimes days and nights—going into seclusion in a cave outside of Mecca, where he was clearly having some sort of spiritual awakening. At some point, there was revelation.

So what happened to him? His spirit opened up. There was some connection to the other dimension of reality that we can't touch and describe scientifically. Something happened so that he started to perceive certain truths and morals, and he put them into sentences. Now, it's up to the believer to decide whether that was dictated to him from on high, or whether there was some participatory element in this experience.

There are other stories that are clearly miraculous. For instance, in the Night Journey, the angel Gabriel takes Muhammad on a winged horse to Jerusalem and then up to the heavens, where he meets previous prophets, including Moses and Jesus. What do you make of this story?

For me, this whole story is a spiritual experience. I have no problem accepting it, just as someone might tell me that he had an extraordinary spiritual experience one night, when he found himself going to heaven and meeting prophets from earlier centuries or millennia. To me, this is the only way to explain it. There's no way I can believe that somebody has been taken to Jerusalem in one night and then up to the seventh heaven and then driven back down on the back of a miraculous creature from Jerusalem to Mecca. Clearly, there is no credence to such a literal description. By the way, I'm one of the few Muslims today or in the past who reject the idea of miracles.

So you don't believe miracles are possible if they defy the laws of science.

That's a theological position one can take. I believe God is in contact or has some relation with His creation. There is a divine presence. But I believe natural phenomena only go through natural laws, and that's why God created natural laws. Otherwise, if every minute He's going to do something different, what's the point of the natural laws?

I also believe that God's relation to us goes through the spirit, not through physics. I can pray and say: "God, please help me. I have an important lecture to deliver tonight." In my mind, the way God could support me—answer my prayer, as we say—is by affecting my spirit and how I would behave. The spirit does not come into the physics and the astronomy that I do; it only comes through my behavior. But when you're dealing with human experience, with the mind—and for believers, the spirit—you're adding extra meaning and understanding.

Do you consider yourself an observant Muslim?
Yes, to a large extent.

So you read the Quran regularly?
Not regularly, but I've read it a number of times.

Do you pray five times a day?
Yes, I pray regularly.

You are an astrophysicist. Do you think there's some design in the universe that led to the creation of stars and planets and, eventually, life?
I don't think science can answer questions about design and purpose, but science can find facts or evidence that help philosophers or religious people to develop a credible answer. That's what is known as the "fine-tuning of the universe"—which is a set of scientific facts that seem to show that the universe has specific parameters, without which life, intelligence, and humans would not have come about or even been possible. Science does tell us that this universe is extraordinary.

Extraordinary in the sense that various physical laws had to be fine-tuned for things to turn out the way they have?
Yes, even for the universe to be interesting—not just for life and humans to be here, but also for there to be galaxies, stars, planets, and water. This universe could have been total chaos. It could have existed for only a fraction of a second, or it could have expanded so fast that there was nothing but cold darkness out there. But the universe has certain parameters that make all this extraordinary existence. Then we get to the evolution of life, which produced extraordinary species and eventually humans.

I believe there was a plan for this universe—what Paul Davies calls a "cosmic blueprint." Now, we can try to be even smarter and ask, "Was there any underlying principle that produced this cosmic blueprint?" We can always take the explanation one step deeper. I also believe there is some meaning to existence and to this universe. It's not an accident that intelligence, consciousness, and life exist. But can we ever determine what the purpose really is? I'm not sure. It may be a question that's way beyond us. It's important that we find meaning—and even construct meaning if necessary. For many people, meaning can be supplied by religion. For others, it can be supplied by their conscious thinking and philosophy. But there must be meaning.

Aren't there a lot of Muslim scholars who are looking for scientific content in the Quran and trying to use this to develop science in the Islamic world?

It's a huge movement. It's by far the most popular cultural trend in the Arab and Muslim world today. Many, many books and web sites that pertain to science are related, implicitly or explicitly, to content in the Quran. There are even references like this in textbooks that my children study.

Just two days ago, I received an email from a friend who said, "Here's this verse that people say refers to black holes. What do you say?" And I replied, "Same old, same old. There's nothing new here." Then just this morning, as I checked my email, this person said, "Can you please explain why it is unacceptable to you that this verse could be referring to black holes?" Some people even look at certain verses of the Quran and take a number here and some letters there, multiply this and divide that, and it gives you . . . ta da . . . the speed of light! These are extraordinary claims. This way of approaching the Quran is completely wrong. Unfortunately, there's a lot of it today.

What about evolution? How widely accepted is evolution in the Muslim world?

You mean, how widely unaccepted! (*Laughs*) Some surveys just came out that looked at attitudes of high school students in several Muslim countries. In most cases, no more than 15 percent of Muslim respondents accept evolution. That's true in most of the Muslim world, including countries like Egypt, Turkey, and Malaysia. What is more shocking, actually, is that this rejection of evolution is not just among the general population.

This is where it's significantly different from the American reaction to evolution. People say to me, "Even the Americans reject evolution, so why are you so shocked? After all, they've had many decades of advanced knowledge, and we're just coming out of our backwardness." But evolution is being rejected equally by educated and uneducated Muslims. This is the key part. If you went to campuses in the United States and interviewed students and professors, you'd get maybe 10 percent who would reject evolution. And this is because of deep fundamentalist beliefs, and even then, they wouldn't express their beliefs openly. But in the Muslim world, you will find a very large majority of students and professors convinced that evolution is wrong.

How do you explain this hostility to evolution in the Muslim world?
The culture is largely creationist, and it's influenced by religious authorities and teachers who all hold the same views. This culture does not encourage people to inquire freely. It says, "Be careful with that stuff. Don't even study it with an open mind." Some students come to me and say, "I heard you the other day talking about all of this, and I was challenged and confused. So I went to the imam and asked him." And I say, "Why did you go to the imam? With all due respect, let's not confuse apples and oranges. You shouldn't go to the imam and ask about evolution, just like you don't come to me and ask about legal rulings in Islamic law."

Do you get into trouble for saying this? It's worth pointing out that you're not teaching at some university in the United States or France. You're in the heart of the Arab world saying some very critical things about Islam.
I get into social trouble. People start disliking me or pointing a finger at me. You know, "He's a liberal or Westerner, an iconoclast."

But this hasn't hurt you professionally?
No, it hasn't . . . fingers crossed. But it would be a different story if I lived in Saudi Arabia, for example. I live in the Emirates, which is a relatively liberal, open-minded country, where people are free to read whatever they want and free to discuss diverse viewpoints.

So a scientist in Saudi Arabia could not say what you're saying?
Not without risk. Serious risk. A university student could go to the administration in Saudi Arabia and say, "We have a professor saying this and that." At
the very least, the administration would investigate. They'd check with students
and colleagues, and if they find that the professor is saying these things, there's
a good chance he'd be fired. In the United Arab Emirates, there's no such
process. In fact, about two years ago, there was a long story in the English-
language newspaper about supporters of Harun Yahya in the Emirates, who
were distributing leaflets and trying to show that there's no evidence for evolution. The news story said evolution was going to be removed from twelfth-
grade biology.

I was stunned. So I wrote a letter to the editor saying that evolution is a
very strongly supported scientific theory, so how could it be removed from
the curriculum? How can these ignoramuses influence the curricula and
you devote a whole page to them? They published my letter, and there was
even another letter that supported me. This would not happen in many other
Muslim countries.

**The Turkish creationist Harun Yahya is widely regarded as the most influ-
ential creationist in the Islamic world. Scientists generally consider him
a crackpot. How much influence does he have?**
His influence is growing. That's the dangerous part. Originally he was just an
interesting, obscure author that nobody had seen, with an interesting web site
and all kinds of videos. But then he started to become more aggressive. He
produced his famous *Atlas of Creation* and mailed it around the world, though
it didn't have much success. But he became more successful by establishing
groups of supporters in different countries, who campaigned locally. They go
to campuses, organize discussions, and distribute leaflets and books against
evolution and other ideas.

And this isn't just in Turkey, but in other countries, too.
Many countries in the Muslim world and the non-Muslim world. I think most
educated Muslims—certainly in Europe and even in the United States—have
heard of Harun Yahya and have seen his books in English, French, or whatever

the local language is. This is why it's a significant cultural phenomenon. It has dangerous implications for science and for education.

But if he's just a crackpot, why not ignore him and just pretend that he doesn't exist? Can you do that?

Absolutely not. That would be the biggest mistake. We cannot leave the stage. Harun Yahya has taken the stage because no one else has. We have a duty to prevent society from being pushed in the wrong direction. We cannot ban him. We need freedom of inquiry and freedom of speech. Let him speak. But let us also speak to present more solid information, and hopefully the people will see what is correct and to be accepted.

Where are the Muslim scientists, especially the biologists, who should be defending evolution?

That's the silent crowd, unfortunately. People don't want to get in trouble. It's already difficult to get a good job. We don't live in free and democratic countries, so one has to preserve whatever comfort and work that one can get. We have not had a culture of debate, so it's very rare for forums to bring in people with different views. And people haven't developed the skill of talking to the public. It was never emphasized. If you're a scientist, what's the point of writing popular articles and books and giving talks? That's not going to get you promoted or get you tenure, so why should you bother? I bother because I feel it is a calling and I feel a moral responsibility. But most people don't see it that way.

Rebecca Goldstein and
Steven Pinker

"I'VE ALWAYS BEEN OBSESSED with the mind–body problem," says the philosopher Renee Feuer Himmel. "It's the essential problem of metaphysics, about both the world out there and the world in here."

Renee is the fictional alter ego of novelist and philosopher Rebecca Newberger Goldstein. In her 1983 novel *The Mind-Body Problem*, Goldstein laid out her metaphysical concerns, which include the mystery of consciousness and the struggle between reason and emotion. As a novelist, she is drawn to the quirky lives of scientists and philosophers. More recently, she has probed various religious ideas in her novel *36 Arguments for the Existence of God*. She's also fascinated by history's great rationalist thinkers. She's written nonfiction accounts of the seventeenth-century Jewish philosopher Baruch Spinoza and the twentieth-century mathematician-philosopher Kurt Gödel.

Perhaps it's not surprising that Goldstein would end up living with Steven Pinker, a leading theorist of the mind. He is a cognitive psychologist at Harvard; she is a philosopher who has taught at several colleges. Although they come out of different disciplines, they mine much of the same territory: language, consciousness, and the tension between science and religion. If Boston is ground zero for intellectuals, then Pinker and Goldstein must rank as one of America's brainiest power couples.

With a series of best-selling books on language and human nature, including *How the Mind Works*, Pinker has emerged as his generation's most influential cognitive theorist. His work on the evolution of language and how humans possess an innate capacity for language revolutionized linguistics. His writing about the nature/nurture debate helped shift prevailing thinking away from seeing human nature as a blank slate.

Pinker and Goldstein share a basic philosophical outlook, but I discovered that their views diverge somewhat when it comes to the "science and religion" debate. In a wide-ranging joint interview, we talked about animals and language, atheism and astrology, Iraq and faith, and their books, Goldstein's *Betraying Spinoza* and Pinker's *The Stuff of Thought: Language as a Window into Human Nature*.

■ ■ ■ ■

Steve, do you think language is what makes our species unique? Is this the defining trait of human beings?

PINKER: It's certainly one of the distinctive traits of *Homo sapiens*. But I don't think language could have evolved if it was the only distinctive trait. It goes hand in hand with our ability to develop tools and technologies, and also with the fact that we cooperate with nonrelatives. I think this triad—language, social cooperation, and technological know-how—is what makes humans unusual. And they probably evolved in tandem, each of them multiplying the value of the other two.

You have a fascinating observation in your book about causation. You say the way we construct sentences, particularly verbs, has a lot to do with how we understand cause and effect.

PINKER: That's right. For example, if John grabs the doorknob and pulls the door open, we say, "John opened the door." If John opens the window and a breeze pushes the door open, we don't say, "John opened the door." We say something like, "What John did caused the door to open." We use that notion of causation in assigning responsibility. So all of those crazy court cases that happen in real life and are depicted on *Law and Order*, where you have to figure out if the person who pulled the trigger was really responsible for the death of the victim, tap into the same model of causation.

I talk about the case of James Garfield, who was felled by an assassin's bullet, but lingered on his deathbed for three months and eventually succumbed to an infection because of the harebrained practices of his inept doctors. At the trial of the murderer, the accused assassin said, "I just shot him. The doctors killed him." The jury disagreed, and he went to the gallows. It's an excellent case of how the notion of direct causation is very much on our minds as we assign moral and legal responsibility.

Rebecca, you've written a great deal about competing philosophical theories of language. Do you think our mind can function apart from language? Or does language define our reality?

GOLDSTEIN: Obviously, much of our thinking is being filtered through language. But it's always seemed to me that there has to be an awful lot of thinking that's done prior to the acquisition of language. And I often have trouble translating my thoughts into language. I think about that a lot. It often seems to me that the thoughts are there and some words are flitting through my mind when I'm thinking. So there's something very separate between thinking and language. But that might vary from mind to mind.

As a novelist, this must be something you think about.

GOLDSTEIN: Very much so. My novels begin with a sense of the book, a sense of the place, and then I have to find the language that does justice to it. Strangely, I find that in my philosophical work as well. And in math; I've done a lot of math. I have the intuition, I'll see it, and then I have to translate it into language. So I've always had a keen sense that thought does not require language.

What do you make of the language studies of various animals—for instance, the bonobo Kanzi, who's learned to piece together simple sentences by pressing lexigrams. Is that real language?

PINKER: It isn't a scientific question whether something is real language. That's really a question of how far you want to extend the word "language." I think the scientific question is: Are the chimpanzees, bonobos, and gorillas who are trained by humans doing something that's fundamentally the same as what children are doing when they first acquire language? I suspect they are quite different. You need experimenters hell-bent on training chimpanzees, whereas with children, you can't help but acquire a language if you're a child in a human community. Indeed, children thrown together in a community that doesn't have a language of its own will invent one in order to communicate with each other. And while it's impressive that chimps have been trained to learn a few dozen or even a couple hundred symbols or signs, the ability to combine them is quite rudimentary and forced.

You each dedicated books to each other, and I'm curious about how your relationship has influenced your work. You've both written about language and human nature, about religion and the power of reason. Do you talk about these things around the dinner table?

GOLDSTEIN: (*Laughs*) Yes, there's no way around it. Our work spills over into our lives, and our lives spill over into our work.

PINKER: But that's not the only thing we talk about.

Would you say your common interests are partly what brought you together?

GOLDSTEIN: Oh yes, completely. Actually, we met through each other's work. I was a great fan of Steve's work. And then I discovered that he had cited me in one of his books. It was my unusual use of an irregular verb. So it was completely through our work and my tremendous interest in Steve's work that we first came to know each other. I don't know if I should say this, but when I first met Steve in the flesh, I said that the way he thinks had so completely changed the way I think—particularly what I had learned from him about cognitive psychology and evolutionary psychology—that I said, "I don't think I've had my mind so shaken up by any thinker since [eighteenth-century philosopher] David Hume." And he very modestly said, "That can't be the case." But it was the case. So I can certainly say that Steve has profoundly influenced the way I think.

PINKER: And I've certainly been influenced by Rebecca as well. Our connection isn't just that we met through an irregular verb, which sounds like the ultimate literary romance of two nerds finding each other. (*Goldstein laughs*)

Rebecca as a philosopher is a strong defender of realism—the idea that there is a real world that we can come to know—which emboldened me to press that theme in my own writings, even though people often say that we just construct reality through language. And the topic of consciousness—how the mind emerges from the body, and what makes the three-pound organ that we call the brain actually experience things subjectively—is a theme that runs through both my nonfiction and Rebecca's fiction and her philosophical writings.

Do you show each other your articles and books as you're writing them?

GOLDSTEIN: Yes, we've each seen each other's work in early drafts and in the final work. But this is the first time I've ever shared my work with anybody while it's happening. I'm very private about my work. So this has been a very new experience for me. Now I'm wondering how I ever wrote any books without having Steve read them.

Are you very open in your criticisms and suggestions about each other's work?

PINKER: Very much. But we're not brutal.

GOLDSTEIN: We can be brutal. (*Laughs*) Sweetly brutal.

PINKER: But yes, we each say, "This isn't working. This joke isn't funny. I don't think your readers are going to understand what you're trying to get at here."

Rebecca, the dedication in your Spinoza book reads, "For Steve, despite Spinoza." Can you explain that?

GOLDSTEIN: Spinoza wasn't a great fan of romantic love. He didn't think that the life of reason had any place for romantic love. And Spinoza's methodology is strictly reductive. He tries to prove everything, starting with definitions and axioms. And he has this rigorous proof that romantic love will always end badly.

Does that mean he did not experience romantic love himself?

GOLDSTEIN: He didn't, as far as we know. There are some rumors about his landlady's daughter, who went to another young man when he gave her a pearl necklace. But no, Spinoza's view about love is all directed toward love of truth and God and nature. It's not directed toward another person. To love another person is to want desperately for them to reciprocate. And that's not something we have complete control over. Therefore, it's irrational. He argues that romantic love just increases your fragility and vulnerability and therefore you ought not to do it.

In your book on Spinoza, you talk about your own religious education in an orthodox Jewish school, and how Spinoza was trotted out by one of your teachers as precisely the kind of heretical thinker that good Jewish girls should avoid. But this seemed to make you especially interested in him. Why do you still like Spinoza so much?

GOLDSTEIN: It's interesting. It's almost like there are two different Spinozas. And I really didn't bring them together until I wrote the book. At my very orthodox all-girls high school, Spinoza was told to us as a kind of cautionary tale: This is what can go wrong if you ask the wrong questions. I was in a school that discouraged one from even going on to college. And philosophy was absolutely the worst thing you could study because it does ask you to question everything. And then there was the Spinoza I came in contact with when I was a professional philosopher. Spinoza is a metaphysician of a very extravagant sort. He wants to deduce everything through pure reason. And that was a kind of philosopher that I was also taught to dismiss and disdain. So both sides of my training—the orthodox Jewish training, the analytic philosophy training—pushed me to dismiss Spinoza.

I like the grandeur of his ambition. He really does believe that we can save ourselves through being rational. And I believe in that. I believe that if we have any hope at all, it's through trying to be rigorously objective about ourselves and our place in the world. We have to do that. We have to submit ourselves to objectivity, to rationality. I think that's what it is about Spinoza. He's just such a rationalist.

Spinoza certainly dismissed the religion he'd been exposed to. Do both of you consider yourselves atheists?

(*Pause*) GOLDSTEIN: Yes.

PINKER: Yes.

GOLDSTEIN: Proud atheists.

PINKER: There, we said it. (*Laughs*)

So you have to hesitate for a moment before you use that dirty word?

PINKER: Atheists are the most reviled minority in the United States, so it's no small matter to come out and say it.

Well, I find it puzzling how the recent atheist manifestos by Richard Dawkins, Sam Harris, and Christopher Hitchens have all turned into best-sellers in a country that's overwhelmingly religious. According to various polls, half of all Americans believe the Bible is the literal truth. A *Newsweek* poll found that 91 percent believe in God. How do you explain the enormous popularity of these books?

PINKER: Part of it is that the people who buy books—at least that kind of highbrow trade book—are not a random sample of the population. The opinions sampled by these polls are probably soft. When people are asked a question, they don't just turn a flashlight into their data bank of beliefs and read out what they see. When people say, "Yes, I believe in God and the Bible," they're kind of saying, "I'm a moral person. I have solidarity with the community of churchgoers that I was brought up in and that I currently belong to." I think that if you were to probe a lot of people's religious opinions, they would not be as religious as the numbers would suggest.

GOLDSTEIN: It would be fascinating, though, to see a poll of the people who are buying the new atheist books and see how they are answering these questions.

PINKER: Well, the question often arises whether these authors are preaching to the choir. Especially since these books make no concessions toward religious sensibilities. It's a full-throated intellectual assault on the concept of God. My sense is that the books are really not aimed at the 91 percent of the people you cited who believe in God, but rather at some minority of people who are wavering, who've been brought up in a religious way but now have some private doubts. They perhaps think that confessing to being an atheist is like confessing to being a child molester. So they're not willing to even think those thoughts. Then they come across a book that seems to vindicate all of their doubts. And that tortured minority of reflective, analytic people from a religious background—perhaps like Rebecca from her religious background—are who the books are aimed at. Julia Sweeney's one-woman show, *Letting Go of God*, would be representative of the kind of person whose mind could be changed by a book like that.

Steve, you recently waded into the controversy over Harvard's proposal to require all undergraduates to take a course called "Reason and Faith." The plan was dropped after you and other critics strongly opposed it. But the people who supported it say that every college graduate should have a basic understanding of religion because it's such a powerful cultural and political force around the world. Don't they have a point?

PINKER: I think students should know something about religion as a historical phenomenon, in the same way that they should know something about socialism and humanism and the other great ideas that have shaped political philosophies and therefore the course of human events. I didn't like the idea of privileging religion above other ideologies that were also historically influential, like socialism and capitalism. I also didn't like the euphemism "faith." Nor did I like the juxtaposition of "faith" and "reason," as if they were just two alternative ways of knowing.

One of your critics in this controversy is Stephen Prothero, a religious studies professor at Boston University who wrote the book *Religious Literacy*. He said, "You can be a very smart person and be very dumb when it comes to religion. Professor Pinker just doesn't get it." Prothero says we have to understand religion to come to grips with hot-button issues like abortion, stem cell research, and gay rights. And he says Iraq is such a mess right now because our leaders in Washington just didn't understand a basic fact about Islam before they launched the war—that Sunnis and Shiites hate each other.

PINKER: I think religion is one of the things you have to understand. But the situation in Iraq is not primarily a theological one. There are just as fierce battles among the various tribes and militias, clans and nationalities. So it's not just a

Shiite–Sunni dispute. The mistake was not being ignorant of religion. The mistake was being ignorant of all aspects of Iraqi society, including family structure, local history, the evolutionary psychology of kinship, and how it reinforces ties of family and clan and kin in Iraq in a way that differs from countries that we're more familiar with. So religion should be part of it. But I don't see why, of all of the forces that go into history—military, economic, sociological, evolutionary, psychological—religion itself should be privileged.

GOLDSTEIN: It depends on what you mean by understanding religion. Obviously, religion is a tremendously powerful influence in history. But I have to say—and I think this is something that Steve and I disagree on—I do worry whether some of the people who are writing the new atheist books understand what it feels like to be a religious person. Do they get what that feels like? And I don't want to say that there's only one kind of religious impulse. There are so many different ways of responding to the world that could be called religious—some of them very expansive and life-embracing, and some of them not. But I think one of the things that made Steve nervous was to pose these two things—faith and reason, religion and science—as alternative ways of pursuing truth. In terms of the pursuit of knowledge, faith is not an alternative mode to science and to reason.

PINKER: Exactly. I would be opposed to a requirement on astrology and astronomy, or alchemy and chemistry. Not because I don't think people should know about astrology. Astrology had an important role in the ancient world. You can't understand many things unless you know something about astrology—the plays of Shakespeare and so on. What I'm opposed to is equating it with reason or science.

But can you really equate religion with astrology, or religion with alchemy? No serious scholar still takes astrology or alchemy seriously. But there's a lot of serious thinking about religion.

PINKER: I would put faith in that same category because faith is believing something without a good reason to believe it. I would put it in the same category as astrology and alchemy.

Those are fighting words!

GOLDSTEIN: (*Laughs*) He said it, not me.

Rebecca, where do you come down on this? Obviously, you've moved away from the religious milieu you grew up in. But do you reject it out of hand, as Steve does?

GOLDSTEIN: I do, intellectually. We get into terrible trouble if we believe sloppily, if we let emotions—and our own view of the way we want the world to be—shape the way we think the world is. This accounts for a great deal of the madness in the world. So I am completely committed to trying to justify everything, and in that regard, I have very little use for faith. However, I know what it feels like to believe without justification. And we all do it. I mean, I believe my children are the most wonderful children ever born. Of course, most parents feel that way. It's a useful thing, perhaps. Could I justify it? Should I even go about justifying my love for them? There would be something wrong with that. So I have more sympathy toward an emotional reaction to the world and some of the more religious reactions.

Steve, you've written about the need for scholars to investigate what you call "dangerous ideas." For instance, do women on average have different abilities and emotions than men? Would society be better off if heroin and cocaine were legalized? Let me suggest another dangerous idea which is not on your list—the idea that the mind is more than the physical mechanics of the brain, that there might be some aspect of consciousness that goes beyond an individual's brain. Is this a dangerous idea?

PINKER: No, it's an idea that probably the majority of the population believes. The more dangerous idea is what most biologists believe, which is that the mind is the information-processing ability of the brain. In the nineteenth century, the idea that there's something to consciousness beyond the functioning of the brain was a serious scientific hypothesis. Scientists as distinguished as Alfred Russel Wallace, the co-discoverer of evolution, and William James, the hero of both Rebecca and mine, were involved in kitschy, séance-like demonstrations trying to contact the souls of the dead. Those experiments failed. We don't seem to be able to communicate with the great beyond.

But there's some dispute on this history. Deborah Blum wrote about this in her book *Ghost Hunters*. James and other scientists searched for proof of the supernatural, and he discounted the vast majority of these psychics. He dismissed virtually all of them as frauds. But there were a few that he couldn't explain away.

GOLDSTEIN: Yeah, his Mrs. Piper. He was very convinced by her. He did want desperately to believe in the afterlife. He had lost a young son, Herman. There's often that tremendous desire. I've lost a sister. I'd love to believe she still exists in the world. I know how powerful that desire is. But that's different from any kind of proof or evidence.

I think virtually all religious believers think the mind cannot be reduced to the physical mechanics of the brain. Of course, many believe the mind is what communicates with God. Would you agree that the mind–brain question is one of the key issues in the "science and religion" debate?

PINKER: I think so. It's a very deep intuition that people are more than their bodies and their brains, that when someone dies, their consciousness doesn't go out of existence, that some part of us can be up and about in the world while our body stays in one place, that we can't just be a bunch of molecules in motion. It's one that naturally taps into religious beliefs. And the challenge to that deep-seated belief from neuroscience, evolutionary biology, and cognitive science has put religion and science on the public stage. I think it's one of the reasons you have a renewed assault on religious beliefs from people like Dawkins and Daniel Dennett.

The neuroscientific worldview—the idea that the mind is what the brain does—has kicked away one of the intuitive supports of religion. So even if you accepted all of the previous scientific challenges to religion—the Earth revolving around the sun, animals evolving, and so on—the immaterial soul was always one last thing that you could keep as being in the province of religion. With the advance of neuroscience, that idea has been challenged.

And yet some prominent scholars of the mind have not adopted the strict materialist position. The atheist Sam Harris, who's a neuroscientist by training, says he's not at all sure that consciousness can be reduced to

brain function. He told me that he's had various uncanny—what some would call telepathic—experiences. And there's the philosopher David Chalmers, who famously distinguished between the "easy" and "hard" problems of consciousness. He's also critical of the materialist view of the mind. He has argued that the physical laws of science will never explain consciousness.

GOLDSTEIN: It's interesting. Actually, my doctoral dissertation was on the irreducibility of the mind to the physical. We have not been able to derive what it's like to be a mind from the physical description of the brain. So if you were to look at my brain right now, I would have to tell you what it is that I'm experiencing. You can't simply get it out of the physical description. So where does that leave us? It might mean that we're not our brain. It might mean that we have an incomplete description of the brain. Our science is not sufficient to explain how this extraordinary thing happens—that a lump of matter becomes an entire world. But the irreducibility doesn't in itself show immaterialism. And you can turn it around and say, look, all the neurophysiology that we have so far shows there is a correlation between certain physical states and mental states. And even a dualist like Descartes said there's a one-to-one correlation between the physical and the mental. So I'm not sure that we've settled this question once and for all.

PINKER: I'm also sympathetic to Chalmers's view. It might not be the actual stuff of the brain that makes us conscious so much as it is the information processing. I don't think Chalmers's view would give much support to a traditional religious view about the existence of a soul. He says that consciousness resides in information. So a computer could be conscious and a thermostat could have a teensy bit of consciousness as well. Still, the information content requires some kind of physical medium to support the distinctions that make up the information. And the Cartesian idea that there are two kinds of stuff in the universe—mind and matter—doesn't find a comfortable home in current views of consciousness, even those of Chalmers.

I know neither of you believes in paranormal experiences like telepathy or clairvoyant dreams or contact with the dead. But hypothetically,

suppose even one of these experiences were proven beyond a doubt to be real. Would the materialist position on the mind–brain question collapse in a single stroke?

PINKER: Yeah.

GOLDSTEIN: Yeah, if there was no other explanation. We'd need to have such clear evidence. I have to tell you, I've had some uncanny experiences. Once, in fact, I had a very strange experience where I seemed to be getting information from a dead person. I racked my brain trying to figure out how this could be happening. I did come up with an explanation for how I could reason this away. But it was a very powerful experience. If it could truly be demonstrated that there was more to a human being than the physical body, this would have tremendous implications.

Many stories of the paranormal turn on anecdotal, often once-in-a-life-time experiences. They fall outside the realm of what scientists can study because they are not repeatable. That raises the question, does science have certain limits to its explanatory power? Might there be other parts of reality that are beyond what science can tell us?

PINKER: It's theoretically possible. But if these are once-in-a-lifetime events, one has the simpler explanation that they're coincidences. Or fraud.

GOLDSTEIN: Or wishful thinking.

PINKER: Statisticians tell us that people underestimate the sheer number of coincidences that are bound to happen in a world governed by chance. That's why it would be essential to do the statistician-proof experiment or the Amazing Randi–proof experiment, showing that it isn't just stage magic. If that could be done, if you could show that someone could know something without it having to go through their sense organs—that you could cut the optic nerve connecting the eyes to the brain and the person could still see—then yeah, everything that I've been saying would be refuted. The fact that we don't have reliable paranormal phenomena, the fact that all aspects of our experience do depend on details of the physiology of the brain, make it a persuasive case that our consciousness depends on the brain.

GOLDSTEIN: Yeah, but what you're saying could be very true. It could be in the nature of the phenomena that it's extremely difficult to reproduce it in controlled experiments. In which case, we'll never know. I think it's a kind of arrogance to say that our science is complete. It's an amazing thing that we can know as much about the physical world as we do know. Why assume that we know everything about the world that there is to know? We've developed through all sorts of happenstance a kind of methodology that allows us to know a tremendous amount. It's an extraordinary thing that we can test and probe nature. And it's yielded amazing secrets. But why assume that this methodology that we're just damn lucky to have been able to stumble upon is going to yield all secrets? Of course, there could be things beyond the reach of science. But could we have any good evidence for accepting it? As soon as you have good evidence, it becomes science. So can there be good evidence for nonscientific propositions? No. Because the minute there is good evidence, it becomes science.

I still have to wonder if the study of neurons, synapses, and brain chemistry will ever be able to explain things like dreams or the creative process.
PINKER: That's a good example of something that's very difficult to study scientifically because it's rare and unpredictable. But it doesn't involve any kind of magic. When you throw together 100 billion neurons with 100 trillion connections, a lot of things are going to happen that are very hard to track down. And I suspect that creativity—we don't call it creative unless it's rare—means that it's going to be hard to study but not impossible. Historians who study creative individuals have uncovered a lot about the preconditions for creativity—for instance, what goes into a Mozart or an Einstein.

They can understand that. But just by looking at the brain itself, will you ever be able to understand the creative mind?
PINKER: I suspect not. In fact, the reason I'm not a neurobiologist but a cognitive psychologist is that I think looking at brain tissue is often the wrong level of analysis. You have to look at a higher level of organization. For the same reason that a movie critic doesn't focus a magnifying glass on the little microscopic pits in a DVD, even though a movie is nothing but a pattern of

pits in a DVD. I think there's a lot of insight that you'll gain about the human mind by looking at the whole human behaving, thinking, and reporting on his own consciousness. And that might be true of creativity as well. It may be that the historian, the cognitive psychologist, and the biographer working together will give us more insight than someone looking at neurons and brain chemistry.

Paul Davies

FORGET SCIENCE FICTION. IF YOU WANT to hear some really crazy ideas about the universe, just listen to our leading theoretical physicists. Wish you could travel back in time? You can, according to some interpretations of quantum mechanics. Could there be an infinite number of parallel worlds? Nobel Prize–winning physicist Steven Weinberg considers this a real possibility. Even the Big Bang, which for decades has been the standard explanation for how the universe started, is getting a second look. Now many cosmologists speculate that we live in a "multiverse," with Big Bangs exploding all over the cosmos, each creating its own bubble universe with its own laws of physics. Lucky for us, our bubble turned out to be life-friendly.

If you really want to start an argument, ask a room full of physicists this question: Are the laws of physics fine-tuned to support life? Many scientists hate this idea—what's often called the anthropic principle. They suspect it's a trick to argue for a designer God. But more and more, physicists point to various laws of nature that have to be calibrated just right for stars and planets to form and for life to appear. For instance, if gravity were just slightly stronger, the universe would have collapsed long before life evolved. If gravity were a tiny bit weaker, no galaxies or stars could have formed. If the strong nuclear force had been slightly different, red giant stars would never produce the fusion needed to form heavier atoms like carbon, and the universe would be a vast lifeless desert. Are these just happy coincidences? The late cosmologist Fred Hoyle called the universe "a put-up job." Princeton University physicist

Freeman Dyson has suggested that the universe, in some sense, "knew we were coming."

British-born cosmologist Paul Davies calls this cosmic fine-tuning "the Goldilocks enigma." Like the porridge for the three bears, he says the universe is "just right" for life. Davies is an eminent physicist who has received numerous awards, including the Templeton Prize and the Faraday Prize from the Royal Society in London. His 1992 book *The Mind of God* has become a classic of popular science writing. But his book *The Goldilocks Enigma* challenges even the most open-minded readers. Without ever invoking God, he argues for a grand cosmic plan. The universe, he believes, is filled with meaning and purpose.

What Davies proposes is truly mind-bending. Drawing on the bizarre principles of quantum mechanics, he suggests that human beings—through the sheer act of observation—may have helped shape the laws of physics billions of years ago. What's more, he says the universe seems to work like a giant computer. Indeed, it is possible that's exactly what it is, and we—like Neo in *The Matrix*—might just be living in a simulated virtual world.

Shortly before our interview, Davies had moved from Australia to set up a research institute at Arizona State University. We spoke about some of the controversies now raging in physics and why he's so determined to find meaning in the cosmos.

■ ■ ■ ■

A lot of scientists get annoyed by talk about the universe being strangely fine-tuned for life. They see this as a sneaky way to bring religion into scientific explanations for how the universe began. Clearly, you have a different perspective. Why are you so interested in the idea that the universe is just right for life?

All my career, I've been fascinated by the fact that the universe looks not just beautiful but in some sense deeply ingenious. It looks like it's been put together in a way that makes it work exceptionally well. I suppose the most striking example is that the laws of physics and the various parameters that go into those laws seem to be just right for life. If they were even slightly different, it's quite likely there would be no life, no observers, and no people like you and me having this conversation.

How many laws of physics have to be just right for life to be possible?
It's a little hard to write down the definitive list, and part of the reason is that we don't yet know what are the truly fundamental set of physical laws. Changing some of those laws by even a tiny amount would wreck the chances for life. Others seem to have a bit more flexibility. Overall, the total number of these coincidences, or special factors, is probably somewhere between a half a dozen and a dozen. I think most scientists would now agree that you couldn't change things very much and still have life.

So for all of these to happen—for instance, for carbon to be formed, for gravity to have the precise strength that it does—you're suggesting that it's more than coincidence that they are just right.
That's right. To just shrug this aside and say, "Well, if it wasn't that way, we wouldn't be here, would we?"—that's no answer to the question. It's just choosing to sweep it under the carpet. And in the case of the carbon resonance, if the strong force that binds the particles together in the nucleus were a little bit stronger or a little bit weaker, that resonance would be at the wrong energy and there would hardly be any carbon in the universe. So the fact that the underlying laws of physics seem to be just right to make abundant carbon, the essential life-giving element, cries out for an explanation.

But most scientists seem to believe it's just a lucky fluke that we're here. They say there's no inherent reason that all of these physical laws happen to have just the right properties so that carbon could form, the Earth could develop, and human beings could evolve.
You're absolutely right. Most scientists would say it's a lucky fluke. And if it hadn't happened, we wouldn't be here, so we won't bother to ask what's going on. Now, that point of view might have been tenable 20 years ago when the laws of physics were simply regarded as just there—as God-given or existing for no reason—and the form they had just happens to be the form they had. But with the search for the final unification of physics, there's been more of a

thrust toward saying, we won't just accept the laws of physics as given. We'll ask, how did those laws come to be? Are they the ultimate set of laws? Or are they just effective at low energies or in our region of the universe?

In the past, these "why" questions—why the laws of physics are the way they are, why the universe began, why we are here—were questions that theologians and philosophers asked. They seemed to be beyond science. But you're saying this is an arena where science can now operate.

Yes, there was a separation of powers—"nonoverlapping magisteria," to use Stephen Jay Gould's expression. In the past, the underlying laws of the universe were regarded as simply off-limits as far as scientists were concerned. The job of the scientist was to discover what the laws were and work out their consequences, but not to ask questions like, "Why those laws rather than some others?" But I think we've moved on since then. Are we just to suppose that these laws were magically imprinted on the universe at the moment of the Big Bang for no particular reason and that the form they have has no explanation?

There are different versions of the anthropic principle. Can you briefly lay those out for us?

Nobody can really object to the "weak anthropic principle." It just says that the laws and conditions of the universe must be consistent with life, otherwise we wouldn't be here. But if we combine it with the multiverse hypothesis, then we're in business. The multiverse hypothesis says that what we've been calling the universe is nothing of the kind. It's just a bubble, a little local region in a much vaster and more elaborate system called the multiverse. And the multiverse consists of lots of universes. There are different ways you can arrange this. One way is to have them scattered throughout space, and each universe would be a gigantic bubble, much bigger than the size of what we can see at the moment, but there would be many, many bubbles. And each of these bubbles would come with its own set of laws.

So the billions of galaxies in our universe still make up just one universe. But in this theory, there would be many such universes.

That's right. Everything as far as our most powerful instruments can penetrate would belong to just one universe—this universe. I call this a "Hubble bubble." So we're talking about a distance out to nearly 14 billion light-years. Everything we see within that one region of space seems to have a common set of physical laws. According to one version of the multiverse hypothesis, if you traveled enough in any direction, you'd reach the edge of that bubble, and there would be a chasm of exceedingly rapidly expanding space, and then you'd come to another bubble. And in that other bubble, maybe all electrons would be a little bit heavier or gravity would be a little bit stronger. There would be some variation. And you would find that in only a tiny, tiny fraction of those bubbles, all the conditions would be right so there can be life. And of course it's no surprise that we find ourselves living in such a life-encouraging bubble, because we couldn't live in any of the others.

The "strong anthropic principle" is far more controversial. What is this theory?

The strong anthropic principle says that the universe must bring forth life and observers at some stage. So even if there's only one universe, it must be the case that this universe will end up being observed by beings such as ourselves. Now, that's much harder for scientists to swallow because it seems to turn everything upside down. Most scientists think that the universe came into existence by some happy coincidence, or maybe from this multiverse selection there were beings who emerged. But these beings don't play a central role even in the multiverse theory. They don't play a creative role, whereas in the strong anthropic principle, the observers are in the central position. They are the ones dictating how the universe is put together. And that seems too much for people to swallow. It gives mind and consciousness a central place in the great scheme of things.

Well, it sounds fairly religious. Let's face it, the most common explanation for how all of this happened is that God set the process in motion so that human beings could eventually evolve.

You could give this either a religious or an antireligious interpretation. The religious interpretation is that God made the universe just as it is in order that life and conscious beings could emerge. The other way, which I suppose would be antireligious, is to say that the emergence of life and observers *causes* the universe to have the laws that it does. In the causal sense, it puts the cart before the horse. It makes the emergence of life and observers later on in the universe have some responsibility for the way the laws come into being at the beginning.

Is this what John Wheeler, the famous theoretical physicist, talked about when he made the case for a "participatory universe"?

Yes. Now we're into another variant of the anthropic principle—which is sometimes called the "final anthropic principle"—where, somehow, the emergence of life and observers link back to the early universe. Now, Wheeler didn't flesh out this idea terribly well, but I've had a go at trying to extend it. This has some appeal because the conventional theistic explanation and the conventional scientific explanation both suffer from the same shortcoming. They attempt to explain the universe by appealing to something outside it. In the religious explanation, appeal is made to an unexplained God who simply has to be there in order for the universe to be created in the form that it has. In the scientific explanation, the laws of physics just happily exist for no particular reason, and they just happen to have exactly the right properties, but it's all unexplained and it's all pushed off to outside of the universe. What appeals to me about John Wheeler's idea is that it attempts to provide an explanation for the bio-friendliness of the universe from entirely within it. Now, the difficult point is that we have to explain why life today can have any effect on the laws that the universe emerged with at the time of the Big Bang.

This sounds like it's coming right out of science fiction. Somehow, future people can go back in time and have some role in creating the universe. It's pretty far-fetched.

It is pretty far-fetched until you stop to think that there is nothing in the laws of physics that singles out one direction of time over another. The laws of physics work forward in time and backward in time equally well. Wheeler was one of the pioneers of this underlying time symmetry in the laws of physics. So he was steeped in the fact that we shouldn't be prejudiced between past and future when it comes to causation. The particular mechanism that Wheeler had in mind has to do with quantum physics. Now, quantum physics is based on Heisenberg's uncertainty principle. In its usual formulation, it means that there's some uncertainty at a later time how an atom is going to behave. You might be able to predict the betting odds that the atom will do this or that, but you can't know for certain in advance what's going to happen. Now, this uncertainty principle works both ways in time. There's no doubt about this. If we make an observation of an atom in a certain state now, then its past is uncertain, just as its future is uncertain.

So one way to think about this is that there will be many past histories that will lead up to the present state of the universe. In the remote past, its state was fuzzy. Now, in the lab, it's all very well to put an atom in a certain state and experiment on it at a later time. But when we're applying quantum physics to the whole universe, we simply can't establish the universe in a well-defined quantum state at the beginning and make observations later. We're here and now. So we can only infer backward in time. It's part of conventional quantum mechanics that you can make observations now that will affect the nature of reality as it was in the past. You can't use it to send signals back into the past. You can't send information back into the past. But the nature of the quantum state in the past can't be separated from the nature of the quantum state in the present.

So you're not talking about super smart beings in the far future who go back in time and somehow fiddle with the laws of physics to create the Big Bang. You're saying this happens just through the act of observation itself, through the fact that human beings or other intelligent beings are aware of the universe.

Right. I'm not talking about time travel. This is just standard quantum physics. Standard quantum physics says that if you make an observation of something today—it might just be the position of an atom—then there's an uncertainty about what that atom is going to do in the future. And there's an uncertainty about what it's going to do in the past. That uncertainty means there's a type of linkage. Einstein called this "spooky action at a distance." It's normally cast in terms of two particles which separate a long way apart, and you perform an experiment on one and the other instantaneously knows what the result is. These experiments have been done many times. It's called "quantum non-locality." But if it works across space instantaneously, then it can work back in time as well.

But what's so hard to fathom is that this act of observation, which has been observed at the subatomic level, would affect the way matter spread right after the Big Bang. That sounds awfully far-fetched.
Well, it's only far-fetched if you want to think that every little observation that we perform today is somehow micromanaging the universe in the far past. What we're saying is that as we go back into the past, there are many, many quantum histories that could have led up to this point. And the existence of observers today will select a subset of those histories which will inevitably, by definition, lead to the existence of life. Now, I don't think anybody would really dispute that fact.

What I'm suggesting—this is where things depart from the conventional view—is that the laws of physics themselves are subject to the same quantum uncertainty. So that an observation performed today will select not only a number of histories from an infinite number of possible past histories, but will also select a subset of the laws of physics which are consistent with the emergence of life. That's the radical departure. It's not the backward-in-time aspect, which has been established by experiment. There's really no doubt that quantum mechanics opens the way to linking future with past. I'm suggesting that we extend those notions from the state of the universe to the underlying laws of physics themselves. That's the radical step, because most physicists regard the laws as God-given, imprinted on the universe, fixed and immutable. But Wheeler—and I follow him on this—suggested that the laws of physics are not immutable.

I'm trying to understand how the laws of physics could change. You're suggesting that they were different 10 billion years ago. How could they change through the act of observation?
I have to explain my point of view in relation to the laws of physics. In the orthodox view, the laws are regarded as just unexplained, fixed, idealized

mathematical relationships. It's an idea that goes right back to Newton—that the universe is governed by these infinitely precise mathematical laws.

This is basically the Platonic view of the universe.

Plato had the view that mathematics lies outside of the physical universe, in a realm that's not part of space and time. It's often called the "Platonic heaven." But there's another view of the laws of physics, which is gaining increasing currency, that has really come about because of the information revolution. So a lot of physicists think that we should regard the laws of physics not as perfect, immutable mathematical forms that just happen to exist for no reason in this Platonic realm, but rather that they're more like computer software.

Let me explain that. When the Earth goes around the sun, we can imagine applying Newton's laws to predicting how it's going to move. That's just like a computer algorithm. If we know the position and motion of the Earth today, we can compute its position and motion this time next year. So the laws of physics could be thought of like a computer algorithm, taking input data, processing it, and delivering output data. That inevitably leads to the analogy that the universe is really a gigantic computer. And many people are enamored of that idea.

So, basically, information is all there is in the universe.

That's right. The universe is just a big information processor. Wheeler calls this "it from bit." Now, if you take that view—that the universe is a gigantic computer—then it leads immediately to the conclusion that the resources of that computer are limited. The universe is finite. It's finite because the speed of light is finite. There's been a finite time since the Big Bang. So if we have a finite universe, we have a computer with finite resources, and hence, finite accuracy. So once you recognize that the universe is a gigantic computer, then you see that the laws of physics can't be infinitely precise and perfect. There must be a certain amount of wiggle room or sloppiness or ambiguity in those laws.

And the key point here is that the degree of error, which is inherent in the laws, depends on time. As the universe gets older, there are fewer errors because it's had longer to compute. If you go back to the first split second after the Big Bang, then the underlying errors in the laws of physics really would have been very large. So instead of thinking of the universe as beginning magically with a bang, and the laws of physics being imprinted magically on the universe with infinite precision right from the word "go," we must instead think of the laws as being emergent with and inherent in the universe, starting out a little bit vague and fuzzy, and focusing down over time to the form that we see today.

There are some obvious questions about the Big Bang. Can we really talk about it coming out of nothing? Don't we have to ask, wasn't there something that caused the Big Bang?

Many people fall into that trap. But Augustine, in the fifth century, pointed out that the world was made with time, not in time. I think he got this exactly right. Of course, most people think that there must have been a previous event that caused whatever event we're talking about. But this is simply not the case. We now know that time itself is part of the physical universe. And when we talk about the Big Bang in a simplified model, then we're talking about not only matter and energy coming into being but space and time as well. So there was no time before the Big Bang. The Big Bang was the origin of time.

People want to ask, "What happened before the Big Bang, or what caused the Big Bang?" But in a simple picture where there's just one universe, the Big Bang can be the ultimate origin of space and time as well as matter and energy. So unless the universe has always existed, you're faced with the problem that time itself comes into existence. And any attempt to talk about causation has to be couched in terms of something that comes after the beginning and not before the beginning . . . because there was no before.

There are some obvious religious implications to all of this. My sense is that a lot of Jews and Christians are actually quite delighted with the Big Bang—the idea that the universe was created out of nothing. It seems to correspond to the story of creation in Genesis.

I think there's a misunderstanding by religious people if they think that creation ex nihilo is anything like the Big Bang. People misunderstand what creation ex nihilo is about. It's not that there existed a God within time who was there for all eternity and then at some particular moment, on a whim, decided, "I'm going to make a universe" and then pressed a button that made the Big Bang. That raises exactly the objection that Augustine was addressing: What was God doing before making the universe? If the universe was a good idea, why wasn't it made an infinite time ago?

I might also say that it's always a bad idea for people to decide what to believe on religious grounds and then to cherry-pick the scientific facts to fit, because these facts are likely to change. And we may find that the Big Bang theory goes out of favor at some point in the future. And then what? Religious people will have backed the wrong horse. So it's fraught with danger to seize on these cosmological ideas. But I personally think we can draw the conclusion that we live in a universe that's deeply imbued with meaning and purpose.

But most scientists would probably say there's no inherent meaning or purpose to the universe. It's an absurd universe. There's a famous quote from the Nobel Prize–winning physicist Steven Weinberg: "The more the universe seems comprehensible, the more it also seems pointless." Weinberg is an atheist who believes there's no ultimate point to human existence. Is he just wrong?

He and I would agree entirely on the scientific facts and would simply draw opposite conclusions from them. It's really an argument about whether the bottle is half full or half empty. Words like "meaning" and "purpose" are human categories, derived from human experience, and so we're projecting them onto nature and saying, well, the best way of understanding the universe is to say it behaves in a purpose-like manner.

You've written that it looks as though the universe's evolution is following a script. This raises the specter of teleology, which is a dreaded word among scientists.

I don't think anyone, including Weinberg, would deny that it looks like the universe is following a script. We call that script the laws of physics. There is no doubt that the universe seems to be following a pattern; we might even use the word "plan." The reason that I feel comfortable using words like "meaning" and "purpose" in connection with the universe is because I don't see them as being very different from words like "mechanism" or "information process-ing." I've said that the universe is like a computer. So the politically correct idea is to say the universe is a mechanism, a machine. That's okay. But to say it's like a living organism with a purpose is not. I just think that's inconsistent.

Are you saying that if you go back to the first few seconds of the universe, somehow the laws of nature were put in place so that intelligent life would arise billions of years later?
I'm not saying that an intelligent designer figured it all out and created the universe with a set of laws that would bring intelligent beings into existence.

You want to stay away from God.
I want to stay away from a preexisting, cosmic magician who is there within time, for all eternity, and then brings the universe into being as part of a pre-conceived plan. I think that's just a naive, silly idea that doesn't fit the leanings of most theologians these days and doesn't fit the scientific facts. I don't want that. That's a horrible idea. But I see no reason why there can't be a teleological component in the evolution of the universe, which includes things like meaning and purpose. So instead of appealing to something outside the universe—a completely unexplained being—I'm talking about something that emerges within the universe. It's a more natural view. We're trying to construct a picture of the universe which is based thoroughly on science but where there is still room for something like meaning and purpose. So people can see their own individual lives as part of a grand cosmic scheme that has some meaning to it. We're not just, as Steven Weinberg would say, pointless accidents in a universe that has no meaning or purpose. I think we can do better than that.

Do you think one reason the multiverse theory has become so popular in recent years is to keep the whole idea of God at bay?
Yes.

Because a lot of physicists seem to be at a loss for how to explain this cosmic fine-tuning. But with the multiverse, you can say there are an

infinite number of universes and we just happen to be lucky to live in one that supports life.

There's no doubt that the popularity of the multiverse is due to the fact that it superficially gives a ready explanation for why the universe is bio-friendly. Twenty years ago, people didn't want to talk about this fine-tuning because they were embarrassed. It looked like the hand of a creator. Then along came the possibility of a multiverse, and suddenly they're happy to talk about it because it looks like there's a ready explanation. Only those universes in which there can be life get observed, and all the rest go unobserved. Notice, however, that it's far from a complete explanation of existence. You still have to make a huge number of assumptions. You need a universe-generating mechanism to give you all these universes. You need a set of laws that can be scattered across these universes, distributed in some way, according to some algorithm. You're no better off than saying there is an unexplained God.

Even the scientific explanations for the universe are rooted in a particular type of theological thinking. They're trying to explain the world by appealing to something outside of it. And I think the time has come to move beyond that. We can—if we try hard enough—come up with a complete explanation of existence from within the universe, without appealing to something mystical or magical lying beyond it. I think the scientists who are anti-God but appeal to unexplained sets of laws or an unexplained multiverse are just as much at fault as a naive theist who says there's a mysterious, unexplained God.

You say in your book that there's another explanation for how the universe is structured. You suggest we may actually live in a fake universe. We could be part of an "ingeniously contrived virtual reality show," like the *Matrix* movies. Do you really think that's a possibility?

Clearly, it's a logical possibility that this entire universe could be a simulation, if we imagine that in 100 or 1,000 years we'd be able to make computers that are sufficiently powerful to simulate consciousness. You need only to believe that consciousness is ultimately a physical process, which in principle we can mimic. Then we clearly have the possibility of building a machine and feeding in electrical impulses to produce this or that sensation. So this raises the obvious question, is there a real world out there? And how do I know that it's not all a gigantic virtual reality show, with my own mental experiences being created by some super-duper computer, so that I'm just living inside this machine? Now, there are a number of philosophers who are enamored of this idea. How would we know from within the simulation that it is a simulation and not the reality? If it's a good simulation, we couldn't know. So we must be open to the possibility that this whole world is in fact a gigantic simulation.

Near the end of *The Goldilocks Enigma*, you say all these explanations about the universe are probably wrong, and "perhaps we have reached a fundamental impasse dictated by the limits of the human intellect." Do you think future scientists will ever resolve these questions?

If future scientists are human beings, they may be stuck with the same problems that we have. The way we think, the way we like to analyze problems, the categories that we define—like cause and effect, space-time and matter, meaning and purpose—are really human categories that cannot be separated from our evolutionary heritage. We have to face up to the fact that there may be fundamental limitations just from the way our brains have been put together. So we could have reached our own human limits. But that doesn't mean there aren't intelligent systems somewhere in the universe, maybe sometime in the future, that could ultimately come to understand. Ultimately, it may not be living intelligence or embodied intelligence but some sort of intelligent information-processing system that could become omniscient and fill the entire universe. That's a grand vision that I rather like. Whether it's true or not is another matter entirely.

Steven Weinberg

STEVEN WEINBERG IS WIDELY REGARDED as one of the world's greatest theoretical physicists. He not only won a Nobel Prize for his groundbreaking work on nature's elemental forces; he's also the rare physicist who is a gifted writer, as he demonstrated in *The First Three Minutes*, his masterful account of the origin of the universe. Weinberg has a special talent for the memorable quote. Among his gems: "The effort to understand the universe is one of the very few things that lifts human life above the level of farce, and it gives some of the grace of tragedy."

So what is it about Weinberg that riles up so many people? No doubt it's his stark atheism, perhaps best summed up by his famous statement: "The more the universe seems comprehensible, the more it also seems pointless." One gets the sense that the great physicist has looked deep into the cosmos and—for all the beauty and majesty he has found there—he's left with an empty bag. If you are looking for some smidgen of existential comfort, stay away from Weinberg. He is the cosmic grinch. That unremitting bleakness can be unnerving, even for secular scientists.

Take physicist Joel Primack, a leading expert on cold dark matter. His book *The View from the Center of the Universe*—coauthored with Nancy Ellen Abrams—is essentially a 380-page response to Weinberg's meaningless universe. Primack is convinced you *can* find underlying meaning in our existence if you just know where to look. Or consider biologist Stuart Kauffman, another nonbelieving scientist who is out to show the limitations of Weinberg's scientific reductionism.

Weinberg's atheism comes across as old school. Unlike Richard Dawkins or Sam Harris, who don't seem to have any need for the solace that religion offers, he admits that a pointless universe is a bitter pill. "It's hard to swallow," he told me. "But human life is irremediably tragic." Weinberg also scoffs at scientists who believe we live in a "designer universe" that's fine-tuned for life, though he's surprisingly open to the possibility of a "multiverse"—the theory that our Big Bang was just one of countless Big Bangs all over the cosmos.

I talked with Weinberg about his quest for a "final theory" in physics, his belief in free will, and his notion that religion is "pretty silly."

■ ■ ■ ■

Many scientists don't care about religion. They simply ignore it as they go about their daily lives. Why have you been so outspoken in your criticism of religion?

I do care about religion. I read a lot of history, so I see the enormous effect that religion has had on history. Science also impacts religion, and I'm interested in the effect that science has outside the laboratory and on our general culture. You can't say science has disproved the existence of God or an afterlife. These are beliefs that are designed to resist disproof. But by explaining more about the world we live in, science leaves less and less for religion to explain. The most important example comes from Darwinism.

You're suggesting many of the old reasons for why people believe in God—for instance, there had to be a designer who created life—just don't hold up in the face of modern science. Is that your main objection to religion?

Some people have certainly used religion to play an antiscientific role. I'm thinking particularly of al-Ghazali, the influential twelfth-century Islamic philosopher who argued that scientific laws don't explain anything. Things happen simply because God wants them to happen. But I'm not that worried about what religion does to science. My objections come mostly from what religion does to people—the endless inquisitions, jihads, and crusades that have risen from religious belief. It's such a sad story even when it hasn't been violent. Just the unnecessary self-denial that people have imposed on themselves, giving up the good things of life in order to worship God. It's a terrible, sad story and I look forward to the day when that story will come to an end.

It sounds like the moral questions are what you find most troubling about religion. And yet religion is supposed to give us the grounding in knowing good from evil.

There are really two questions: Do you believe in what religion teaches? And why should you care? On the first question, I see no reason to believe what religion teaches because it doesn't fit my scientific picture of the way the world works. I regard all the arguments for the truth of religious teaching as empty and unreliable. The other question, quite apart from whether or not you believe it, is what effect religion has on the world. It might be that religion has terrible effects and yet its teachings are true, or that religion is wonderfully beneficial but its teachings are false. But the real reason I don't believe in religion is that it's pretty silly.

Did you grow up in a religious family?

No. My parents identified themselves as Jews and insisted that I go through some of the rituals. But it was more a matter of ethnic self-identification. As far as I know, they had no particular religious belief. I didn't believe the teachings of the Jewish religion, but I had a vague idea that there had to be a God. But by the time I was 10 or 12, it just seemed increasingly silly, so I became completely unreligious. The stories told by different religions, whether it was Judaism, Christianity, or the Norse myths, were so transparently the creations of fertile imaginations that I couldn't take them seriously.

Weren't some of your relatives killed in the Holocaust? Has that affected your thinking about how religion deals with the problem of evil?

Well, I didn't know them, but the Holocaust poses the classic problem of theodicy. If God is good and powerful and all-knowing, why does He permit something like this? This is a powerful reason for not believing the conventional picture of God. I know there are explanations that have to do with free will, but how do you explain cancer? Is that free will for tumors? After the terrorist attacks of 9/11, which killed some 3,000 people, a number of people said their faith in God was shaken. That remark seemed rather silly to me. Surely they knew about much more disastrous events: millions of people killed in the Holocaust, or hundreds of thousands killed in tsunamis, or tens of millions killed in epidemics. We didn't need 9/11 to tell us this is a cruel world.

You have been quoted as saying, "Good people will do good things and bad people will do bad things. But for good people to do bad things, that takes religion." What did you mean?

There are so many examples of people who were led by their religion to do terrible things. One was St. Louis, the king of France, who was by all accounts a wise and benevolent ruler, concerned with the welfare of his subjects to an extent that was quite unusual for the thirteenth century. And yet he started a war of aggression against the Arabs, what is known as the Seventh Crusade, because of the religious imperative to regain the Holy Land. There are any number of people who have been influenced by their religion to do terrible things, though I also have to admit that some people have done wonderful things under the influence of religion.

I don't know much about the Muslims who blow themselves up in crowded markets or fly airplanes into tall buildings. I probably wouldn't describe them as good people. I think they're motivated by twisted hatred, but they're also motivated by their religion. Many have said they look forward to the reward of going to paradise after their death and being entertained by comely virgins. And it's the public position of many Islamic countries that Muslims who abandon Islam deserve to be executed.

It seems to me that acts of evil are often situational. Many Nazi guards were devoted to their wives and children, but they had no problem killing Jews. Their minds had been poisoned. But it's not clear they were intrinsically bad people.

No, although it's hard for me to avoid that conclusion. And though Hitler was not a serious Christian, anti-Semitism in Germany and throughout Europe certainly has its roots in Christianity. You see the working out of traditional Christian anti-Semitism in the horror of the Holocaust. But it is often pointed out that the worst regimes of the twentieth century were not theocratic regimes.

Right. We could mention the atrocities committed by the regimes of Hitler, Stalin, and Mao.

And Pol Pot. But there's a broader point to make. Though in no sense Christian, these regimes share something with religion. They mobilize large numbers of people to work together with a great feeling of solidarity to serve a grand idea— some overwhelming ideology—which is supposed to answer all questions. In the case of the Nazis, it was racial purity and the mastery of the German race. In the case of Stalin, it was the dictatorship of the proletariat. This is very similar to religions that provide an all-embracing code of morality and conduct, as well as answers to why the world is the way it is. Whether it's religious or secular, this kind of big truth is something people should be wary of.

There are no big truths that should govern human behavior. There are a lot of little truths. We should be nice to people when we can. We should have a few people we love and are loyal to. We should try to tell the truth as much as we can, even to ourselves. These little truths are really what make life worth living.

Let's talk about your own field of physics. There are plenty of physicists who have used religious language to describe the universe. Paul Davies titled one of his books *The Mind of God* to talk about the structure of the universe. Einstein famously said, "God does not play dice with the universe." What do you make of this God talk?

It varies from one person to another. In a letter to a friend, Einstein explained that he did not believe in a god who cared about human beings. For him, God was a synonym for harmony and order in the universe. When Einstein says "God," he's really talking about the laws of nature or the fundamental principles that govern the universe, without anything remotely resembling a personal God.

There does seem to be a battle now between atheists and religious believers over who gets to claim Einstein. He certainly didn't believe in a personal God, but some people think he was essentially a deist. Judging from various statements he made, he seemed to believe that God set the laws of nature in motion.

Well, I'm not particularly concerned with arguing about what Einstein meant. He was a great physicist—certainly the greatest physicist of the twentieth century and one of the greatest of all time. But we don't take Einstein as an authority in matters of physics. No one today would quote Einstein as an authority on general relativity, because we now understand it better than Einstein did. In fact, this is one of the differences between science and religion. Scientists don't have that kind of sacred authority whose word is taken as the ultimate answer.

But it does bother me when Einstein is appropriated by the religious. Clearly, what he meant by "God" is so vague and so far from conventional religion that it seems to me a misuse of the word. I probably have more sympathy with traditional religion on this matter than Einstein would. The concept of God is one that's been terribly important historically. It's had a fairly definite historical meaning. Of course, people have argued endlessly about the attributes of God, but there were common features: God was conscious, God was powerful, and many people thought God was benevolent, though it's certainly not an ordinary kind of human benevolence. If you're not going to use the word "God" in something like its historical meaning, then I don't think you should use the word. You're just trying to sound more religious than you actually are.

So you're bothered by religious language that's used in a metaphorical sense.

If it's clearly a metaphor, then it doesn't bother me. But it's this fogginess about whether it's a metaphor or whether you really mean it. My goodness, when someone sneezes, I say, "God bless you." I don't really mean it.

I'm actually surprised you do say that.

(*Laughs*) Oh, it's hard to avoid. That's harmless. But there's this shadow zone, where you sort of take the word seriously but don't mean what's historically been meant by it. That's just confusion. And it represents a defensiveness, a desire not to be called an atheist when that's what you actually are. So I wish Einstein had not used the word "God," but I don't really care what he thought.

Throughout the years, you've been very quotable. There's another famous quote: "The more the universe seems comprehensible, the more it also seems pointless." What did you mean by that remark?

There's nothing we've learned about the universe that suggests any ultimate purpose. I don't mean that we should then go out and jump off a cliff. There are things we can invent to give life a point—like loving each other, finding beauty in the world, and trying to work out the laws of nature. I don't mean that life is pointless and therefore we shouldn't treasure it. But we create whatever point there is.

I've talked with some cosmologists who don't believe in God but still react quite negatively to that quote of yours. Basically, they can't stomach the idea that we live in a meaningless universe. That doesn't bother you?

It bothers me very much. It's hard to swallow. I would much prefer to think that we're part of a cosmic drama. But human life is irremediably tragic. We have the tragedy of not being part of a cosmic drama, of knowing that we are the result of millions of years of random events shaped by the impersonal process of natural selection. We have the tragedy of knowing that our finest impulses, such as love, are heavily dictated by glands which evolved in order to produce certain behaviors—for example, so that we take care of our children so they survive and carry on the genes. It's all rather tragic that we don't cut a large figure in the universe. At the same time, we have to treasure the love that we have for each other and our children. It's difficult to treasure things that have no objective value. It's not an easy philosophy to follow.

What about the big existential question: Why are we here? Do you wonder about that?

I think the only real question is why the universe is here. Why are the laws of nature what they are? Sure, I wonder about it. We can answer all sorts of other questions. For instance, we can explain why there are atoms by referring to the principles of electrodynamics and quantum mechanics. But even if we reach a so-called final theory, we'll be left with the question: Why is that true? And part of the human tragedy is that we'll never have a satisfying understanding of why the world is the way it is.

There's a related question: Why *is* there a world? I've suggested that we may get closer to an explanation by showing that the laws of nature cannot be slightly modified in any way without leading to logical inconsistencies. And to some extent, we're already there. The laws of physics are rather rigid. If you start fooling around with the principles of quantum mechanics, you'll get nonsense, like negative probabilities or infinite quantities resulting from perfectly sensible questions. We may be able to answer why the world is not slightly different, but I don't think we'll ever be able to answer why it isn't completely different or why we don't simply have no world at all. We'll always be faced with an irreducible mystery. It's just something we have to live with.

Some physicists talk about a "designer universe" and point to various laws of physics that seem to be fine-tuned for life. They say it must be more than coincidence that gravity has the precise strength that it has, that the carbon atom—the essential ingredient for life—was able to form billions of years after the Big Bang, that the strong nuclear force has just the right strength to create hydrogen. And the list goes on. Are these examples of a bio-friendly universe?

Clearly, the universe is bio-friendly, because we're here. The question is whether or not this is remarkable. Some of these examples of fine-tuning are exaggerated. For example, you mentioned the carbon nucleus. If it didn't have a certain energy level, carbon wouldn't be synthesized in stars—or at least not to any great extent—and then it would be much harder for life to arise. That energy level has to be within a narrow range for carbon to be synthesized. Well, there are good arguments for why it has to be in that range that don't involve any fine-tuning of constants.

There are better examples of the fine-tuning of the laws of nature. To me, the most impressive is the fact that the "dark energy" that drives the expansion of the universe is vastly less than some of the contributions we can calculate. Now, that in itself is not a paradox because there are other contributions we can't calculate that could cancel the ones we can calculate. But the cancellation would have to be unbelievably precise—good to 56 decimal places. So that's an example of remarkable fine-tuning. Opinions differ about how to solve that problem. We don't know at present, but one thing that's been proposed—that would also be a solution to any of these other fine-tuning problems—is that our Big Bang didn't form the whole universe. The universe actually consists of Big Bangs that go on here and there, everywhere, time without end.

This is the idea of a "multiverse."
It's probably a misuse of words. I think "universe" should be kept as the word that means everything, but that's the language that has developed. We can easily imagine theories in which different subuniverses within the multiverse have different laws of nature. The values of constants, like the dark energy constant, would vary from one Big Bang to another.

So in many of these subuniverses, probably the vast majority of them, there would be no life. They would be dead universes. We just happen to live in one that's conducive to life.
Of course, the fact that we live in one that's conducive to life is not surprising, because we couldn't live in the others. The multiverse theory is highly speculative. But if it is correct—and it may well be—it removes the sense of wonder about why the laws of nature and the value of physical constants are suitable for the appearance of life.

The multiverse theory has really gained currency among cosmologists over the past decade. But some people say the multiverse has become popular because so many scientists hate the so-called anthropic principle, which they see as a sneaky way to bring religion into scientific explanations for how the universe began. If there are billions of universes out there, it's easier to account for the bio-friendly one that we just happen to live in.
If the anthropic principle means the laws of nature must allow for the appearance of intelligent life, yes, scientists do hate that. It reverses the historical progress of science, which does not regard intelligent life as fundamental to nature but rather as something that's risen through evolution. The multiverse makes the anthropic principle unnecessary. But I don't think that's why the multiverse idea came along. There were developments in mathematical physics that led to the popularity of the multiverse.

One was the chaotic cosmology of Andrei Linde, which at first had nothing at all to do with anthropic reasoning. It just recognized that it was quite natural that the same quantum fluctuations that produced our Big Bang—if the initial state of the universe was entirely chaotic—would go on producing Big Bangs eternally. The different Big Bangs would appear to lead to different laws of nature. And other physicists have discovered that string theories have a vast number of solutions. Michael Douglas and his collaborators have estimated it as something to the order of 10^{500}; that's a 1 with 500 zeroes.

If there are so many possible solutions, doesn't that make string theory absurd?

It's not absurd if that's the way it is. What is absurd is the idea of finding the answer by going through each solution one by one. But we're not prevented from studying this enormous set of solutions statistically. The discovery that there is a huge number of solutions to string theory had nothing to do with any philosophical liking or disliking of the anthropic principle. It's just a mathematical development of string theory.

There's also an older theory that goes back decades to the work of Hugh Everett, when he was a graduate student at Princeton. He developed an interpretation of quantum mechanics that many of us find more plausible than Bohr's Copenhagen interpretation. In Everett's theory, when we make a measurement of which possibility is actually realized—for example, whether the electron spin is up or down, or Schrödinger's cat is alive or dead—what happens is not that the wave function collapses but that we become part of that wave function that's found by the experiment. And all of these different parts of the wave function continue to exist. So there's one universe in which the experimenter has discovered that Schrödinger's cat is alive and another universe in which the experimenter has found that Schrödinger's cat is dead. Quantum mechanics is continually producing an unbelievable variety of sub-universes in a multiverse.

I have to say, this idea of parallel universes seems utterly fantastic.

Yeah, it does to me, too. I have to admit it. But the Bohr interpretation is even worse: the idea that there's a distinction between the measuring apparatus—which is intrinsically classical and not quantum mechanical—and the thing observed—which is quantum mechanical—and the measuring apparatus forces the wave function collapse to one result or another. That introduces a kind of dualism between most of nature, which is quantum mechanical, and the observers, who are not, which I find absolutely unacceptable. I'd rather believe in the Everett interpretation. My hope is that someone will find a way to modify quantum mechanics to eliminate the patent violation of common sense of the Everett interpretation without going to the absurdity of the Bohr interpretation. But we don't have that yet. I'm not happy with our present understanding of quantum mechanics.

But I do wonder if scientists can ever prove the existence of these sub-universes outside our own subuniverse. And if they can't, is this really science? Or have we entered the realm of metaphysics?

We don't prove theories by observing every structure described by those theories. Our proof comes when theories predict enough that is then verified experimentally, which gives us confidence in the theories. For example, no one will ever observe a quark. Our understanding of quarks is entirely based on the fact that the theory of strong forces works very well in other respects; it accounts for lots of things that we can measure, like the way colliding electrons and positrons produce showers of strongly interacting particles at very high energy. That kind of experiment verifies the modern theory of strong nuclear forces without anyone ever seeing a quark.

Presumably, we'll never see the other parts of the multiverse. But if we have a theory that requires the existence of a multiverse, and if that theory is verified in other ways, then we'll believe it. We don't have that yet, and I'm not saying we should accept this as part of established science. But I can imagine a time when we'll have a modern version of string theory that's sufficiently well verified. It may predict the existence of a multiverse, which we'll then believe without being able to see the other subuniverses. That's the way science works. You never verify every prediction of the theory. For example, our present theory of nature predicts things beyond the reach of telescopes, beyond what we'll ever be able to see in the universe. With the way the universe is expanding, there are galaxies we will never observe. And yet we don't really have any doubt that they exist and that they behave according to certain rules.

Do you think scientists will ever come up with a theory that explains precisely how our universe began?

I think it's quite possible. We're well on our way. This is really a golden age of observational cosmology. Through studies of microwave background radiation and the large-scale structures of galaxies, we now have a degree of precision in our understanding of how the universe evolved that would have been unthinkable a few decades ago. We can now say that the age of the Big Bang is 13.7 billion years, plus or minus 0.2 billion years. We also have a theory of inflation that takes us back to the origins of the Big Bang and is increasingly well verified by observation. That doesn't answer the question of how it began. But I can believe that within the lifetime of people now living we'll have a theory which settles this question. It may also be much further away, maybe 1,000 years away. But I don't think it's outside the range of human intelligence.

Let me ask a more philosophical question: Do you think we live in a deterministic universe?

Yes and no. (*Laughs*) Quantum mechanics describes the evolution of the universe in terms of a wave function, which evolves deterministically. Nevertheless, quantum mechanics has a lot to do with probabilities. The probabilities come in when you make measurements—for example, whether a particle is here or there, whether a spin is up or down, whether a cat is alive or dead. Your measurements can only be described probabilistically. My conception of free will is simply that our actions rise out of our volition. I decide that I want to scratch my head, so I scratch my head. That doesn't rule out a deterministic picture of nature, because our volition itself undoubtedly comes from something else. We may want to scratch our head for reasons beyond our control.

So we at least think we have free will.

I think we do have free will. We all experience the act of doing things because we want to do them. The question of why we want to do things is a murky one. In a sense, the question of free will is divorced from the question of determinism. You know, this relates to legal arguments about punishment. Should criminals be punished because they do evil things, like murder? My feeling is yes, they should be punished. Now, you might say their desire to murder is either because of inherent propensities they inherited at birth or because of childhood experiences over which they had no control. That's all true. But the fact that they want to commit some evil act is enough to merit punishment. People have to get the rewards and punishments resulting from their actions, even though the desire to do those things is not entirely under their control.

Stuart Kauffman

STUART KAUFFMAN HAS PLENTY of experience tilting at windmills. For years he has questioned the Darwinian orthodoxy that natural selection is the sole principle of evolutionary biology. As he put it in his first book, *The Origins of Order*, "It is not that Darwin is wrong but that he got hold of only part of the truth." In Kauffman's view, there is another biological principle at work—what he calls "self-organization"—that "co-mingles" with natural selection in the evolutionary process.

A physician by training, Kauffman is a widely admired biologist; in 1987, he was a recipient of a MacArthur "genius" award. He is also one of the gurus of complexity theory, and for years was a fixture at the Santa Fe Institute, a renowned scientific research community. He later moved to the University of Calgary to set up the Biocomplexity and Informatics Institute.

If this sounds heady, it is. Getting Kauffman to explain his theory of self-organization, "thermodynamic work cycles," and "autocatalysis" to a nonscientist is challenging. But he is at heart a philosopher who ranges over vast fields of inquiry, from the origins of life to the philosophy of mind. He's a visionary thinker who's not afraid to play with big ideas.

In his book *Reinventing the Sacred*, Kauffman has launched an even more audacious project. He seeks to formulate a new scientific worldview and, in the process, reclaim God for nonbelievers. He argues that our modern scientific paradigm—reductionism—breaks down once we try to explain biology and human culture. This has left us flailing in a sea of meaninglessness. So how do we steer clear of this empty void? By embracing the "ceaseless creativity" of nature itself, which in Kauffman's view is the real meaning of God. It's God without any supernatural tricks.

Kauffman is now in his seventies, and his advancing age may partly account for the urgency he seems to feel in grappling with life's ultimate questions. When I spoke with him, I found him in an expansive mood as we ranged over a host of big ideas, from the prospects of creating life in a test tube to the need for a sacred science.

■ ■ ■ ■

You've suggested we need a new scientific worldview that goes beyond reductionism and incorporates a religious sensibility. Why?
The first thing to say is that the current scientific paradigm has done extraordinarily good work for at least 350 years. The reigning paradigm of reductionism takes a little bit of explaining. It goes back to the Greeks in the first century C.E., and then it really explodes at the time of Newton, who had three laws of motion and a law of universal gravitation. With Newton comes the idea of a deterministic universe. In fact, he took himself to be doing the work of God. The theistic god who reached into the universe and changed its course gave way during the Enlightenment to a deistic god, who wound up the universe at the beginning and let Newton's laws take over. It was the clockwork universe.

So the idea is that if you understand the laws of the universe, you can plug in all the variables and predict what the outcomes will be.
Exactly. It finds its clearest explanation in the French mathematician Pierre-Simon Laplace, at the time of Napoleon, who said if you knew the masses and velocities of all the particles in the universe, then you could compute the entire future and past of the universe. As the Nobel laureate physicist Steven Weinberg says, once all the science is completed, all the explanatory arrows will point downward from societies to people to organs to cells to biochemistry to chemistry to physics.

And if you can explain the laws of physics, Weinberg thinks you can explain everything else.

Right. He also says we live in a meaningless universe. Those are the fruits of standard reductionism. And the majority of scientists remain reductionists. It's comforting in that the entire universe is seen to be lawful; we can understand everything, from societies to quarks. Yet a number of physicists, including the Nobel laureates Philip Anderson and Robert Laughlin, feel that reductionism is not adequate to understand the real world. In its place, they talk about "emergence." I think they're right. Now, these are physicists. I'm talking as a biologist.

This seems to be a fundamentally new scientific framework. Can you explain what emergence is?

There are things that we just can't deduce from particle physics—life, agency, meaning, value, and this thing called consciousness. The fact is that we can act on our own behalf and make choices. So agency is real. With agency comes value. Dinner is either good or bad. There's consciousness in the universe. We may not be able to explain it, but it's true. So the first new strand in the scientific worldview is emergence.

And that new scientific view has no room for reductionism?

Right. In physics, and in the meaningless universe of Steven Weinberg, there are only happenings. Balls roll down hills but they don't do anything. "Doing" does not exist in physics. Physics cannot talk about values, because you have to have agency to have values. So let's talk about agency for a moment.

You and I are having an interview right now. We're acting on our own behalf and we're changing the world as we do so. The physicist Philip Anderson has a charming way of putting it. He says if you doubt agency, just look at the anguished expression on your dog's face when you say, "Come." When I used to call my sweet dog Windsor, he would give me a sidelong glance. I think he was thinking, "Well, I've got more time here." Finally, I'd say, "Come, Windsor!" And he'd come.

I don't doubt agency in my dog Windsor. And once you've got agency—and I think it's sitting there at the origin of life—then you've got food or poison, which I call "yuck" and "yum." And once you've got food or poison, it is either good or bad for that organism. So you've got value in the universe.

Are you rejecting Weinberg's famous comment: "The more we comprehend the universe, the more pointless it seems"?
I profoundly believe that Weinberg is wrong. I also happen to think that Weinberg is utterly brilliant. He's one of the best defenders of the pure reductionist stance. But once you've got agency, you've got meaning. This is the beginning of a change in our scientific worldview. Agency is real, so meaning is real in the universe. Value is real, at least in the biosphere. And these things can't be talked about by physicists.

So the reductionist model breaks down when we're talking about how life evolves. This is unpredictable.
Absolutely. This idea is frightening at first, but then utterly liberating. For 3.8 billion years, the biosphere has been expanding from the origin of life into what I call "the adjacent possible." Once we're at levels of complexity above the atom, the universe is on a unique trajectory. It's doing something that it's never done before.

To take one example, I argue that the evolutionary emergence of the human heart cannot be deduced from physics. That doesn't mean it breaks any laws of physics. But there's no way of getting from physics to the emergence of hearts in the evolution of the biosphere. If you were to ask Darwin, "What's the function of the heart?," he would have said it's to pump blood. That's what Darwin meant by adaptation. But there may be other causal consequences of the heart, or any other part of you, that are of no functional significance in the current environment but may become useful in a different environment.

Isn't this called a Darwinian preadaptation?
Yes. And when a preadaptation happens, a new function comes to exist in the biosphere and can change the history of the planet. We just don't know ahead of time what the relevant selective environments are. This is just stunning when you think about it. We cannot say how the biosphere will evolve.

The same is true for our technologies, our economy, our culture. We didn't have the faintest idea what would happen with the invention of writing or the invention of tractors. These were Darwinian preadaptations at the technological level. This is the creativity of the universe that we're participating in right now. We literally don't have the faintest idea what the biosphere is going to invent in the next million years, or what technology is going to invent in the next 40 years. Who foresaw the Web 50 years ago?

It seems that one of your big goals is to explain the origin of life. You have devoted much of your career to trying to work out a science of self-organization. Can you explain this?

It's harder than you think. I wrote a whole book, *The Origins of Order*, and I very carefully never defined self-organization. My own life work asks if there might be laws of self-organization that are sources of order in biology quite apart from natural selection. For most biologists, the only source of order is natural selection. But we don't need DNA or RNA to get molecular reproduction. People have already made self-reproducing systems. Reza Ghadiri at the Scripps Research Institute took a string of amino acids and used it to replicate itself.

But the second part has to do with self-organization. I worked out a mathematical theory, which says if we have a large enough diversity of molecules and chemical reactions, so many reactions will be catalyzed that you'll get some form of collective autocatalysis popping out of the soup. The mathematics has been proved, but it still needs to be shown experimentally. For years, I've been probing laws of self-organization that co-mingle with natural selection and give rise to the order we see. And we're not very far, experimentally, from creating life all on our own.

One of the great mysteries of science is consciousness. Virtually all scientists assume the mind is formed by neural circuits in the brain, while religious traditions typically see a direct connection between the human mind and God. Do you accept either of those views?

Nobody has the faintest idea what consciousness is. In the Western tradition, St. Augustine said the human mind is directly connected to the mind of God.

The dualism of Descartes distinguished between mental substances and physical substances. Now, contemporary neurobiologists and computer scientists believe that if you have a sufficiently complex computing system—like neurons or logical gates in a computer—then it would become conscious.

But I'll tell you my own bias. I think it's possible that the mind really is associated with quantum mechanics. Now, a good physicist will say, "That's just nonsense. Quantum behavior will disappear in 10^{-15} second, so it can't happen." Well, there are recent theorems in quantum computing that say that's not necessarily so. The question is, can you get sustained quantum coherent behavior at body temperature in something like neurons? Nobody knows.

Are you saying there's no way that computer scientists in the future will be able to reproduce the human brain? That computers will not be able to create consciousness?

Roger Penrose wrote a book called *The Emperor's New Mind*. He looked at this argument for artificial intelligence, and he said it's just bunk. I think he's right. I've fallen in love with the idea that consciousness has something to do with being poised forever between the quantum world of possibilities, where nothing actual happens, and the transformation of that—whether it's the collapse of the wave function or decoherence, where something actual happens in the world.

If this is related to consciousness, it provides an intellectual framework in which we can understand the mind acting on matter. Quantum mechanics is astonishing because it's not causal. It just happens. Maybe the mind is acausal. Maybe the mind is nonalgorithmic. I don't want you to take this very seriously. It's just Stu Kauffman getting old and thinking weird things. But it may be true. And even if my arguments are right, it still doesn't tell us what consciousness is. I don't have any idea. Nor does anybody else, including the philosophers of mind.

You call yourself a secular humanist. But you also say we need to reinvent the sacred. What do you mean by that?

Once one gets beyond reductionism, it leads to a radically new scientific worldview, which changes our place in the universe as human beings. We are

not meaningless chunks of particles spinning around in space. We are organisms with meaning in our lives, and the way the biosphere will evolve is ceaselessly creative. The way the economy evolves is ceaselessly creative in ways
that cannot be predicted ahead of time. That's why five-year plans don't work.
The same thing for human culture.

**Okay, we can't predict what's going to happen. But I'm still trying to figure
out why you invoke religious language. Why do we need a new understanding of God and the sacred?**

First of all, because of global communications and commerce, a global civilization of some kind is emerging. But there's also a natural retreat by some
people into religious fundamentalism, and people are killing each other. So
I think a shared sacred space across all of our traditions will lead us to
coalesce around a sense of what is sacred—for example, all life on the planet
and the planet itself. I hope we can find our way to a global ethic, beyond
just the love of family, a sense of fairness, and a belief in democracy and free
markets.

**Historically, God has had a very specific meaning, particularly in the
Western tradition. It refers to an all-powerful, transcendent reality. Can
you really take such a loaded word and give it a new meaning?**

Maybe. I have a very explicit reason for wanting to use the word "God." It's
the most powerful symbol humanity has created. We have been worshiping
God or gods at least since the sacred Earth mother 10,000 years ago in
Europe. In the Abrahamic tradition, our sense of God has evolved. For
example, the Israelites 4,500 years ago had Yahweh, who was a ferocious
warrior, a law-giving God. That's a very different god than the one that Jesus
spoke of, a God of love. So our sense of God just in the Abrahamic tradition
has evolved.

The question is whether we choose to take our most powerful, invented
symbol and use it in a new way to mean the creativity in nature itself. Is
it more astonishing to believe in a God who created everything that has
come to exist—planets, galaxies, chemistry, life, and consciousness—in six
days? Or is it even more astonishing and awesome to believe what is almost

certainly the truth: namely, that all of this came to be all on its own? I think the second.

Most scientists talk about the origins of the world strictly through naturalistic means. Why are you so determined to invoke "God"?

"God" carries with it a sense of awe, reverence, and wonder that no other symbol carries. It's a choice. Can we give up the creator God—the all-powerful, omnipotent, all-loving God who confronts us with the problem of evil—and instead find reverence for a ceaseless creativity in the unfolding of nature? I think we can. I also feel parts of the religious person's sense of awe. I sense the solace that prayer to a transcendent God brings. But I don't believe in a transcendent God. I do believe in this new scientific worldview.

Forget the "God" word for a second and just try to feel yourself as a co-creating member of the universe. It changes your stance from the secular humanist lack of spirituality to a sense of awed wonder that all of this has come about. For example, I was sitting on my patio and started thinking about the trees around me. I thought I'm one with all of life. If I'm going to cut down a tree, I better have a good reason. It's not just an object. It's alive. Then I thought about the river I'm sitting next to. I can dam the river if I want to. But I'm going to change the ecosystem downstream from it and change the planet.

So even without talking about God, this new scientific worldview brings with it a sense of membership with all of life and a responsibility for the planet that's largely missing in our secular world. In a materialist society, being spiritual is—if not frowned upon—what you do in the privacy of your own mind, because there's something flaky about it for those of us who don't believe in God.

It sounds like your God is equivalent to nature.

I'm saying God is the sacredness of nature. And you can go a step beyond that. You can say that God is nature. That's the God of Spinoza. That's the God that Einstein believed in. But their view of the universe was deterministic. The new view is that evolution of the universe is partially lawless and ceaselessly creative. We are the children of that creativity. One either does or does not take the step of saying God is the creativity of the universe. I do. Or you say there is divinity in the creativity in the universe. If we can't transform our secular humanist, consumerist worldview into one in which we have this sense of responsibility, awe, and wonder for the planet and all life, then we can't invent a global ethic. Yet we need it to create a transnational, mythic structure to sustain the global civilization that's emerging.

You are Jewish, but you've said you can't accept the God of Abraham. Have there been occasions in your life when you wish you could?

Sure. I don't believe in God, but I seem to thank Him a lot. It's not logical, but it feels right. Of course, Jews don't believe in heaven and hell. I've lived a lot more than half my life. Death is frightening. It would be wonderful to be able to believe in a heaven so that when I die, I could see my daughter, who was killed more than 20 years ago. I wish I could, but I don't. I think when I die, I die. But it would be nice to believe the other.

Your daughter Merit's death must have been a wrenching experience. Did that pull you in a religious direction?

In one sense. There's an ancient Aramaic prayer that's perhaps 5,000 years old. It's the Kaddish, the prayer for the dead. When Merit died, it mattered enormously to me as a nonobservant Jew, but a member of the Jewish community, that the Kaddish be said for my daughter.

Now, it's worth pointing out that Neanderthals buried their dead. Why did they bury their dead? The need to reach out in these spiritual directions is antique in us. You can see it in the struggle that's going on right now among religious fundamentalists. Fundamentalist Islam is appalled at the materialism and secularism of the West. Some kind of awakening to the spiritual part of being human seems to me just essential. And this goes beyond where science can go.

I'm struck by how you and a few other secular scientists—like the cell biologist Ursula Goodenough, the cosmologist Joel Primack, the psychiatrist George Vaillant—are all appropriating the language of religion to explain what happens in the natural world. Do you see this as an emerging movement?

I hope so. It is a historical fact that new spiritual or religious movements often appropriate the holy sites of older ones. For example, Notre Dame in Paris is built on a holy Druid site. And in northern New Mexico, there are holes in the ground, called sipapus; the Pueblo believed that the first people came up to the surface through these holy sipapus and populated the Earth. When the Spaniards conquered the Indians, they built their churches on the sipapus. And one of them is the glorious sanctuary of Chimayo, not far from Santa Fe, with holy dirt and crutches and wheelchairs in it. It's said that if you take the holy dirt from the sipapu, it's healing. Even though I don't believe in it, there's something wonderful about the fact that thousands of people do truly believe that dirt in the sipapu has healing powers.

Clearly, you don't accept traditional beliefs about God. But are you carving out a different space from atheists, especially those scientists who are atheists?

I absolutely am. Take Richard Dawkins's book *The God Delusion*. It's a very good book. And I know Richard, and he lays out the atheist case well. It appeals to the billion or so of us who do not believe in a supernatural God, and who've hidden in the corners, particularly in the United States, where religion is so widely adhered to. But it will do no good whatsoever in bridging the gap between those who do believe in some form of God and the secular humanists like Dawkins and myself who do not. We need something else.

Well, Dawkins does not want to bridge that gap. He wants to convince those religious believers that they're wrong.

Absolutely. But I think Richard is wrong. Not that there's a supernatural god. I think that there's something else. I think the creativity in nature is so stunning and so overwhelming that it's God enough for me, and I think it's God enough for many of us if we think about it. You see, Richard's view, and those of the new atheists, is simply not going to reach out and persuade those who hold to the standard Abrahamic religious views to consider something else. Whereas I hope what I'm saying may help create a new kind of sacred space.

You're rejecting the whole notion that science deals only with the physical world, while religion and philosophy deal with value and meaning. Do we need to redefine both religion and science?

Yes, we do. Reductionist science can't talk about meaning. But we are beyond reductionism. And it goes beyond science. C. P. Snow wrote a famous essay in 1959 called "The Two Cultures," decrying the fact that science and the humanities were split apart. In other words, we can have either Einstein or Shakespeare, but we can't have them both in the same worldview. I think that's the fruit of a stark reductionism. But there's an opening wedge for us to have both Shakespeare and Einstein. Maybe we had that in the ancient world, but we haven't since science burst forth 350 years ago. There's something new for us to invent because science isn't the only gold standard for finding out about the world. Shakespeare told us about human beings in a profound way. Great novelists are telling us about the world. That's a very different worldview than what we've had for the past 350 years.

Jane Goodall

JANE GOODALL HAS AN ICONIC status like no other living scientist. For decades, she has lived in the public eye, as we've watched her evolve from curious ingenue to celebrated sage. By now, she is so widely admired that it's easy to forget how she once rattled the cages of the scientific establishment.

At a time when wildlife biologists were taught that animals didn't have minds or personalities, Goodall wrote vivid accounts of David Greybeard, Flo, and the other chimpanzees she studied in Tanzania's Gombe Stream National Park. She was the first scientist to observe that chimps not only use tools but make tools. She was the first to discover that chimpanzees hunt other animals. In three decades of field study, she revolutionized the study of primates and forced people to rethink what it means to be human. As Stephen Jay Gould said, "Jane Goodall's work with chimpanzees represents one of the Western world's greatest scientific achievements."

Goodall's appeal, though, has always stretched beyond her scientific accomplishments. Partly it stems from those old National Geographic shows of the lone white woman out in the bush with these wild apes. The cultural critic Donna Haraway once wrote, "There could be no better story than that of Jane Goodall and the chimpanzees for narrating the healing touch between nature and society," though Haraway went on to say that our fascination with Goodall also played on Western stereotypes about Africa: "It is impossible to picture the entwined hands of a white woman and an African ape without evoking the history of racist iconography."

Goodall has remained a fascinating figure partly because she has always kept one foot outside of mainstream science. She is an outspoken advocate of animal rights and also the rare scientist who talks openly about mystical experiences—from her transformative encounters in the wild to a ghostly vision she once had of her dead husband. Now in her seventies, Goodall is a larger-than-life figure who looms over the field of primatology. Today, she spends less time with her beloved Gombe chimps than traveling the world as a UN messenger of peace, campaigning for environmental causes and promoting her Roots & Shoots program for young nature lovers.

I caught up with Goodall after she received the Leakey Prize, awarded to "scientists who transcend the boundaries of their disciplines." The prize was fitting because it was the famed paleontologist Louis Leakey who gave Goodall her first big break.

■ ■ ■ ■

Back in 1960, you seemed to be the most unlikely candidate to revolutionize our understanding of chimpanzees. Why did Louis Leakey pick you to do this field study?
He told me later that he deliberately picked somebody with no university training because he wanted to send somebody into the field with an unbiased mind. Back in the early sixties the ethologists of Europe were very reductionist. Complex behavior was not really accepted. Of course, I hadn't been taught that animals didn't have personalities and feelings. I hadn't been taught that only humans had minds. And so I merrily just recorded what I saw, rather than worrying about what I ought to be seeing.

Did you have much scientific training when you first went to Gombe?
I didn't have any. None. I left school at 18. I got a course of training as a secretary. I got a job in London with documentary films and then decided I had to get to Africa when I was invited by a school friend. So I left my job in London, which didn't pay very well, went home, worked as a waitress, saved up my wages and tips, got a fare to Africa, and there, I met Louis Leakey.

But if you had been a Ph.D. biologist, do you think you wouldn't have noticed the chimpanzees' personalities and feelings?

I can't imagine that because I grew up with animals. I had a teacher, who was my dog. But I might have become intimidated by this male-dominated discipline had I been through college. Who knows? I'm not someone who easily gets intimidated. I knew that chimps had personalities, minds, and feelings. And I had a wonderful supervisor who taught me how to express myself so that the more rigid scientists couldn't tear me apart. I was very naive at first.

What did your supervisor teach you?

I wrote that Flo had a baby and the baby's eldest sister, Fifi, was very protective of that baby. And if other youngsters came up, she was jealous. She chased them away with bristling hair and screams of anger. Robert Hinde said, "You can't say she was jealous because you can't prove it." I said, "Well, okay. But I know she was jealous. So what shall I say?" And he said, "I suggest you write, 'Fifi behaved in such a way that, had she been human, we would say she was jealous.'" Now, that is so brilliant. He taught me how I could protect myself and at the same time express what I believed to be true.

As I've read the accounts of your early fieldwork at Gombe, I'm struck by how much time you were out in the field, alone with the chimpanzees.

It was absolutely amazing. It wasn't only a beautiful place, surrounded by this timeless world, but also, everything I saw with the chimpanzees was new. I mean, how lucky can you get?

Didn't they just run away from you when you first approached them?

Oh yeah. They'd never seen a white ape before and they were horrified. They vanished into the bushes. Fortunately, one of them—I named him David Greybeard—lost his fear before the others and came to my camp, where he found some bananas. And it was because of him that the others gradually began to lose their fear. So it was as though he helped me open a door into a magic world.

Some of your early discoveries—that chimpanzees use tools—involved David Greybeard. Can you describe the first day you saw this?

It had been raining. I was pushing through some tall grass and suddenly I saw this dark shape hunched over the golden soil of a termite mound. I peered through the bushes with my binoculars and saw a hand reach out and pick a piece of grass. I could see him pushing it down into the termite mound. After he left, I went over there and saw termites crawling over the surface of the mound. There were some stems lying around, so I poked them down and the termites bit on them. A couple of days later, not only did I see David Greybeard using the tools but actually stripping leaves from a twig, therefore making a tool. That was the exciting thing. Up until then, it was thought that only humans used and made tools. We were defined as man the toolmaker.

You also discovered that chimpanzees hunt. Did anyone know this before you saw it?

No Western scientist knew. I think the local people knew. But it was very exciting the first time I saw it. They hunt young pigs, young bushbuck, and they share the prey after they've had a successful hunt. They beg, with gestures like we use. And the meat is shared.

Some years later, you found that chimpanzees can be a lot more aggressive than people had known. Some of your colleagues saw that chimpanzees will even hunt and kill other chimpanzees.

That was very disappointing to find that, just like us, they have a dark side. The first accounts were of male chimpanzees patrolling the boundary of their territory and catching a female from a neighboring social group—a stranger— and subjecting her to such a violent attack that she later died of her wounds, and taking her baby and killing it. It was a total shock. Soon after that, the community divided. The smaller group took up residence in the south of the range. And four years later, the males of the larger community systematically hunted down, attacked, and killed all of the breakaway males—seven of them— and two females.

These were all chimpanzees that had once lived together. They had been intimate with each other.

It's like a civil war. And civil wars in human society are the worst. This was horrible.

How do you explain what happened?

I think it was territorial. The southern community had taken over part of what had once been shared range. As soon as the southern community was annihilated, the northerners moved back into the territory with their females and young. It's very human, isn't it?

It must have made you wonder about how violent humans can be. What conclusions did you come to?

When I first started publishing the descriptions of those attacks—that four-year war—various scientists suggested that I didn't need to publish it. They said that if I publish this, certain people will use this information to show that aggression is hardwired. Certainly, if you look at human behavior around the world, you have to admit that we can be very aggressive. So it goes back to Louis Leakey's premise when he sent me: If we find behavior common to chimpanzees and humans today, perhaps it was present in our common ancestor six million years ago. If that's so, perhaps violence has been with us all the way through human evolution.

But does that mean that war and violence are inevitable? I would argue not, because we have also evolved this amazingly sophisticated intellect, and we are capable of controlling our innate behavior a lot of the time. Chimpanzees equally show tendencies of love, compassion, and altruism, so we have these from our ancient past as well.

It's striking that Louis Leakey picked three women to lead pioneering primate studies: you with chimpanzees, Dian Fossey with gorillas, and Biruté Galdikas with orangutans. Was that just coincidence?

No, not at all. He felt that women made better observers, and he liked working better with women. So he deliberately chose women.

Do you think he was right?

If you look at women in an evolutionary perspective—and I compare chimp mothers with human mothers—you find that a mother needs to be patient. Otherwise her children won't do very well. A woman needed to understand the needs of a nonverbal creature—our children before they can speak. And women, even if they've been subjugated, have been quick to recognize the little communication signals in a household to prevent arguments before they blow up—to keep children out of the way of irritable men. So all those characteristics would be useful.

And when I began, most women didn't have careers. So you could afford to go sit in a forest and expect that a white knight would come along with shining armor and gather you up and look after you for the rest of your life. Whereas men, they were the breadwinners. They had to finish their field research, get a Ph.D., and get a job.

There was another convention back in the sixties. Scientists were not supposed to get emotionally involved with the subjects they studied. It seems that you violated that rule in your study of chimpanzees.

I didn't know about that when I began. I'd just done biology in high school. But I'd watched animals all my life, long before I watched chimpanzees. And I think having empathy with the creature you're watching is an immensely powerful tool. It gives you a platform from which you can start asking questions. Especially with chimpanzees, our nervous system is almost identical. Their brain is just a little bit smaller.

You were studying mother–infant interactions of chimpanzees, and then you had a child of your own. You raised him at Gombe while you were doing these field studies. Did you learn anything about raising your own son from the chimpanzees you studied?

I'm quite sure I did. I really looked on Flo as a role model. She was patient and supportive. She was protective but not overprotective. She could impose discipline when she wanted. She provided a nice secure base for her kids. And she supported them when they got into difficulties. That's a hallmark of a good mother. But looking back on it, my own mother raised me much the same way, so I don't know if I really learned from Flo.

You've written about the death of Flo and the impact it had on some of her family members. How did it affect her son Flint?

Flo, at the time of her death, looked older than any other individual we've observed at Gombe. She was probably close to 50. Chimpanzees don't have a menopause, and it's interesting to consider how useful menopause is in a long-lived species. Because Flo gave birth to an infant when her previous child, Flint, was only four and a half, she didn't have the strength to wean Flint. She didn't have the strength to nurture this embryo inside her and push Flint toward independence. So when he threw violent tantrums, she allowed him to suckle and to ride on her back. And then, when the infant died at six months, Flint was still sleeping with her, and she just took him back and treated him as though he was an infant. So he developed this strange, abnormal dependency on his old mother.

When she died, he was eight and a half years old, but it seemed he simply couldn't cope without her. And he showed signs of clinical depression. He rejected food, he rejected the approaches of other chimps. And in this state, which I can only describe as grief, his immune system weakened. He fell sick and was dead within a month of losing Flo.

He was simply too sad to live anymore.

He was too sad. I'll never forget seeing him about five or six days after she died. He climbed very slowly up a tree. He was already a little sick, and he got to a nest, which he'd shared with his mother about two weeks earlier. He just stood there looking at that nest. You can only wonder what was going on in his mind. Then he turned around and walked very, very slowly along the branch, climbed down to the ground, and curled up in a little heap. It was heartbreaking. We sat with him, we offered him food, but he did get some sickness and we couldn't help him.

You had known Flo for many years. How did her death affect you?

I sat with her body. We found it at the edge of the stream, and I sat there during the day and also during most of the following night—to see the reaction of other chimpanzees, and also, I didn't want the pigs to eat her. It was like losing an old friend.

Your research showed that chimpanzees have sophisticated emotional and mental capacities, which raises a big question: How unique are human beings?

It's the explosive development of our intellect that sets us apart. I personally believe that this happened because we, and only we, have developed the kind of language that enables us to teach about things that are not present, to tell stories, learn from the past, plan the distant future, and perhaps most important of all, gather together a group of people to discuss a new idea. That has really stimulated the growth of the intellect.

So if this is what makes us more human than anything else, makes us the most intellectual being that's ever walked the planet—able to arrange the environment to suit our needs, able to create technology to go to the moon—then why are we destroying our only home? That is so unintelligent of us.

Do we need to revise our definition of consciousness so that it includes the great apes?

Maybe we should include the great apes. Maybe we should extend certain rights to them that we agree are human rights. I'm always pushing for human responsibility. Given that chimpanzees and many other animals are sentient and sapient, then we should treat them with respect. But we don't even treat each other with respect. We have all these barriers between cultures and religions and nations, and between us and the natural world.

What are the moral implications of treating other animals with more respect—especially sentient beings like the great apes?

We should not be torturing them in medical research labs in five-foot by five-foot prison cages. We should not be taking them from their mothers and dressing them up for circuses of entertainment. We should not be buying and selling them like slaves for pets. And we shouldn't be killing them for food or for the live-animal trade in the African forests. But we're doing many of those things to our own species as well. It doesn't make either of those things better.

When you were at Gombe, did you find yourself wondering what was going on inside the minds of chimpanzees?

Constantly. We can guess what they're thinking, but how do they think? Are they thinking in pictures? How do you think without words? I spent ages wondering about that.

Were there any particular moments when you felt like you got a better understanding of that?

One moment was very special. That was when I was sitting in the forest with David Greybeard and I picked up a fruit and held it out to him. He turned his head away and I put my hand closer. He turned, looking directly into my eyes, and reached out, took the fruit and dropped it. He didn't want it. He then very gently squeezed my hand, which is how chimpanzees reassure each other. So in that moment, we communicated with a language—or in a way—that seems to predate words, perhaps in a way that was used by our own common ancestor millions of years ago. It was an extraordinary feeling. It was bridging these two worlds.

You seem to be very drawn to the idea of knowing the world without language or words.

I am fascinated by it. I always have been. We think with words. But when we don't think with words, I think we come close to what mystics might describe as a mystical experience. I don't think words would come into that.

Did you have mystical experiences at Gombe?

Yeah, sometimes. But it's awfully hard to describe, because words aren't there. It's a feeling of complete oneness with the natural world, and being able to hear it better and sense it better and smell it better and be better.

Can you tell me about one of those moments?

One was when I'd been following a little group of chimpanzees and I was wet. In the evening, they climbed up into this tree, which had beautiful lime green shoots. The sun behind them was making them shine and the trunks of the trees were still wet and shining black ebony. And the chimpanzees' coats were black ebony shot with little gleams of chestnut. The smell of ripe figs was strong in the air. Then this beautiful male bushbuck appeared with his coat dark with the rain, his spiraled horns gleaming, and just stood there. It seemed I could hear the insects loud and clear, much differently than usual. And the birds. And each leaf with its pattern of veins. It was incredibly vivid, being at one with that beautiful world.

It sounds like you lost your sense of your own self.

That's it. Totally losing sense of one's own self. That's the only way I can really study animals. Because if I'm on my own, I forget that I'm there. I'm with them. I'm not considering that I'm there. I'm just considering them.

In your book *Reason for Hope*, you speculate that chimpanzees might also have spiritual lives of their own. You've written, for instance, about a beautiful waterfall they go to. You suggest that they may even have some experience of awe.

Well, they sometimes pass there when they go from A to B, but it's what happens when they're near that. You can hear the roar of the falling water. It falls about 80 feet. The chimpanzees, usually the males, will bristle a little bit with excitement. And as they get near, they start these rhythmic displays, swaying from foot to foot, often upright. They may climb the vines and push out into the spray. And afterward, they may sit watching the water as it falls, watching as it flows past them. What is it? What is this strange substance which is always coming and always going and always here? You can't help feeling that if they had a language like ours, they could discuss whatever feeling it was that led them to these dramatic displays, which would turn into some kind of animistic religion. Watching these displays, you can't help feeling that it must be something that we would describe as awe or wonder or amazement, which can turn into the worship of things that we don't understand.

It makes you wonder if our own ancestors millions of years ago had similar experiences.

I would bet they did. I think we still do. But we immediately describe them with words.

Has that made you wonder about the origins of religion?

Yes, I think it probably originated something like that. Because we have language, because we like to explain everything, we describe experiences in terms of a spiritual or religious experience. Whatever is inside us that makes who we are feel different from our mind, we call a soul or a spirit. And if we have souls or spirits, then I suspect that chimpanzees do, too. I've always felt that if I had to describe what it is, I would say it's a little spark of a great spiritual power that I felt so strongly around me when I was out in the forest alone. Probably that little spark is in all living things. And it's we, with our passion for describing everything, that decided to call it a soul or a spirit.

It's unusual for a scientist of your stature to be so upfront about your own spiritual views. You've written about how you were raised in an open-minded Christian family. How has your sense of spirituality evolved over the years?

I don't spend that much time being introspective, believe it or not. All I know is that I grew up not questioning God because that's how you are. God was there like the birds and the wind. Then I was in Gombe, spending all that time alone out there with nature, and just feeling a very strong sense of something other than me that was out there.

You've also written about a transformative experience you once had at Notre Dame in Paris. What happened there?

It was not a peaceful time of my life. I went there early in the morning, just as the sun was coming in the great rose window. And it was Bach's Toccata and Fugue in D Minor from the organ that suddenly filled the cathedral. There was a wedding, though I just heard this music. You know, I can't accept that the humans who built that amazing cathedral and wrote that music, and the people who'd prayed there for hundreds of years, I couldn't accept that it was all chance—little bits of matter dancing around that suddenly somehow turned into this amazing experience. Therefore, if it wasn't chance, then it was antichance, which means something like God. But as I'm not a theologian or a philosopher, I don't really have the words to explain what I mean.

You seem to be convinced that there's some underlying purpose to our existence and to the universe.

That's what I really strongly feel. And I feel that for some extraordinary and peculiar reason, I have been almost pushed to do what I've done. I look back over my life and see the stages that led seamlessly from one to another to another. I suppose I could have said "no" and chosen a different way. But it just seemed inevitable to bring me to what I'm doing now, which is crazy, really.

What do you say to all those biologists who think it's just an evolutionary accident that human beings ever evolved?

I don't get into discussions with them because I don't really care. I just feel this way myself. It helps me to believe there's a purpose. I don't want to argue with them. I don't really mind what they believe.

But you're taking me away from everything I'm trying to do now, which is trying to get people to roll up their sleeves. People often ask me, "Okay, do you believe in creation or God?" And I always say quite honestly that how we got to be who we are is so much less important than getting together to get ourselves out of this horrendous mess that we have put the planet in. We're reaching the point of no return. We've got to roll up our sleeves. We've got to take action. We can't afford to sit back and philosophize too long about how we got to be the way we are.

But it's so rare for a scientist to talk about these things. You've written, for instance, about a remarkable experience you had, a vision of your husband Derek after he died. Can you describe what happened?

Yes, it was extremely strange. I'd gone back to Gombe, because it's very peaceful to be out in nature with chimpanzees who aren't questioning you or sympathizing with you. They're just getting on and being and doing. You get this feeling of the cycles of life and death. But I was woken up at night and there was Derek talking to me, very happy. I couldn't see him. At least I don't know if I could, because all I remember is waking and thinking, "I've got to write this down. It's fantastic." And then this feeling that you get when you're about to faint, this roaring in the ears. And then, I don't know if I fell asleep again or what, but I started remembering. And when I started remembering, the roaring came back. So I went to sleep again, and I couldn't remember anything he'd said. I'd vividly remembered what happened, but I couldn't remember any words.

I talked to a very strange lady—a medium—who said exactly the same thing had happened to her when her husband died. She had tried to get out of bed to write it down, and had gone into a coma and nearly died. So I said, "Goodness, don't get out of bed if it happens again!" And I asked, "What do you think it was?" She said, "I don't know, but maybe I was trying to move from one plane to another." You know, I'm not going to go deeply into exactly what happened. I don't know. All I know is that something happened which gave me this strong feeling that there is something that continues after we die.

And you're convinced that wasn't just a dream you had?
No, it wasn't a dream. And it was strange that she had exactly the same feeling. Of course, we read these books about lights at the end of tunnels, and the *Tibetan Book of Living and Dying*. I've been with so many people who accept this absolutely as a matter of fact.

I'm willing to bet that you get a lot of flak from scientists for talking publicly about this kind of thing. Do you worry about that?
No, I don't care. I never have. And I think it's very helpful for a lot of people who do have a religion that they find my books extremely helpful.

Today, you are more an activist than a scientist. You travel constantly, talking about environmental concerns and animal rights issues. What do you see as the biggest impact you can have right now?
I always think there are two. One is going back to my roots. Because I had this opportunity to work with chimpanzees, it has given people a different way of looking at animals and understanding them better. And the other one is working with youth and giving people hope. There's hope when we realize that every one of us makes an impact on this planet every single day. We have a choice as to what we buy, what we eat, what we drink, what we wear, how we get from A to B, how we interact with people and animals. These small changes in lifestyle can add up to the kind of change that we need.

How have some of these issues played out in your own life—what you eat, what you buy, what you wear?

In the early seventies, I read Peter Singer's book *Animal Liberation*. Once I learned what factory farms did to cows and pigs and hens, I was totally horrified. I looked at the piece of meat on my plate and I thought this is symbolic of fear and pain and death. I never ate another piece of meat. I'm not a vegan. I'm a vegetarian. And try to think about buying a cheap garment. Was it cheap because it involved child slave labor? Have products that you just pick up off a shelf caused destruction to the environment? If we would try to think about the consequences of our actions, it would make a big difference.

How are the chimpanzees at Gombe doing now?

Not that well. There were 150 in three communities when I arrived. The main study community is in the middle of a long, thin strip of forest, and it's about the same as it always was. But to the north and the south, where chimps have come up against cultivated fields which now completely surround the tiny 30-square-mile park, those communities have dwindled. So there are only a total of about 100 chimpanzees at Gombe today.

We're trying to ensure their future by working with the people living around the park. They are very poor people. They can't afford to pay for food elsewhere, so they've degraded the land. We can't really hope to save the chimps unless we can improve the lives of these people. So now we're in 32 villages with our Take Care program. We provide information about farming practices most suitable to this degraded land, information and help for water systems and sanitation, we provide microcredit for groups of women so they can start their own small environmentally sustainable projects, scholarships for girls so they can stay in school—concentrating on women because all around the world, family size drops as women's education improves.

The final piece in all of this is that up in the high hills a very good coffee is grown. I was able to persuade some coffee roasters—primarily Green Mountain coffee roasters—to come and test the coffee, buy it, help to improve the farming practices for harvesting and storing the coffee, and provide a good price for the first time. As a result, the villagers are setting aside between 10 and 20 percent of their village land for regeneration of forest or protection of the last little patches. We've done it by deliberately helping them in the way that they wish, not going in and telling them what a bunch of white people want to do, but with our Tanzanian team listening and asking, "What would make your lives better?" It didn't start with conservation at all. It was health and their children's education. That's where we began. Now these people are our partners. They're fascinated by the chimpanzees. They realize it's part of their heritage. They realize it's because of the chimpanzees that we're there in the first place. They're grateful and they're putting land aside for the chimps.

What advice do you have for kids who would like to do what you did—to become a naturalist and study animals?

Don't just learn virtually. Don't just learn from your TV screen. Go out and watch. Even if you're in the middle of an inner city, you can grow things and watch how they grow. You can study pigeons or trees out in the streets. There's always a way of getting out there and feeling the Earth, and learning something about the natural world. It's so important.

Epilogue

AN INTERVIEWER IS BY PROFESSION, and often by nature, someone who prefers asking questions to answering them. Ask enough questions on a particular topic, however, and sooner or later people expect you to form your own opinions. "So," friends and colleagues ask, "what do you think about science and religion? Where do you stand in this debate?"

I confess that I have struggled with how to answer. Partly because I'd prefer to let these interviews speak for themselves, but also because at a deeper level, what drew me to the science and religion debate in the first place—indeed, what continues to draw me—is its resistance to any clear-cut, definitive answer. Spend enough time thinking about some of these subjects—from the origins of the universe to profound mystical experiences—and you're likely to find at least a few of your assumptions becoming less, rather than more, certain.

The debate over science and religion is extraordinarily difficult to resolve because it demands expertise in so many different areas—from neuroscience, evolutionary biology, and theoretical physics to theology and the world's religions. Frankly, there isn't a single individual who has this kind of encyclopedic breadth of knowledge. There's more than just scholarly or scientific knowledge at stake here: Personal faith and lived spiritual experience are part of the story as well. This is not a subject that should just be left to the experts. I've come to believe that not only is there no shame in saying "I don't know" in the face of such complexity but that the very experience of not knowing, of casting aside at least a few of one's former certainties, is intellectually exhilarating and probably good for the soul.

Of course, we all have our own biases and personal contexts. Some of mine are no doubt apparent in the questions I've asked in these interviews. I know that I've been swayed at times by my own hunches and personal experiences, as well as by my family background. I come from a long line of Congregationalists and missionaries on both sides of my family. The virtues of public service were drilled into me at an early age, but strangely, talk about God didn't make much of an impression on me until adolescence. Maybe it was just teenage rebellion, but at around the age of 12 or 13 I concluded that the arguments for God's existence simply didn't add up. After a series of explosive arguments with my mother, I stopped attending church. My parents themselves left their Congregational church a few years later, dabbled in the human potential movement, and went on to found an eco-spiritual community in rural Wisconsin. I remained the family skeptic, a role that doubtless had something to do with my later choice of profession.

Over the years, I drew a line between religion and spirituality. Religion conjured up unpleasant memories of stultifying church services and Sunday school stories about the miracles of Jesus. Spirituality, on the other hand, seemed far more intriguing. I devoured books about Buddhism, Jung's collective unconscious, shamanism, and the Gnostic gospels—looking, I suppose, for the sort of "perennial philosophy" that Aldous Huxley once celebrated. Meanwhile, my parents' New Age crowd embraced modern mysticism with wholehearted fervor. It looked like fun, but I could never manage to suspend my disbelief for very long. If only I were less of a rationalist, I thought, I, too, could transcend quotidian life for more exalted states of consciousness. Alas, the journalist in me kept resisting.

I have come to regard that line between religion and spirituality to be far more permeable than I once thought. I've found myself particularly drawn to stories of ecstatic mystical experiences, like those about St. Francis of Assisi. A few years ago, I made a brief Franciscan pilgrimage through the hill towns of Umbria and Tuscany. I can't exactly explain my fascination with St. Francis, though certainly the stories about him are a large part of the appeal—how he preached to birds and tamed the man-eating wolf of Gubbio. According to legend, he also joined the Fifth Crusade in Egypt as a Christian missionary, but then—against all odds—befriended the Muslim sultan, a nephew of the great Saladin. What's most fascinating about Francis is his own life story. Once a dissolute playboy who went off to battle in search of glory, Francis later embraced God and became a wandering pilgrim. He was so popular that crowds would converge on him and even tear at his habit, hoping to touch a living saint. The stories about him are full of miracles: healing the sick and crippled, turning water into wine, and most dramatically, receiving the stigmata during one radiant night on the mountaintop at La Verna.

To really feel the spirit of St. Francis, his old hermitages and small churches are the places to go. I visited San Damiano, just below the walls of Assisi. This is the spot where Jesus supposedly first spoke to Francis from a cross inside a crumbling church. I asked a Franciscan friar there if he thought Jesus really spoke to Francis. "For me, it is not so interesting whether he heard the voice in the church or in himself," Brother Louis told me. "But I believe in miracles. I believe that miracles also happen in our time. I think the world is greater than what we can understand."

Later, I drove to the Carceri above Assisi, a few steep miles up Mt. Subasio and a world away from the hordes of tourists in the town below. A few Capuchin friars still live at the Carceri, where the doorways are so tiny that I had to crouch down to climb through them. Outside the hermitage, I found a trail of breathtaking beauty along the mountain ridge, and at the end of the path, a tiny outdoor chapel that was filled with handwritten notes tied to crosses, offering prayers and thanks to Francis.

If there's such a thing as sacred ground, I certainly felt it there. But I have puzzled over why I—a lapsed Christian—responded so strongly to this experience. I've never had much tolerance for proselytizers, and there's no doubt Francis was a religious zealot out to save souls. But he didn't seem to possess a shred of self-righteousness. By all accounts, he radiated joy, even though he lived in almost constant physical pain. A friar at the Celle, the convent outside Cortona, told me something fascinating. He said Francis thought of Jesus as his lover. It helps explain the ecstasy that he so clearly experienced throughout his life.

My own life could hardly be more different. I know I'll never feel that kind of religious rapture. No matter how much I yearn for the divine—and for all my skepticism, I do envy the mystics and their single-minded devotion to God—I am rooted in another world, a realm of earthly pleasures and more-subdued reflection and intellectual struggle.

Christianity is the religious tradition that has wrestled most vigorously with the fraught relationship between religion and science. But in recent decades, many Muslims have also entered the fray. There is widespread skepticism about evolutionary science throughout the Islamic world. In 2006 *Science* magazine found that of 34 countries surveyed, the country most opposed to evolution is Turkey. (The United States came in right behind Turkey.) Turkey is a particularly fascinating case. Perhaps the most secular Muslim country, it has also experienced the strongest backlash against Darwinian thinking.

In 2008 I traveled to Turkey with the International Reporting Project. Shortly before I set off on this trip, I sent an email to Istanbul to see if Islam's leading creationist would be available for an interview. Would Harun Yahya, the scourge of Richard Dawkins and founder of a global media empire, be free to talk? Actually, I wasn't sure it was worth the trouble. Hiring a guide for a day in Istanbul would run $300, plus more for a translator. But when Yahya's assistant called me from Istanbul—it couldn't have been more than three minutes after my query—she offered to send a driver to pick me up at my hotel on the other side of the city. And the translator? No problem—they would supply one.

Later, I came to realize this was all part of Yahya's new "charm offensive," as one Istanbul journalist described it to me. Harun Yahya, the pen name for Adnan Oktar, gets some seriously bad press in the West. Newspapers across Europe and the United States have covered his ongoing legal troubles, including charges of extortion and sexual abuse, and the response has been scathing. Now he is trying to position himself as the go-to critic of evolution . . . or at least a thorn in the side of modern science.

It may be tempting to dismiss Yahya as a crackpot, but he runs a sophisticated media operation, with perhaps several hundred members, that distributes books, articles, videos, and web sites around the Muslim world. Several years ago he mailed, unsolicited, a visually stunning 13-pound, 800-page *Atlas of Creation* to thousands of scientists, doctors, museums, and research centers in Europe and the United States. The cost of this publicity stunt, if that's what it was, had to be staggering.

The great mystery is where Yahya's Science Research Foundation gets its money. No one knows, although speculation runs from Saudi donors to wealthy Turks whose children have joined the secretive group. Whoever funds it, the organization seems to have the kind of wealth and influence that Christian creationists can only dream of. Yahya's teachings aren't confined to a religious subculture in Turkey. They are part of the mainstream. Creationist stories are now popping up in high school science textbooks, and some government officials in the AKP, the ruling Islamic party, freely criticize evolution. In Ankara, the government's point man on religious issues, Mehmet Gormez, told me, "All the holy texts say human beings are created by God. I think evolutionary theory is not scientific, but ideological." The Quran doesn't have a detailed origins story like the six days of creation found in Genesis, but it does say Adam was created out of clay in a heavenly paradise and later banished to Earth, along with Eve.

I had no idea what to expect from my meeting with Adnan Oktar, though it didn't seem like the smartest idea to be driven halfway across Istanbul for a 10 P.M. interview. My driver, Emre, quickly put me at ease. Dressed in jeans and sneakers, he picked me up at the hotel, and we chatted amiably on our drive to the Yahya compound. As we neared our destination, he pulled off the road and in hopped our translator, a dapper young man in a suit with a cultivated British accent. Soon they were joking about their respective English-speaking accents. Emre assured us that girls preferred his. This wasn't exactly my image of die-hard Islamic fundamentalists.

We finally arrived at a sprawling modern house on the Asian side of Istanbul. Glass doors led out to a swimming pool, and a huge plasma TV screen hung over a low-slung couch. But the biggest surprise was to find that I had walked onto a stage set. Bright klieg lights beamed down on our interview chairs, which were carefully arranged to show off four editions of *Atlas of Creation*, all in different languages. Several men were waiting to operate the three video cameras and high-tech recording gear. It turned out I wasn't the only one taping this interview.

After 20 minutes of sound checks, Adnan Oktar made his grand entrance. He is a burly man with slicked-back hair and a carefully trimmed beard, and he wore his trademark white suit with a black T-shirt. He was gracious throughout the hour-long interview, but the weirdness of the evening quickly emerged. When I asked how so many evolutionary biologists could be wrong, Oktar replied, "We need to talk about the Masons' role because Masons manage the world through a scientific dictatorship." When I suggested that scientists would be surprised to hear this, he said that's because the Masons' "essential characteristic is that they act secretly and they are invisible."

I asked Oktar about his legal troubles. In 2008, he was sentenced to three years in jail for extortion and running a crime gang, a conviction he is appealing. Earlier he had been charged with drug possession and sexual assault, but both cases against him fizzled. (In the 1980s, he spent 10 months locked up in a mental institution.) In response, he launched into a rambling account of how he and his friends had been threatened with torture and death: "If you were given electricity or were tortured, you would sign the documents which were put in front of you. This is what we did. We would be dead otherwise." Oktar said he had faced many assassination attempts and then recounted how he was once framed on a drug charge by a policeman who had slipped cocaine into his kabob. Why has he been targeted? "Because I'm fighting against Darwinism, communism, and other terrorist organizations." So Darwinists are terrorists? Their work is "a Satanic plot" that nurtures terrorism around the world, "like the development of mosquitoes in mud or in ponds. So many fascist and communist leaders have stated very clearly that they have been affected by the teachings and ideals of Darwinism." (It's true, at least, that Oktar has both powerful enemies and powerful friends.)

By this point my head was spinning—just where could I take this interview?—but I kept wondering why Oktar would bother doing interviews with Western journalists like me. Just how would he benefit from this coverage? I got the answer once I asked him to assess his own influence. With the publication of *Atlas of Creation*, Oktar claimed that "Darwinism had come to an impasse for the first time in history." He then pulled out a loose-leaf notebook filled with clippings from major European newspapers and magazines and proceeded to quote from them: *Liberation* had referred to "the book that created a great panic"; *Stern* had likened his book to thunder; and *La Stampa* had run the headline "Farewell Darwin." The lesson was clear, according to Oktar: Most Europeans had lost their belief in Darwinism.

So this was it: Any publicity, no matter how bad, would confirm Harun Yahya's status as a global player in the evolution wars. Would we be better off simply ignoring him? Probably not. Yahya has already grabbed the spotlight, not just in Turkey but in Muslim communities around the world. His organization is adept at filling the vacuum where support for evolution is weak, and many scientists in Islamic countries are now wary of defending evolution. What's needed is more public engagement, especially from Muslim scientists and religious figures willing to confront him. But will a freewheeling discussion of modern science persuade people to give up creationism? That's anybody's guess.

I have not included interviews with creationists or intelligent design advocates in this book because their science simply isn't credible. At the same time, I don't believe that science offers the only paradigm for determining what is real. It's possible that certain strange and even bizarre experiences could reveal a great deal about the nonmaterial world—or at least some dimension of reality that is beyond the physical world now known to science. We often don't have to go far to hear about such experiences. Nearly every family seems to have a "mystery tale" tucked away in its collective memory. In my own family, there are several. I grew up hearing some crazy stories about paranormal experiences.

When I was eight, my family lived for a year in Fortaleza, a Brazilian city with a strong cultural tradition of the occult. At one point, my mother became very ill, even partially paralyzed, and she developed an unrelenting sense of dread. Her doctors couldn't find anything physically wrong, but she heard through the grapevine that the local Macumba high priestess had cast an evil eye on her (apparently because she had unwittingly offended the woman). My own mother was possessed by an evil spirit! She was told that she needed to have the demon cast out of her. My parents went to a spirit medium in a beach-front favela and after a ritualistic exorcism, lo and behold, she immediately felt better. To this day, my mother can't explain what happened—whether it was indeed the removal of an evil spirit or simply the power of suggestion.

Another story came from my mother's father, though he usually brushed it off out of embarrassment. A firm rationalist, he spent his career as an engineer at General Electric and was highly skeptical of anything that smacked of the paranormal. As the story goes, when he was 16, his family was very anxious about the condition of his grandfather, who was gravely ill. One day he was alone in the living room. All of a sudden, he heard an odd sound and looked up to see the picture of his grandfather knocking against the wall where it was hanging. Somehow, he knew instantly that his grandfather had just died. As a budding scientist, he also noted the time this happened. Later, a telegram arrived confirming the news. The time of death given was the exact time he had seen the picture move. Many years later, when my grandfather told me the story, he shrugged it off, saying he had no explanation for what happened.

Frankly, I have no idea what to make of these stories, but I suspect that they have something to do, subconsciously, with my unwillingness to believe that the modern scientific paradigm has the monopoly on truth. Perhaps this is one reason I'm drawn to consider whether there is a dimension to consciousness that goes beyond our individual brains. That's a question that also preoccupied one of my heroes, the pioneering psychologist William James.

Questions about the paranormal usually fall outside the debate over science and religion, but I consider them pertinent because they challenge the materialistic assumptions of science. In fact, Steven Pinker says his materialist understanding of the mind would crumble if a single paranormal experience like telepathy or a clairvoyant dream were ever proved. Such stories also pose an epistemological problem: Do these anecdotal, one-of-a-kind experiences have any place in the scientific understanding of reality? One response is to acknowledge that certain paranormal phenomena may indeed occur, even if they fall outside the domain of science. In other words, the scientific method, which depends on testable theories and repeated observations, may not provide the only evidence for determining what is real. This seems to be the position taken by scientists as diverse as Jane Goodall and Sam Harris. Of course, even if we accept the possibility of some nonmaterial reality (or at least nonmaterial by today's scientific standards), it still reveals nothing about the existence of God, the soul, or any kind of cosmic consciousness. But I would like to make a plea for the spirit of open-minded inquiry.

In fact, that spirit animates this collection of interviews. It grew out of my own curiosity about a host of scientific and spiritual questions. Will science ever explain the birth of the universe or the mystery of human consciousness? What might the word "God" mean if we came to it fresh today, free of centuries' worth of accumulated baggage? For that matter, can science and religion ever be truly reconciled? As to the last question, I am still working out my own answer.

Acknowledgments

MY GREATEST DEBT IS TO THE 21 PEOPLE who generously shared their time and intellectual passions in these interviews. One of these scholars, Ron Numbers, also provided invaluable practical advice that helped with the publication of this book. Sixteen of these interviews originally ran in the online magazine *Salon*. The book would not exist without the support and expert editorial guidance of my two editors at *Salon*—first, Hillary Frey, and later, Kevin Berger, who created the *Atoms and Eden* column as a forum for my interviews. A hearty thanks as well to Dan Engber, my editor at *Slate*, where a longer account of my article about Harun Yahya originally appeared.

Excerpts of these interviews were broadcast nationally on the public radio show *To the Best of Our Knowledge*. I am indebted to Wisconsin Public Radio for giving me the freedom and encouragement to turn this material into a book. I especially want to thank my talented colleagues at *To the Best of Our Knowledge*, who were unfailingly supportive of this project throughout its four years of gestation. They didn't flinch—at least I don't think so—as I pursued my obsessions about religion and science, even as we labored to put out new radio shows every week.

The Templeton-Cambridge Journalism Fellowship in Science & Religion gave me a wonderful opportunity to explore this subject in depth during the summer of 2006. Many thanks to the project's directors then, Julia Vitullo-Martin, Fraser Watts, and Russell Stannard, as well as my fellow journalists for an incredibly stimulating three weeks in Cambridge. I am also grateful to the International Reporting Project for sponsoring my trip to Turkey. Working with Oxford University Press has been a great pleasure. I am thankful to my editor, Cynthia Read, and to the others who brought this book into the world, especially Molly Balikov, Christine Dahlin, Lisa Force, Jamie Taratoot, Brian Hughes, and Sarah Russo.

Various people provided encouragement and practical advice, and others told me about pertinent books, articles, and noteworthy thinkers. Thanks especially to Eric Paulson, Susan and Edmond Strainchamps, Raphael Kadushin, Peter Sobol, David Lagerman, Ann Shaffer, and Taner Edis. My parents, Lisa and Belden Paulson, played a crucial role in the genesis of this book, not only through our many animated conversations—even though they didn't always agree with my conclusions—but more important, through their lifelong commitment to exploring uncharted territory.

I am profoundly grateful to my family for their support, patience, and love, all of which made this book possible. Katie and Nicky have spent sizable portions of their young lives hearing me talk about this project. I can imagine that "science and religion" has not always been their favorite subject, especially when I disappeared for long hours to prepare for one or another interview. This book is dedicated to my wife, Anne Strainchamps. She has been my partner in all sorts of ways for more than two decades. She's a brilliant writer and radio producer, and she has—at one time or another—been my editor, sounding board, and fellow explorer in life's great mysteries. And not least, she's been there for Katie and Nicky when I was unavailable. Thank you, Anne!